Business Management Controls

A Guide

Business Management Controls

A Guide

JOHN KYRIAZOGLOU

IT Governance Publishing

Every possible effort has been made to ensure that the information contained in this book is accurate at the time of going to press, and the publisher and the author cannot accept responsibility for any errors or omissions, however caused. Any opinions expressed in this book are those of the author, not the publisher. Websites identified are for reference only, not endorsement, and any website visits are at the reader's own risk. No responsibility for loss or damage occasioned to any person acting, or refraining from action, as a result of the material in this publication can be accepted by the publisher or the author.

Apart from any fair dealing for the purposes of research or private study, or criticism or review, as permitted under the Copyright, Designs and Patents Act 1988, this publication may only be reproduced, stored or transmitted, in any form, or by any means, with the prior permission in writing of the publisher or, in the case of reprographic reproduction, in accordance with the terms of licences issued by the Copyright Licensing Agency. Enquiries concerning reproduction outside those terms should be sent to the publisher at the following address:

IT Governance Publishing
IT Governance Limited
Unit 3, Clive Court
Bartholomew's Walk
Cambridgeshire Business Park
Ely
Cambridgeshire
CB7 4EA
United Kingdom

www.itgovernance.co.uk

© John Kyriazoglou 2012
The author has asserted the rights of the author under the Copyright, Designs and Patents Act, 1988, to be identified as the author of this work.

First published in the United Kingdom in 2012
by IT Governance Publishing.

ISBN 978-1-84928-428-8

FOREWORD

Business Management Controls is a practical guide and reference for the business person who needs to implement, or improve, business controls. This hands-on guide is clearly organised and arranged by functional business area. John Kyriazoglou has written a detailed overview of controls in a complete, easy-to-follow format. This book is a great companion to *IT Strategic and Operational Controls* (2010), and extends his work and expertise beyond information technology, to the entire organisation.

As a professor of strategic management, and a frequent consultant to entrepreneurial ventures, including those at various stages of new venture creation, this book is a detailed reference for businesses at all stages. It will be of particular benefit to those growing concerns that need to better organise and control their many systems, as well as the mature business that wants to streamline various operations for cost-containment and strategic positioning for the future.

In the first part (*Chapters 1* to *3*) of this book, Kyriazoglou sets up the role of managers in setting controls to reach their goals and to ensure a company's longevity. The book considers a company's strategy, as well as its organisational structure in choosing and developing a control system. Of the functions of management all business students learn – planning, organising, leading, directing, and controlling – control is often an overlooked function. Whilst not as popular in the academic and popular-press business literature in today's global economy, with more pressures for compliance, cost management and business continuity planning, control has taken on more importance to executives the world over.

Kyriazoglou does a thorough job of clarifying the various controls an organisation and its leadership must consider – directive, preventive, detective, corrective and compensating controls. This book is a complete framework for internal controls, as well as implementation approaches. Managers must decide on the controls most appropriate for their organisation, given its strategy and macro environment. One of the key benefits of this book is the various recommendations in the tables and text boxes. They guide managers and suggest practical options.

For the entrepreneur just starting a company, *Chapter 4* provides detailed examples of a written business strategy, as well as clear goals and objectives to emulate or adapt. Often businesses do not allow proper time for planning, and these steps are overlooked. *Chapter 4* is a concise review of the steps, but more importantly, the questions to ask in the strategic management process.

Financial and production controls (*Chapters 5* and *6*) provide detailed explanations of the various financial statements and budgeting processes. Examples of measures to track and assess are included for the new manager to consider, or as a refresher or new viewpoint, for the seasoned manager.

Chapter 7 on IT governance controls illustrates Kyriazoglou's expertise in IT, and his various roles and responsibilities in the IT field. With today's emphasis on succession planning, sustainability, business continuity and disaster planning, the section on back-up and disaster recovery plans is especially helpful. The recommendations are clear and concise, for example, 'Recent IT research has shown that data volumes, e-mail traffic and other network transactions, grow in an increased mode every year. CIOs and board directors must be vigilant, and implement the required IT and information governance controls, to ensure that their organisations are safe and secure in the new web-based environment'.

The book continues with an additional chapter on business data management controls (*Chapter 8*) and even recommends various business record keeping systems and policies and procedures manuals. Suggestions, including limiting the number of file formats used and the use of standard templates, are helpful for any business person who uses electronic data.

With his vast technical knowledge, Kyriazoglou doesn't neglect the human components, and considers the human factors in applying business management controls (*Chapter 13*). He separates these into 'hard' and 'soft' controls. Soft controls consider the tone at the top, the culture, the morale, and even integrity and ethical values.

The third and fourth parts (*Chapters 10* to *13* and *Chapters 14* to *16*) of this book, move to the implementation and auditing of various business controls, and include frameworks, as well as a case study for review. The balanced scorecard method forms the basis for the third section, considering financial, as well as customer perspectives. Kyriazoglou covers key tools of total quality management and other performance frameworks (*Chapter 10*) and compares them for the reader.

Planning is often easier than implementation, and the implementation chapters are clear, with action steps highlighted for the reader to follow. The theme of business continuity planning (*Chapter 14*) also resonates throughout the book. As a recent victim of a tornado that devastated the South East United States, I better understand the need for operational procedures in a disaster. Few businesses devote the time to think about these issues, but with global climate change and a host of other potential disasters, this book reminds us all of the importance of a business continuity management process and back-up, and of the need to restore policies and procedures. Kyriazoglou even provides an example of a 10-step back-up and restore policy.

The case study in *Chapter 15* considers ways to use controls to mitigate fraud and other business risks, and uses examples from the Italian firm, Parmalat, as well as Lehman Brothers from the US, along with other business examples from around the world.

The book concludes with the roles and responsibilities of participants in business management controls (*Chapter 12*), as well as the various types of audits performed for management controls (*Chapter 16*). The checklists, numbered lists, and issues to consider, are presented in a step-by-step format for managers to follow.

This book is complete, but easy to follow, without unnecessary detail. Managers have so little time and Kyriazoglou readily understands this with his lists, examples, and recommendations. For the reader who needs additional background or detail, he has included links to websites for more information. Thus the book can be customised for the skills, needs, and expertise of the reader.

Business control documents, policies, procedures, plans and checklists referenced in this book are included in the *Business Management Controls Toolkit*, also authored by John Kyriazoglou. These are customisable, pre-written documents that will prove invaluable for the manager. For

Foreword

companies struggling to develop key policies for their
employees, and for compliance postings and corporate
handbooks, the toolkit includes a sample privacy of
information policy, an information sensitivity policy, a
statement of security and safety controls for personal
computers, a confidentiality policy, a statement on
password controls, a statement on business management
controls for laptops and smart devices, a social media plan
and an ethics policy.

Whilst all businesses know on an intuitive level that they
need such statements and policies posted and disseminated
to all their global employees and units, few organisations
take the time to develop them, because they are difficult to
create from scratch, and require background research.

This book has done the research for the manager, and even
indicates where customisation of the policies should occur.
A manager or executive could easily copy and adapt the
policies very quickly for their organisation.

This book is indeed as a guide, or almost a workbook, that
all business managers should follow. It reminds us of the
various tasks all organisations must consider in the
managerial function of control, however, too many
overlook or forget these policies, often to their detriment.

As the work of business continues to evolve, controls are
predicted to become even more critical in the future.
Kyriazoglou has created a concise guide to eliminate much
of the worry over controls, and offers an action plan, with
steps and recommendations for the manager to follow.

Dr Marilyn M Helms
Sesquicentennial Chair and Professor of Management
School of Business

Foreword

Dalton State College
E-mail: *mhelms@daltonstate.edu*
Website: *www.daltonstate.edu/faculty-staff/mhelms*

PREFACE

'There is nothing so easy but that it becomes difficult when you do it reluctantly.'

Pythagoras, ancient Greek philosopher (about 570 to about 495 BC)

The first decade of the 21st Century has brought upon all of us an array of very perplexed issues and problems which are, by their own nature, very difficult to manage and resolve to any level of satisfaction: continuing world financial crises, new technical developments, starvation of over one billion people, increased terrorism, new corporate insider and cyber threats, organised crime operations across many countries, parallel and informal economies, ecological disasters, along with deforestation and pollution, increasing regional wars and upheavals, new corporate governance, compliance, accountability and reporting regimes, etc.

As Richard Chandler has said[1] 'Societies are not static. They change over time. The most obvious changes result from economic and social processes that are constantly in flux. Expanding trade, technological innovation, new fashions and new forms of entertainment, seem to transform the world before our very eyes. Habits, cultural traditions and values change more slowly. Yet changes in these more intimate areas of life are just as important for progress and

---

[1] See page 3: *Galileo Report – The World in 2010*, Chandler, Richard (2012), www.richardchandler.com.

xi

prosperity as economic trends'. All these impact on our lifestyle and mode of operation.

The new lifestyle (*modus vivendi*, in the sociological vernacular) enforces upon all of us a new set of operational factors and transactional characteristics in our societal and human interactions; a new socio-economic operating mode (*modus operandi* in the sociological vernacular).

This set of social interactions is permeated and driven by several socio-technical factors and functional characteristics, such as: globalisation of markets; liberalisation of markets; services economy; lack of governance controls in international fiscal and financial markets, transactions and activities;[2] very fast developments in the fields of information technology, communications, biology, medicine, management, etc; information plurality, diffusion and potential information over-loading, as well as the increased role of knowledge on a global scale;[3] increase of the leverage and focus on the needs of customers, the so-called customer-focus approach in all dealings; new developments and trends,[4] as well as new risks on a global scale;[5] differentiation of the needs, and increase of the expectations, of better provision of services to citizens, the so-called citizen-based service approach in all public-sector exchanges and transactions;

---

[2]See also: *ACFE 2010 Global Fraud Study*, available at: www.acfe.com/rttn.aspx.

[3] See also: *The Diplomacy of Knowledge*, Johnston, David, Governor-General of Canada, Globe and Mail Newspaper (17 February 2012), www.theglobeandmail.com/news/opinions/opinion/the-diplomacy-of-knowledge/article2341017/).

[4] For more see: *Galileo Report – The World in 2010*, Chandler, Richard (2012), www.richardchandler.com.
[5] See also: *Global Risks, 2011* – Sixth Edition, World Economic Forum, (January 2011), www.weforum.org/.

and reduction and de-strengthening of the traditional government model of a large central organisation, to a model of organisation based on a de-centralised approach.

All of these are interacting and inter-connecting in different sets, and make up a new social, compliance,[6] economic, technological, moral and political framework, within which society, economy, enterprises, government, non-profit organisations, communities, citizens, etc, operate and function productively. New, and more complicated roles, are being created for the state (central administration, regional forms of government, local governments, etc.), for the business entities (small size, middle size, large size, conglomerate, international enterprises, etc.), and for organisations of the main public sector and related public regulatory authorities, with greater expectations for improved quality of life, and socio-economic advancement and development, in all industrial sectors and socio-economic environments.

All these new, and very quickly developed roles, are required for:

1 Quicker and more effective service (in relation to costs and benefits).
2 Better management and more efficient use of global resources.
3 Better (ethical, ecologically-friendly) resource management by all industries, in all countries.
4 Continuous improvement in the quality of products and services provided, in social and citizen participation, in

[6] See also: *Ten Things UK/EU Compliance Officers Must Do in 2012*, Hammond, S, London (9 January 2012), http://accelus.thomsonreuters.com/solutions/regulatory-intelligence/compliance-complete/.

the commitment to democratic institutions and customer services, for all stakeholders (people and organisations).

5 Minimisation, if not total reduction, of social, public sector and business fraud and corruption.

6 Better understanding of what has gone wrong in private and public organisations, and what must be done to get things right.

All these mean that we need, at least at the business level, to develop new, and more effective ways and means, to manage and control private and public organisations, as we live in a human-centric, complicated, interconnected and fraud-prone turbulent world. As Tom Peters,[7] the noted American writer on business management practices has said: 'Excellent firms don't believe in excellence – only in constant improvement and constant change'.

The consideration of all these provided me with the inspiration and motivation to write this book, and describe various ways to improve internal controls in business entities (private, for profit companies), and, therefore, make them more effective, efficient, beneficial to society and stakeholders, accountable and protected.

This book defines and identifies the various types of controls, with specific examples (over 300 in terms of: policies, procedures, management plans, etc.) in all core business functions, such as: governance, strategic, operational (finance, production, IT, data governance, business continuity, etc.) and compliance controls; describes various frameworks for designing and implementing them (BSC, CAF, etc.); discusses the BSC

---

[7] See:*www.tompeters.com/*.

approach in more detail; and presents examples of compliance and performance measures, the counterparts of strategic and operational controls in the areas of finance, corporate governance, production, IT, etc.

This book includes specific case studies of applying controls to mitigate fraud and other corporate risks. These are complemented by a set of example plans, policies and audit programmes that may be customised to suit the needs of any organisation, which can be found in the *Business Management Controls Toolkit*. This provides more specific and practical guidance to any business person, manager, audit professional, etc, who needs to implement, audit, or improve business controls, for his or her business organisation.

A set of 21 practical 'how to' recommendations are also offered to guide (possibly) the manager wishing to apply these controls in his or her corporate environment. This short guide outlines business management controls in four parts, 17 chapters, 21 recommendations and over 200 controls (plans, frameworks, methodologies, policies, procedures, audit tools, job descriptions, terms of reference, etc.), in the following way:

Part A: Establishing the Internal Controls Environment

Chapter 1: Business Management Controls Framework

Chapter 2: Enterprise Governance Controls

Chapter 3: Risk and Compliance Controls

Part B: Main Types of Strategic and Operational Controls

Chapter 4: Strategic Management Controls

Preface

Chapter 5: Financial Management and Accounting Controls

Chapter 6: Customer Sales and Production Management Controls

Chapter 7: IT Governance Controls

Chapter 8: Business Data Management Controls

Chapter 9: Business Intelligence and Espionage Controls

Part C: Implementing Business Management Controls

Chapter 10: Business Performance Management Frameworks

Chapter 11: Implementing Business Management Controls

Chapter 12: Roles and Responsibilities of Participants in Business Management Controls

Chapter 13: Human Factors in Applying Business Management Controls

Part D: Enhancing Business Operations

Chapter 14: Business and IT Continuity Management Controls

Chapter 15: Case Studies: Applying Business Management Controls to Mitigate Fraud and Other Risks

Chapter 16: Auditing Business Management Controls

Chapter 17: Final Conclusion

Appendix 1 contains a list of the business management controls referenced within this book (plans, policies, procedures, checklists, etc.). These controls are contained in the *Business Management Controls Toolkit.*

xvi

Preface

The material, concepts, ideas, plans, policies, procedures, forms, methods, tools, etc. presented, described and analysed in all chapters and appendices, are for educational and training purposes only. They are based on the experience of the author, and on the resources identified in the notes, as well as in the bibliography. These should only be used as an indicative base set, and should be customised by each organisation after careful and considerable thought as to the needs and requirements of each organisation, taking into effect the implications and aspects of the legal, national, religious, philosophical, cultural and social environments, and expectations, within which each organisation operates and exists.

I hope that this book may assist you in executing your business management activities more efficiently, and in understanding, managing and controlling your company in a better way.

I will enrich, and keep this book up to date, with articles and other management and audit-relevant material (e.g. posts with my opinion on current controls issues, case studies with specific control applications, audit programmes, audit checklists, etc.) related to business management controls which I will be including in my business management knowledge repository (my blog and my free SSRN papers at the SSRN site).

Blog: *http://businessmanagementcontrols.blogspot.com/*

SSRN Free Publications: *http://ssrn.com/author=1315434*

Also, educational material, in terms of a set of 100 multiple choice questions (and answers), can be sent, free of charge, to any educator using this book.

Preface

The potential audience of this book includes managers, auditors and professionals, and anyone interested in how assets, transactions, operations, systems, activities and investments of organisations (private and public) may be protected, managed, monitored, controlled, audited and improved more effectively and more efficiently. These persons include, as an example:

1 Board directors, audit committee members and C-level executives.
2 Corporate managers at all levels (senior, financial, production, compliance, risk, data privacy, IT, etc.).
3 Auditors (internal, external, IT, etc.).
4 IT managers and staff (systems development, computer operations, technical support, etc.).
5 Professionals (e-crime experts, fraud examiners, internal controls professionals, security and risk professionals, business consultants, governance professionals, corporate performance experts, human resources advisers, etc.).
6 University students at all levels (undergraduate and graduate) of accounting, finance, internal auditing and business administration.

In conclusion, this book is a clear, practical guide. It will transform your working practices, and save you time and money! This guide will give you a clear understanding of the way business management controls work. It can:

1 Improve your business control practices.
2 Help you develop, customise, assess and implement your own controls better.
3 Show you how to develop more streamlined and successful working practices.

4 Show you how to enable, facilitate, and protect your business operations in a more effective way.

John Kyriazoglou, CICA, BA (Hons)

jkyriazoglou@hotmail.com

ABOUT THE AUTHOR

John Kyriazoglou, CICA, BA (Hon – University of Toronto, Canada), is an International IT and Management Consultant, with over 35 years' on-the-job experience, in both the private and the public sector, in a wide variety of companies, industries and economic sectors, in several countries (Canada, England, Switzerland, Luxembourg and other European countries, Saudi Arabia, etc.). He has taken over 70 courses in all aspects of management and IT, and has attended, and given presentations, in over 25 international conferences.

John has worked in a variety of roles and responsibilities, such as: Managing Director of EDP/IT services company, Senior IT Manager, Group EDP/IT Internal Audit Manager, Acting MIS Director, Senior management consultant to various boards, in a variety of clients and projects, in both the private and the public sectors.

John has published over 20 articles in professional publications, has served in numerous scientific committees, is a member of the Institute for Internal Controls, Inc. (US), and other professional and cultural associations, and is giving courses on IT auditing, security and electronic crime prevention.

John's recent book, published by IT Governance, is *IT Strategic and Operational Controls (2010)*, *www.itgovernance.co.uk*, and a complete list of his books and works is contained at *http://johnkyriazoglou-works.blogspot.com/*.

About the Author

John's volunteering efforts include mentoring, coaching, and founding and supporting cultural societies.

See John's online profile at: *www.linkedin.com/pub/john-kyriazoglou/0/9b/919*, and his blog, at: *http://businessmanagementcontrols.blogspot.com/*.

John welcomes queries and communication about all issues related to his work and his books, and can be contacted at: *jkyriazoglou@hotmail.com*.

ACKNOWLEDGEMENTS

I'm most grateful to Dr Marylin M Helms, Sesquicentennial Chair and Professor of Management (Dalton State College, US), who had the disposition and stamina to go through my first draft, and provide very helpful comments and improvements, and a Foreword.

I am most obliged to Richard Leblanc, PhD, Associate Professor-Law, Governance and Ethics, York University, Toronto, Canada; David Newcomer, Owner, Express Employment and Entrepreneur, Macon, Georgia, US, and George Bass, QC, Vice President, General Counsel and Secretary, The Wawanesa Mutual Insurance Company, Winnipeg, Canada, who had the time, and expended their full energy, to go through my first draft, and offer valuable comments and improvements.

My sincere thanks also go to several of my previous employers and associates, and to the many senior management staff of my clients, for their assistance and support, and for making it easy for me to support them in various projects on business consulting, IT, internal audit and e-crime seminars.

I offer my sincere thanks to the staff of the publisher: Alan Calder, Vicki Utting and Alexandra Thurman, for their undivided attention and spirit. I would also like to thank the reviewers of this book for their feedback: Chris Evans, ITSM specialist; Brian Johnson, CA Technologies and ir. H.L. (Maarten) Souw RE, Enterprise Risk and QA Manager, UWV (National Employee Benefits Administration).

Acknowledgements

I'm most obligated to my Canadian Alma Mater, Woodsworth College, of the University of Toronto, Canada, my inspirational beacon, nourishing source, and fostering mother of my knowledge and intellectual base.

I'd like to thank my family for bearing with me during this wonderful, but very long and enduring task. My wife, Sandy, for her full understanding, support, patience, love, motivation and friendship. My wonderful Chris, for his most inquisitive mind, love and support. My lovely princess, Miranda, and her Dimitri, for their supportive affection and love, humorous spirit, and positive persistence in the journey of life. And last, but not least, to the seventh gift bestowed upon me by the Almighty, my always exquisite and supreme Queen of my life, my granddaughter, the blue-eyed, lovely and admirable, Melina.

John Kyriazoglou

CONTENTS

Contents

Contents

Contents

Contents

Contents

CHAPTER 1: BUSINESS MANAGEMENT CONTROLS FRAMEWORK

'Apply yourself both now and in the next life. Without effort, you cannot be prosperous. Although the land may be good, you cannot have an abundant crop without cultivation.'

Plato, Ancient Greek Philosopher (427–347 BC)

Chapter overview: This chapter, the first chapter of Part A: Establishing the Internal Controls Environment, describes the role of controls, and proposes a business management controls framework which enables, facilitates, and supports you, in designing, and implementing, effective controls to operate all your business functions and control systems. Two controls (business management controls framework and business management controls system manual) are noted, and a recommendation (Recommendation 1: Create and implement a controls framework to satisfy your needs) is offered for your consideration.

Introduction

'The companies that survive longest are the ones that work out what they uniquely can give to the world, not just growth or money, but their excellence, their respect for others, or their ability to make people happy. Some call those things a soul,' is a famous quote by management guru, Charles Handy. But how are all these to be achieved by organisations, in the most optimal way?

Controls, managers, internal control frameworks, business management controls, and performance and compliance measures, are the most crucial components towards reaching these goals, and making companies most beneficial to all.

The role of control in management activities

Business management controls, in general, and governance, strategic and operational controls, in particular, facilitate the process of defining strategic and operational goals, and monitoring the measurement and reward aspects of performance and compliance of private corporations and public organisations.

This process of business management control ensures:

1 Effective and efficient operation of the organisation.
2 Effective implementation of strategy.
3 Practical measurement and comparison of actual vs. expected results, in relation to predefined strategic and operational targets, risks identified and assessed.
4 Fit-to-purpose solutions, by analysing issues and problems, implementing specific solutions, and carrying out corrective and improvement actions for the achievement of expected business performance and corporate compliance requirements.

Control is one of the managerial functions like planning, organising, staffing and directing. It is an important function, because it helps to check the errors and to take the corrective action, so that deviation from standards is minimised, and stated goals of the organisation are achieved in a desired manner. According to modern concepts, control is a foreseeing action, whereas earlier concepts of control were used only when errors were detected. Control means 'to check, verify, regulate'.[8] Control in management means setting standards, measuring actual performance and taking corrective action.

Business management control in a corporate environment, can be defined as a systematic effort by business management to compare performance to predetermined standards, plans, or objectives, in order to determine whether performance is in line with these standards, and presumably, in order to take any remedial action required to see that human, and other corporate resources, are being used in the most effective and efficient way possible in achieving business goals and specific corporate objectives. Planning is a process by which an organisation's objectives, and the methods to achieve those objectives, are established; and controlling is a process which measures and directs the actual performance against the planned objectives of the organisation. Planning and control are instituted via business management controls.

Business management controls are implemented by managers and control activities, while serving the purposes of primary, support and external parties' activities of business entities (organisations) of the private sector.[9]

The word **manager** comes from 'manage', which means 'to handle' (from Latin *manus* 'hand', from Greek *mane* 'hand'). In today's tough, dynamic, resource-tight and uncertain economy, a company (or organisation) needs

---

[8] From Anglo-French, *contreroller*, 'exert authority', from Middle Latin, *contrarotulus*, 'a counter, register', from Latin, *contra-* 'against' + *rotulus* 'wheel'.
[9] For controls related to public organisations, see: OECD (1996), *Management Control in Modern Government Administration: Some Comparative Practices*, Sigma Papers, No. 4, OECD Publishing, *http://dx.doi.org/10.1787/5kml6gb4gn32-en*.

strong managers to lead its staff towards accomplishing business goals. But managers are not only leaders. They are problem solvers, co-ordinators, communicators, cheerleaders, and planners as well. And managers don't come in one-size-fits-all shapes or forms. Managers fulfil many roles, and have many different responsibilities at each level of management within an organisation.

Organisations abound in today's society. Groups of individuals constantly join forces to accomplish common goals. Sometimes the goals of these organisations are for profit, such as franchise restaurant chains or clothing retailers. Other times, the goals are more altruistic, such as non-profit churches or public schools.

But no matter what their aims, all these organisations share two things in common: they're made up of people, and certain individuals are in charge of these people. These are the managers.

Managers appear in every organisation, because organisations want to succeed. These individuals have the, sometimes unenviable, task of making decisions, solving difficult problems, setting goals, planning strategies, and rallying individuals. And those are just a few of their responsibilities.

To be exact, managers manage themselves, administer and co-ordinate resources effectively and efficiently to achieve the goals of an organisation, manage context, manage relationships, and manage change. In essence, managers get the job done effectively, especially if they manage both themselves and other people very well.

No matter what type of organisation they work in, managers are generally responsible for the performance of a group of people. Contrary to what some management gurus[10] are claiming (i.e. that managers only administer while leaders envision, etc.), practice has shown that effective managers are also good leaders. Thus, as leaders, managers create, inspire, motivate, and encourage their people to reach common organisational goals (at the general level), such as bringing a new product to market in a timely fashion; and also reach specific objectives, such as improve profits by a certain percentage, by the end of a given time period.

To accomplish these general goals and specific objectives, in an organisational setting of efficient provision of products and services to the world, managers:

1 Use their human resources, inputs, methods and systems, to create outputs which can be translated into products and services for customers.
2 Need a control system, control activities, specific business management controls (governance, risk, compliance, strategic, operational) and a business management controls framework, as noted next.

Choosing a business management control system to match the strategy, operations, culture, expectations and structure of an organisation, offers board, and management, a number of important challenges. Board and management must select business management controls that provide a framework to monitor, measure, and evaluate accurately, whether or not it has achieved its business goals and strategic objectives. The usual financial, sales, and production (output) controls, must be backed up with

---

[10] For example, Warren Bennis in his book *On Becoming a Leader*, others as noted in *http://changingminds.org*.

behaviour controls (or soft controls) and organisational culture, to ensure that the organisation is achieving its goals in the most efficient and effective way possible. In general, these controls should reinforce one another, and care must be taken to ensure that they do not result in unforeseen consequences, such as competition amongst functions, divisions, projects, and individuals. Many senior managers point to the difficulty of changing organisational culture when they talk about re-engineering their organisation, so that it can pursue new strategic goals. This difficulty arises because culture is the product of the complex interaction of many factors, such as top management, organisational structure, and the organisation's reward and incentive systems.[11]

Types and role of business management controls in supporting business activities

Business management controls are implemented by control activities, which are actions established by policies, procedures, practices, and other automated or manual means, methods, algorithms and systems. The usual types of controls are: directive controls, preventive controls, detective controls, corrective controls and compensating controls.

---

[11] For more details, see Chapter 12 of *Strategic Management*, Hill, Charles WL and Jones, Gareth R, Houghton Mifflin Company (2002).

Directive controls

The purpose of directive controls is:

1 To inform all participants in the activities of the organisation, how the specific business entity will function in various governance issues.
2 To instruct (direct) company resources and stakeholders, about how to handle a variety of governance and management issues of the organisation.

These controls mainly relate to formulating guidelines, declarative statements for company vision, mission, values, etc, as well as corporate policies and procedures in all business functions (governance, risk, production, finance, IT, etc.). These are crafted, and installed, by top management, to enable, promote and facilitate ethical behaviour, social accountability, effective and efficient corporate performance, and compliance with internal and external regulations.

Preventive controls

Preventive controls attempt to deter, or prevent, undesirable events and acts from occurring. They are proactive controls that help to prevent a loss, errors or omission. Examples of preventive controls are: tone at the top and other human factors, defined as 'soft controls' (understanding of the organisation by the Board, culture, structure of reporting relationships, morale, integrity and ethical values, operational philosophy, trust, ethical climate, empowerment, corporate attitudes, competences, leadership, employee motivation, expectations, openness and shared values, information flow throughout the organisation, and emotional contracting), executing corporate procedures (formulating them is considered a directive control), customer and vendor credit checks, job descriptions, data entry checks, personnel hiring controls, segregation of duties, proper authorisation schemes, adequate documentation, firewalls, security guards, anti-virus software, IPS system, training on security and other management issues, and physical security controls over company assets, like cash, ownership records, back-up computer data files, contracts, patents, business records, works of art, etc.

Detective controls

The purpose of detective controls is to search for, and identify errors, and uncover problems after they have occurred, and to detect undesirable acts. Examples of detective controls are: random checks of compliance, spot-checking of customer account and business transactions, bank account reconciliations, observations of payroll distribution, budget and project variance analyses, periodic physical inventory counts, computer passwords, transaction edits, system monitoring, IDS, IPS, anti-virus, regular supervisory review of activities, and reports, and audits (internal and external).

Corrective controls

Corrective controls are designed to prevent the recurrence of errors. Examples of corrective controls are: coaching, counselling and providing training to staff, backing up and recovering data and systems, correcting data in systems, using quality inspection techniques, taking disciplinary actions, upgrading operating and application software, posting reversing journal entries in accounting systems, correcting procedures, etc.

Compensating controls

Compensating controls are internal controls that are intended to reduce the risk of an existing, or potential, control weakness. Examples of compensating controls are: investigating exceptions, errors, shut-downs, irregularities and discrepancies, reviewing a random or critical sample of transactions, reviewing actions, reports, etc, of all transactions executed by the employee who can perform all key activities of a business transaction, comparing cash and other assets to accounting records and other company-maintained data, reviewing all registers, logs, audit trails, and security incidents, etc.

Business managers must choose the right mix of all these control activities (detective, preventive, etc.), and implement them to suit their corporate environment. But in order to do this, they must analyse their business activities, and decide what role the control activities should play in their unique and specific business operational framework.

Business management is defined as 'The activities associated with running a company, such as controlling, leading, monitoring, organising, and planning', according to Business Dictionary.[12]

Business management is what business managers do. Business managers enable and support their organisations in reaching their targets, making more money, and becoming more beneficial. Businesses make money by delivering some value to their customers that the latter are willing to pay for, either directly as consumers, or indirectly as citizens and taxpayers.

---

[12] For more, see: *www.businessdictionary.com*.

The role of business management controls and related control activities is to provide an integrated set of governance, risk, compliance, strategic and operational controls and performance measures. This also includes compliance indicators to support, and facilitate, the operation of the primary, the support, and the external parties' activities of a business entity, and to enable the prosperity and longevity of an organisation to the benefit of all.

Primary activities are the activities of the organisation that are directly concerned with the creation, provision and delivery of products and services to customers, in alignment with the overall corporate strategy. These primary activities are, in most general cases:

1 **Inbound logistics:**[13] activities concerned with receiving, storing, and distributing the inputs to the products and services offered.

2 **Production operations**: concerned with all those production processes that transform the various inputs into final products and services, such as manufacturing of products, provision of services, assembly, testing, packaging, locating the process, facilities and plant, etc.[14]

3 **Outbound logistics**: concerned with all those activities associated with collecting, storing, and getting finished products and services to customers, or bringing customers to the service.

---

[13] For more, see: *Logistics: An Integrated Approach*, Quayle, Michael and Jones, Bryan, Cambridge Academic (2002).
[14] For more, see: *Operations Management*, Heizer, Jay H, Prentice-Hall (2010).

4 **Marketing**: concerned with those activities that make products and services, and their benefits, known to the customer.

5 **Sales**: those activities associated with selling products and services, according to a pricing strategy, to the customers, at a fixed location, over the Internet, via sales networks, etc.

6 **Maintenance service**: all those activities associated with maintaining and improving the performance of products and services after they have been sold, such as installation, repairs, training, customer support, etc.

Support activities are the activities of the organisation that help to improve the economy, efficiency, and effectiveness of the primary activities of the organisation, in alignment with the overall corporate strategy. These are all the systems, policies and procedures that enable and facilitate the primary activities of the organisation, such as administration, finance, human resource management, planning, IT, quality control, security, purchasing, research and development, and general senior management, etc.

External parties' activities are the activities of the organisation that are directly involved in managing the relations and transactions of the organisation with its external partners, in alignment with the overall corporate strategy, and the primary and support activities of the organisation. These are customer relationships, distributor relationships, vendor relationships, joint venture projects, and outsourcing relationships.

All these organisational activities require controls, in order to be executed in the most effective way. This is the role of business management controls.

Business management controls are usually expressed by the institution, design, and implementation of internal control frameworks, standards, rules, guidelines, policies, procedures, practices, declarative statements, activities, etc, and a set of organisational, strategic and operational controls. All these are usually monitored by performance measures and compliance indicators, with the facilitation of a performance management system and a compliance programme and action plan.

Business management controls are made up of governance, risk, compliance (collectively termed GRC), strategic and operational controls. GRC controls are required as a prerequisite, so that strategic and operational controls achieve their purpose. GRC controls relate to organisational, enterprise or corporate governance, administration, compliance, risk, human resource management, and other overhead functions of organisations, such as legal, purchasing, compliance, data management, business continuity, etc. Strategic controls relate to strategy. Operational controls relate to operational activities like finance, production, IT, etc.

The concept of organisational control is implicit in the bureaucratic theory of Max Weber.[15] Associated with this theory are such concepts as 'span of control', 'closeness of supervision', and 'hierarchical authority'. Weber's view tends to include all levels, or types of organisational control, as being the same. More recently, writers have tended to differentiate the control process between that which emphasises the nature of the organisational or

---

[15] For more, see: *The Protestant Ethic and the 'Spirit' of Capitalism,* Weber, Max, Baehr, Peter R, and Wells, Gordon C, Penguin (2002).

systems design, and that of operations. To illustrate the difference, we 'evaluate' the performance of a system to see how effective and efficient the design proved to be, or to discover why it failed. In contrast, we operate and 'control' the system with respect to the daily inputs of material, information, and energy.

In both instances, the elements of feedback are present, but organisational control tends to review, and evaluate, the nature and arrangement of components in the system, whereas operational control tends to adjust the daily inputs.

The direction for overall organisational control comes from the general strategic goals and strategic plans of the organisation. General strategic plans are translated into specific performance measures, such as share of the market, earnings, return on investment, budgets, customer satisfaction, etc.

The process of organisational and strategic control is to review, and evaluate, the performance of the system against these established norms. Rewards for meeting, or exceeding standards, may range from special recognition, to salary increases or promotions. On the other hand, a failure to meet expectations may signal the need to reorganise (organisational control), change strategic direction, or redesign (strategic control).

Performance measurement of private and public organisations is the basis for the development of a business management control system. The standardised model of the balanced scorecard framework offers management a dynamic tool for the development of such a business management control system. This system measures all the critical dimensions of organisational performance (financial, customers, internal corporate processes, and employee learning and innovation – *see Chapters 10 and 11*).

In contrast to organisational and strategic control, operational control serves to regulate the day-to-day output relative to schedules, specifications and costs, by the formulation of policies, and execution of corresponding procedures (for example, is the output of product or service the proper quality, and is it available as scheduled?).

The purpose of organisational and strategic control is to see that the specified function is achieved. The objective of operational control is to ensure that variations in daily output are maintained within prescribed limits. It is one thing to design a system that contains all of the elements of control, and quite another to make it operate true to the best objectives of design. Operating 'in control' or 'with plan', does not guarantee optimum performance. For example, the plan may not make the best use of the inputs of materials, energy, or information – in other words, the system may not be designed to operate efficiently. Some of the more typical problems relating to control, include the difficulty of measurement, the problem of timing information flow, and the setting of proper standards.

Operational control systems are designed to ensure that day-to-day actions are consistent with established plans and objectives. It focuses on events in a recent period. Operational control systems are derived from the requirements of the business management control system.

Corrective action is taken where performance does not meet standards. This action may involve training, motivation, leadership, discipline, or termination. The differences between strategic and operational control are highlighted by reference to a set of main fundamental differences between strategic and operational management, as depicted next. Strategic management is very ambiguous, most complex, organisation-wide, most critical to long-term survival, and has long-term implications. Operational management, on the contrary, is less ambiguous, less complex, specific to functions, less critical to long-term survival, and has short-term implications.

These business management controls, as practice has shown, require an overall internal controls framework, so that they can function in the most optimal way.

Proposed business management controls framework

Internal control, according to the latest COSO draft guidance document,[16] 'is a process, effected by an entity's board of directors, management and other personnel, designed to provide reasonable assurance regarding the achievement of objectives in the following categories: effectiveness and efficiency of operations, reliability of reporting, and compliance with applicable laws and regulations'.

Business management controls and their performance measures follow this approach. These may be designed and implemented by models, such as the BSC, discussed in this book (*see Chapters 10 and 11*). Compliance measures may be designed and implemented by internal control frameworks, such as COSO Framework (*www.coso.org*), The Sarbanes-Oxley Act (*www.soxlaw.com*), COBIT® (*www.isaca.org*) and BIS Framework (*www.bis.org*), briefly described next, but not the main subject of this

---

[16] See: *www.ic.coso.org*.

book, and monitored by the Corporate Governance, Risk and Compliance (CGRC) System, discussed in *Chapter 3*.

COSO is the internal control framework developed by the Committee of Sponsoring Organisations of the Treadway Commission. COSO was created in 1985, to sponsor the National Commission of Fraudulent Financial Reporting (or the 'Treadway Commission'), in order to explore issues in fraudulent financial reporting.

The Sarbanes-Oxley Act (SOX) is a US law that requires the chief executive and chief financial officers of public companies to attest to the accuracy of financial reports (Section 302), and requires public companies to establish adequate internal controls over financial reporting (Section 404). Passage of SOX resulted in an increased focus on IT controls, as these support financial processing, and therefore fall into the scope of management's assessment of internal control, under Section 404 of SOX.

COBIT® focuses primarily on efficiently and effectively monitoring information systems. The framework emphasises the role and impact of IT control, as it relates to business processes. This control model can be used by management to develop clear policy and good practice for control of IT. The BIS framework for internal controls for banks, is used mainly by banks, and was developed by the Bank for International Settlements (BIS).

On the basis of COSO and other internal control frameworks, management, with the possible assistance and support of external experts, must, for efficiency and effectiveness reasons of the organisation, craft, and implement, a business management controls framework, according to the goals, demands, objectives, needs, external regulations and expectations of all stakeholders of the organisation, and taking into consideration the thoughts and activities of all participants in its affairs and operations.

Such an internal controls framework, made up of control processes at five levels of business operation, interconnected and integrated to function as a whole, is proposed[17] in *Figure 1*.

Figure 1: Business management controls (BMC) framework

Level of business operation	Examples of business management control processes
First level (Organise)	Set up: 1. Board, management and committee roles, structure and responsibilities. 2. Business functions and resources. 3. Standards, policies and procedures, 4. Internal controls framework and manual.
Second level (Envision)	Institute: 1. Corporate culture, vision, mission and values. 2. Strategy, goals,

[17] The business management controls framework is considered the first control, for the purposes of this book, and it is termed BMCF Control 1: Business Management Control. 1. All other controls described in this book will also follow a similar numbering method.

	objectives and targets. 3. Performance framework and management. .
Third level (Govern)	Implement: 1. Strategy. 2. GRC (governance, risk and compliance) controls. 3. Operational controls (purchasing, finance, IT, data, security, fraud, etc.). 4. Personnel administration, including segregation of duties, compensating controls, etc. **5.** Management and compliance reporting.
Fourth level (Audit)	Carry out: 1. Monitoring controls. 2. Internal audits. 3. Self-assessments. 4. External audits. 5. Regulatory audits.
Fifth level (Augment)	Compare organisation to external entities: 1. Studies by external

	experts.
	2. Certify personnel.
	3. Certify organisational components (structure, service quality, policies and procedures).
	4. Corporate social responsibility, including community involvement, etc.
	5. Soft controls.

The business management controls framework (BMCF Control 1) will be complemented by a business management controls system manual (BMCF Control 2).

Business management controls system manual (BMCF Control 2)

The contents of this manual, as an example, will include:

1 Purpose and objectives
2 Scope and applicability of internal controls
3 Management and staff responsibility
4 Details of business management controls.

The detailed control activities, and associated control procedures, are documented in the specific, corporate policies and procedures manuals, and related control practices of all departments of the organisations.

The business management controls framework, and the control activities that enable its full operation, are usually complemented by a set of performance measures and compliance indicators, which are monitored by management, to ensure the good effect of all these controls.

Performance measures and compliance indicators

The role of performance measures and compliance indicators is to support, and enable, the easy monitoring and reviewing of all types (financial, production, etc.) of business management controls functioning in a given organisation.

A performance measure is a description of what is measured, to determine the extent to which objectives and outcomes have been achieved, and to what level. Some examples of performance measures are stock market price, return on investment, return on assets, number of coding errors found during formal testing, number of test case errors, number of changes to customer requirements, etc. Performance measures can also be used in risk management, as in many cases a company may be able to track the status of a risk using existing key performance indicators (KPIs); for example, an organisation's voluntary attrition rate, often monitored by HR as part of its talent management responsibilities, may do double duty as a key risk indicator for talent risk.[18] The use of key risk indicators is one of the BIS recommendations for sound operational risk management, and thus an essential component of the Basel II framework.[19]

---

[18] See also *www.isaca.org* for more information on the concept of key risk indicators.
[19] See *www.bis.org* and The Sarbanes-Oxley Act (*www.sox-online.com/basics.html*).

A compliance indicator denotes:[20]

1 Whether plans, policies, procedures, etc, exist, or not.
2 Whether these are followed, or not.
3 Whether the organisation complies, or not, to the specific state laws, industry standards and ethics codes, such as SOX Act, data privacy laws, banking regulations, ISO standards, etc. Some examples are corporate security policy not crafted, IT security policy not formulated, etc.

Conclusion

In order for business entities to be beneficial and effective to society, its shareholders and stakeholders, and survive in the long-term, they must improve, if not excel, as regards their market share, competitiveness, financial results, use of capital and other resources, productivity, customer satisfaction, quality, innovation and ethics, amongst other things. They usually achieve these by managing and controlling, using a set of business management controls in the most optimal way, all the primary (logistics, production, sales, marketing, etc.), support (administration, finance, human resource management, IT, quality control, security, purchasing, etc.), and external parties' activities (customer relationships, distributor relationships, vendors, etc.) of the organisation. The controls identified in this chapter (business management controls framework (BMCF Control 1) and business management controls system manual (BMCF Control 2)) are considered to be part of the first

---

[20] For more on compliance, see: *Compliance Management for Public, Private, or Non-Profit Organisations*, Silverman, Michael G, McGraw-Hill (2008).

level (organise level) of business operation of the BMC framework (*see Figure 1: Business management controls framework*) that can be deployed to protect organisations against fraud, asset abuse, reputational damage, and other risks they may be faced with, while enabling them to reach, and improve, their performance and compliance objectives and targets.

In closing, management must decide, on the basis of a study, and given the particulars of their organisation and its operating environment, which framework, controls, risk assessment and performance management model (business model) they should use for their organisation.

A general business operating model, conceptualised as 'C^1P^4 Model (C one, four Ps)', and applicable to all types of companies (small, medium and large), will have five dimensions: C^1P^4 Model (C one, four Ps), 'C^1' for customers, 'P^1' for people, 'P^2' for property, 'P^3' for production and 'P^4' for performance, as noted in *Table 1*.

Table 1.1: General business operating model

Business model dimension	Description
C^1: CUSTOMERS	All activities related to identifying, selling, and delivering products and services, and in managing and servicing your customers.
P^1: PERSONNEL	All activities related to hiring, utilising, managing and handling your employees.
P^2: PROPERTY	All activities related to managing and protecting your assets (money, other financial assets, buildings, plants, machinery, furniture, computers, information systems, knowledge repositories, patents, etc.).
P^3: PRODUCTION	All activities related to producing (your own) or distributing (from others) high-quality products, and optimising your production processes, including, as needed, the provision of effective services to customers and the market.
P^4: PERFORMANCE	All activities related to measuring, monitoring, and improving the performance of your company.

It is your role, and your duty as a manager, leader or board director, to establish, and operate, an internal controls framework for your business entity.

BMC framework recommendation

Recommendation 1: Create and implement a controls framework to satisfy your needs

The key points to consider in assessing this recommendation for your business environment are:

1 Managing a business, small, medium or large, is quite a difficult and strenuous task.

2 Senior executive management must understand corporate management, compliance, strategic and operational controls, and their manifestations and impact, and employ the right internal control framework, and its components, to suit the specific aspects of the organisation they manage.

3 As a minimum control, you may use the example of the internal controls framework and manual depicted in this chapter (business management controls framework (BMCF Control 1) and business management controls system manual (BMCF Control 2)) and change, improve, amend, craft, and implement your own, to suit your needs, company size, compliance requirements, and business operating environment and culture.

4 At the level of each business function (finance, IT, sales, production, etc.) you will need specific controls to implement the proposed BMC framework, as defined in each chapter in part B (main types of strategic and operational controls), such as:
   a.   Management responsibility controls.
   b.   Standards, codes, policies and procedures.

c.   Business transaction and information processing systems (manual or computerised).

d.   Business performance measures and compliance indicators.

All of these will be coupled by

a.   Governance, risk and compliance controls (*see Chapters 2 and 3*).

b.   Business records filing systems (*see Chapter 8*).

c.   Implementing business management controls (four chapters in Part C).

d.   Enhancing business operations controls (three chapters in Part D).

CHAPTER 2: ENTERPRISE GOVERNANCE CONTROLS

'Nothing is more active than thought, for it travels over the universe, and nothing is stronger than necessity, for all must submit to it.'

Thales, Ancient Greek Philosopher (624–546 BC)

Chapter overview: This chapter, the second chapter of Part A: Establishing the Internal Controls Environment, deals with enterprise governance controls which provide the necessary support for your risk, compliance, strategic and operational controls to function properly. Also, several governance controls (such as regulatory, philosophy, corporate policies and procedures, etc.) are noted, and a recommendation (Recommendation 2: Establish enough and current governance policies and procedures to satisfy your needs.) is offered for your consideration.

Introduction

'The only man I know who behaves sensibly is my tailor; he takes my measurements anew each time he sees me. The rest go on with their old measurements and expect me to fit them,' is a famous quote by George Bernard Shaw.

This provides the inspiration for managers to be on top of things:

1 To establish the governance, administration, strategic, operational and compliance mechanisms and controls, so

that they can drive strategic and operational performance for better results.

2 To measure properly, with specific types of compliance and performance measures, at each business function level, to ensure that targets are met, if not surpassed.

3 To ensure that rules and regulations are complied with, so that they make their organisations more effective, and more beneficial to society.

Enterprise governance controls are discussed in this chapter. Risk and compliance controls are discussed in the next chapter. Strategic, operational, and other controls, are described in other chapters.

Purpose and types of enterprise governance (EG) controls

The purpose of enterprise governance controls is to provide an integrated set of governance, administration, human resource, and compliance and performance controls and measures, to support, and facilitate, the operation of the primary (inbound logistics, production operations, etc.), the support (administration, finance, etc.), and the external parties' (vendors, distributors, etc.) activities of the organisation, and enable the prosperity and longevity of the organisation. EG controls are usually expressed by the institution, design and implementation of frameworks, standards, rules, guidelines, policies, procedures, practices, declarative statements, activities, etc, and are monitored by performance measures, and by compliance indicators, with the facilitation of a performance management system, and a compliance programme and action plan.

Enterprise governance controls and performance management and reporting controls, are required as a prerequisite, so that strategic and operational controls achieve their purpose. Enterprise governance controls relate to corporate governance, administration, human resource management, and other overhead functions of organisations (e.g. risk, legal, purchasing, etc.). Performance management and reporting controls relate to performance issues. Strategic controls relate to strategy. Operational controls relate to operational activities, such as finance, production, IT, etc. The usual types of enterprise governance controls, and their performance measures, are described next. Strategic and operational controls are presented in other chapters.

Enterprise governance controls

Enterprise governance sets limits and boundaries. The objective of enterprise governance controls is to set boundaries on various investment and business alternatives by board directors, managers and staff of the organisation, and to establish limits on acceptable behaviour for both organisations and their stakeholders (board members, management, staff, shareholders, regulators, authorities, customers, citizens, auditors, etc.[21]). Organisations are established and run by people with the support aspects, review activities and facilitation tools of various internal and external mechanisms, such as corporate governance, internal controls, internal auditing, external auditing, regulatory authorities, etc.

---

[21] See also: *International Good Practice Guidance, Evaluating and Improving Governance in Organisations*, February 2009, issued by: *www.ifac.org*.

In terms of enterprise governance, the most critical mechanisms for internal control are:

1 Board and executive management controls, regulatory controls, corporate philosophy controls, organisational controls and administration controls; discussed in this chapter.
2 Segregation of duties and functions; discussed in this chapter.
3 Board of Directors, auditing and remuneration policy; detailed in *Chapter 12.*

Board and executive management controls

Specific organisations are usually established in a given socio-economic environment and sovereign state framework, by shareholders, stakeholders, governments, larger corporate enterprises, and communities, etc. to serve specific goals and objectives. These are managed, controlled, and run by boards and executive management, by using corporate governance mechanisms and internal control, such as the Board of Directors, auditing, segregation of duties and functions, remuneration, managers, committees, compliance, etc, as described in more detail in *Chapter 12* (Roles and Responsibilities of Participants in Business Management Controls).

These relate to: the Board of Directors (EGOV Control 1), audit committee (EGOV Control 2), managers (EGOV Control 3), personnel benefits committee (EGOV Control 4), operating Staff (EGOV Control 5), internal auditors (EGOV Control 6), external auditors (EGOV Control 7), data privacy officer (EGOV Control 8), advisory and regulatory third parties (EGOV Control 9) and stakeholders (EGOV Control 10).

Only the role, and the performance measurement aspects of both the Boards and executive management, are described in this chapter, in order to give you, the reader, a good idea of how boards and management should (or may) manage things better.

Role of the Board of Directors: The Board of Directors (EGOV Control 1.1) for private companies, or senior executive committee for non-profit and public organisations, is usually responsible for oversight of the specific company or organisation, as well as the development, and approval, of all business policies and strategies. This includes maintaining an effective executive management team to manage the organisation, its operations and people. The Board must ultimately hold executive management accountable for execution of all plans and activities.

The goals of your board should include understanding, measuring, and improving the performance of the senior management team, and ensuring the long-term survival of your specific organisation in the most optimal way. When your company performance needs to improve, your board should take all actions to motivate and drive senior management to reach the expected results more effectively. Where senior management fails to improve, or does not perform according to the expectations of the Board, the Board should be capable of terminating and/or replacing top executive management, as necessary.

Role of executive management: Management in all business activities and operations, and for all types of enterprises (private, non-profit, public, etc.), is the act of getting people together, and directing them to accomplish desired long-term strategic goals, and time-specific strategic and operational objectives of the organisation they manage, using available resources, efficiently and effectively. The role of executive management (EGOV Control 2.1) includes establishing, planning, organising, leading, managing, staffing, reviewing, and controlling a complete organisation, or one or more of its functional parts, and its resources (human, financial, technological, natural, research, data, etc.), or a process, or a project, or a set of activities or operations, etc, for the sole purpose of accomplishing a predetermined business goal.[22]

To manage the current affairs of the organisation, and ensure its long-term survival, both boards and executive management, must measure, and monitor, the performance of the organisation, as regards the issues of:

1 Market share and competitiveness.
2 Financial results (profitability, waste, etc.).
3 Use of capital and other resources (environment, information, data, patents, etc.).
4 Productivity, customer satisfaction, quality, innovation, and ethics (executive management values, employee morale, social responsibility, company reputation, etc.).
5 Benefits to economy, society and local community.

The achievement of the performance of organisations by boards and executive management, can be measured by:

1 Completing evaluation forms, surveys and questionnaires.

---

[22] For more, see: *Management*, Drucker, Peter, HarperCollins USA (2008) and *Management*, Daft, Richard L, South-Western USA (2010).

2 Collecting comments from colleagues and outside experts.
3 Tracking performance on company goals.
4 Monitoring the completion, and timeliness, of regulatory directives.
5 Attending board meetings.
6 Taking director training programmes.
7 Maintaining a favourable relationship with regulatory authorities.
8 Establishing, and achieving, business development goals.
9 Avoiding conflicts of interest.

Specific examples of such measures are included later in this section.[23]

Regulatory controls

Your usual regulatory controls (EGOV Control 11) include:

1 Setting up, from a legal perspective, your business entity, according to the laws, tax, customs, and other codes and statutes of the national state in which your specific business entity will operate and do business.
2 Implementing a set of procedures to manage the various legal organisational issues, such as corporate minutes, book administration, issuing stock, registering with the various authorities, setting up the organisation, obtaining licences to operate, obtaining tax and customs codes, reviewing agreements, representing the organisation in courts, etc.

---

[23] See also my blog: *http://businessmanagementcontrols.blogspot.com/*.

3 Establishing, and implementing, management roles, a management structure, and a board structure for managing the affairs of your company.
4 Implementing policies to align with the legal and religious systems, the regulatory frameworks, and various international and national regulations and guidelines that affect the operating environment of your company.

Management philosophy and operating style controls

The typical philosophy controls (EGOV Control 12) of organisations include:

1 The vision, mission, and value statements, crafted and communicated to all stakeholders of the organisation.
2 The development and implementation of a corporate social responsibility policy.
3 The development and implementation of a corporate ethics set of practices, made up of an ethics policy (*see Chapter 3*), an ethics office, an ethics committee, an ethics officer, and an ethics programme for the organisation.

Establishing your own philosophy controls will motivate your people, and drive your whole company to perform better.

Organisational controls

The usual organisational controls (EGOV Control 13) of organisations[24] include:

1 The development and implementation of charters for the Board of Directors, and the various corporate committees (for audit, risk, benefits and personnel, information technology, financial issues, and business continuity, etc.).

2 The development and implementation of corporate policies (for financial accounting, customer relations, fraud and theft, community relations, health and safety and environment management, for performance management, internal audit, risk management, business continuity, compliance, etc.).

You need organisational controls regardless of the type and size of your company. Establishing them, will enable all your business functions to run more efficiently.

Corporate administration controls

You also need corporate administration controls, regardless of the type and size of your company, to run your business operations. Corporate administration controls[25] (EGOV Control 17) are the non-financial, non-information technology and non-production controls, that usually encompass the following activities of the organisation: human, marketing, sales, customer support, forms and

---

[24] For more, see: *Organisation Theory and Design*, Daft, Richard et al, South-Western (2010).
[25] For more, see: *The Design and Implementation of Administrative Controls: A Guide for Financial Executives*, Fertakis, John P, Quorum Books (1989).

records management, etc. These are concerned with the development of procedures for operational efficiency, and with adherence to organisational policies.

Administration controls include (as an example): departmental terms of reference, corporate policies and procedures manual, files, documents and records management procedures, confidential information release procedures, management reporting procedures, asset protection procedures, legal procedures (for the operation of the organisation as a legal entity), administrative office controls, physical security controls, mail controls, EDI controls, facsimile transmission controls, daily activities controls, forms register, etc.

The most critical administration controls, within the scope of this book, are:

1 HRM controls and corporate policies and procedures manual, described in this section.
2 Files, documents and records management procedures (*see Chapter 8*).
3 Confidential information release procedures
4 Management reporting procedures (described later).
5 Asset protection procedures (described in operational controls chapter).
6 Legal procedures (see regulatory controls paragraph).

Human resource management (HRM) controls

The purpose of human resource management controls (EGOV Control 14) is not to specify the goals, but to standardise the way of reaching them. Rules standardise behaviour and make outcomes predictable. These are instituted by managers after the organisation structure is established.

Examples of human resource management controls are: human rights policy, benefits and personnel committee, personnel administration procedures (described later), job descriptions, employee management policies and procedures handbook, HR hiring and dismissal system, HR planning system, HR performance management system, benefits and incentives system, HR computerised information system, soft controls (described in *Chapter 6*) and personnel management controls.

As a minimum level of control in this area, each organisation should craft, and implement, personnel administration procedures.

Personnel administration procedures

In addition to whatever general administration controls are exercised at the level of the organisation, the additional management controls for all personnel (EGOV Control 15) should include (as an example):

1 Screening of personnel during the hiring process.
2 Valid employment contracts and job descriptions.
3 Appropriate supervision by management.
4 Skills planning.
5 Authorisation controls (a set of defined levels of authorisation for purchases, expenses, invoices, payments, contracts, investments, hiring and firing of personnel, transaction processing, file and records management activities, archiving of critical records, reports, and data, etc.).

6 Segregation of personnel duties (described in this chapter).
7 Rotation of duties.
8 Vacation taking.
9 Adoption of ethical standards.
10 Employee documentation (job application, job description, resume, records of participation in training events, salary history, records of disciplinary action, and documents related to employee performance reviews, coaching, and mentoring).
11 Health and safety procedures.
12 Employee performance review.
13 Ethics and compliance procedures.

Segregation of duties and functions

Segregating (also called separating) duties (SEGD Control 1) is a very critical, corporate governance mechanism. It involves assigning specific responsibilities for certain key duties between board members, directors, managers and other individuals, so that each individual's responsibility is well within the moral and operating bounds of both the organisation and society, and not conflicting with, but contributing to, the organisation's goals and objectives. This mechanism can also separate the number of functions, or processes, that one division, or department, completes within an organisation. Creating well-defined roles also keeps the organisation flexible, ensuring that operational changes, or new hires, can be made without interrupting current operations. In the current business environment, segregation of duties (SOD) is a fundamental and crucial element of internal control in modern enterprises and organisations. It is also one of the most effective internal controls in deterring, preventing, combating and minimising errors, resource abuse, and potential employee fraud.[26] Segregation of duties and functions contributes to an organisation's system of checks and balances. In segregating functions, one manager should not be responsible at the everyday operational level, for both IT and finance, or for both IT and HR, or for both administration and IT, etc, as it is the case, from practical experience in many small and medium-size companies and organisations. In segregating duties, no employee should be responsible for two or more of the following five activities, in each business process, noted below. The term SOD is already well known in financial accounting systems. Companies of all sizes understand not to combine roles, such as receiving cheques (payment on account) and approving write-offs; depositing cash and reconciling bank statements; approving time cards and having custody of pay cheques, etc.[27] SOD is fairly new to the IT department, and a high portion of Sarbanes-Oxley internal control issues come from IT (for more, see: *www.soxtoolkit.com/index.htm*). In information systems, the segregation of duties helps to reduce the potential damage from the actions of one person. Your IT or end-user department (e.g. finance, etc.) should be organised in a way that achieves adequate separation of duties. According to ISACA's segregation of duties control matrix,[28] some duties should not be combined into one position. This

---

[26] For more, see: *Principles of Fraud Examination*, Wells, Joseph T, John Wiley and Sons (2010).
[27] For more, see: *Accounting Information Systems and Internal Control*, Vaassen, Eddy et al, John Wiley and Sons (2009).
[28] For more, see: *CISA Review Manual 2008*, Chapter 2, page 112, *www.isaca.org/cisabooks*.

matrix is not an industry standard, just a general guideline suggesting which positions should be separated, and which require compensating controls when combined.

To maintain proper SOD, no employee should be responsible for two or more of the following five activities in each business process:

1 **Record keeping**: Creating and maintaining your company's departmental records, including updating manual files, computerised information systems files and corporate-wide databases, preparing source documents, software code, performance reports, invoices, etc.

2 **Authorisation**: Reviewing and approving your company's transactions (payments, purchase orders, invoices, etc.).

3 **Asset custody**: Managing, accessing and controlling your company's physical assets, including implementing software changes to application systems and production data, managing back-up copies of application data, corporate application and other software, handling patents and other research findings and results, etc.

4 **Reconciliation**: Executing business transaction assurance processes to confirm that your business operations, transactions and activities are proper (valid, accurately reported, in compliance with rules and regulations, and in accordance with the company's goals and objectives), or in balance, including bank reconciliation, financial, and other corporate performance reporting.

5 **Managerial review**: Providing assurance that controls are in place, and operating as designed; that appropriate individuals are authorised, and actually verify transactions, and that high-level reviews for unusual or unreasonable activity are carried out.

Segregation of duties may be designed and implemented by various methods and approaches, and an action plan (as the one noted in *Chapter 15*). When, depending on your company's size and location, duties or business functions cannot be segregated, due to various reasons (e.g. resource availability problems, resource job constraints, etc.), compensating controls should be considered.

Compensating controls are internal controls that are intended to reduce the risk of an existing, or potential, control weakness. If a single person in your company can carry out and conceal errors, and/or irregularities, in the course of performing their day-to-day business activities, they have been assigned SOD incompatible duties. Compensating controls can be preventative, detective, or monitoring controls that are executed by independent, management-level employees, who do not have custody, record keeping, authorisation, or reconciliation responsibilities for the specific business process. Examples of SOD controls and various types of compensating controls that can be implemented by an independent, management-level employee, to address not having adequate segregation of duties in a business function, process or department, of your company, are described in *Chapter 15*.

Corporate policies and procedures manual

All these enterprise governance policies and controls, require, in the daily activities of your company, a set of specific policies and procedures (Corporate Policies and Procedures Manual: EGOV Control 16) to be established and executed, so that the staff of your company know what to do in each standard case, and also how to handle specific abnormalities, depending on the issue they have to manage and resolve. Also, how to manage risks, prepare and issue corporate performance reports (in accordance to internal and external standards, etc.).

These enterprise governance procedures may be developed by the functional corporate committees (audit, finance, IT, etc.) and ratified by the Board of the company, before they are put into operational status. Procedures are normally documented in detailed corporate procedures manuals.

Your corporate policies and procedures manual (EGOV Control 16) would usually contain policies, rules, and procedures, for the following core issues of your business entity (i.e. issues that apply on a universal basis to all private and public entities): corporate administration, human resources, regulations, finance, risk, asset management and protection, and performance management.

Other similar controls (described in *Chapter 6*) that complement a corporate policies and procedures manual are:

1 Business operational manuals (EGOV Control 16.1).
2 Business forms manuals (EGOV Control 16.2).
3 Business raw data retention procedure (EGOV Control 16.3).
4 Business records system (EGOV Control 16.4).
5 Compliance records system (COMP Control 6).

The design, writing and implementation of these procedures, should be controlled by a central administration function, such as policies, procedures and forms department (EGOV Control 16.1). These procedures should be based on a set of national and international[29] government standards and guidelines, such as Health Insurance Regulations, Age Discrimination Guidelines in Employment, Disabilities Act, Civil Rights Act, Employee Retirement Income Security Act, Labour Standards Act, Family and Medical Leave Act, Immigration Reform and Control Act, Occupational Safety and Health Act, Rehabilitation Act, Data Privacy Legal Framework, Tax and Pension Records Retention Requirements, Tax and Customs Code, etc.

Enterprise performance management and reporting controls

Governance, risk, compliance, strategic and operational performance measures, via the performance management system, monitor the implementation and effectiveness of an organisation's strategies (overall business, as well as functional, such as sales, production, IT, etc.); determine the gap between actual and targeted performance; and determine organisation effectiveness, quality of products and services, and operational efficiency.

Performance management may be deemed as:

1 The calculation of achievement, used to measure and manage quality of products and services.
2 The level of attainment of an objective, in comparison to a given effort.
3 The act of measuring, or the process of being measured.

---

[29] Such as: UN, UN Global Compact: *www.unglobalcompact.org*, EU, OECD, etc.

Performance management and reporting controls include the following.

Performance management system

The performance management system (EPMR Control 1) is established by the performance management process.[30] This includes:

1 Formulating, and setting up, the performance measurement system (e.g. BSC at the corporate level), and other complementary quality systems (more about these in *Chapters 10 and 11*).
2 Entering the performance data into your BSC, and other performance systems.
3 Carrying out the required performance analyses, including relating actual performance statistics to strategic and operational targets, conducting benchmarks, and comparing your company's performance to other competitors, etc; linking these to the GRC information system outcomes which measure your performance in terms of governance, risk and compliance (description below).
4 Developing, and deploying, a business dashboard system (EPMR Control 2),[31] so that you can have instant visual and reporting information of all your performance data, by all your scorecard (e.g. BSC), GRC, quality and compliance systems

---

[30] For more on performance management, see: *Harvard Business Essentials: Performance Management: Measure and Improve the Effectiveness of Your Employees*, Luecke, Richard, Harvard Business School Press (2006).
[31] For more information and examples, see: *Dashboard Demystified: What is a Dashboard?*, Hetherington, Victoria (2009) and *http://dashboardspy.com/*.

5 Setting up a corporate rewards system (EPMR Control 3).

A good performance system must communicate strategy, must measure performance in real time, must offer an integrated performance project management capability, and must acknowledge, and enable, emotional contracting with all your staff, which is so vital for linking individual commitment and activity to the attainment of your company's plans and goals.

Business management reporting procedure

This procedure (EPMR Control 4) is needed to manage the data collection, analysis, production and distribution of management reports of the organisation, such as weekly financial reports, cash flow reports, budget vs. actual reports, departmental performance reports, interim financial statements, payroll, personnel issues, safety and health issues, production issues, customer problems, security incidents, compliance issues, etc. These procedures should be based on a set of national and international[32] government standards and guidelines, such as financial accounting reporting standards, auditing standards, employment, health and pension laws, insurance regulations, tax and customs code, corporate performance management system, board executive guidelines, etc. The specific forms and reports that must be designed, and used, by each organisation, to execute these procedures, may be standard financial statements, standard cash flow reports, standard budget reports, standard performance reports, etc.

---

[32] Such as: UN, EU, OECD, *www.ifrs.com*, *www.fasb.org*, *www.xbrl.org*, etc.

2: Enterprise Governance Controls

Enterprise governance performance measures and compliance indicators

Performance measures and compliance indicators (EPMR Control 5), to complement all these enterprise governance controls, are noted next. **Enterprise governance performance measures (EPMR Control 5.1)**: the percentage of board members with a finance background, amount of training budget for board members per year, increased percentage of the market, and the number of reviews of strategic plan.

Enterprise governance compliance indicators (EPMR Control 5.2): departmental terms of references exist (or not), administrative procedures exist (or not), management reporting procedures exist (or not), and internal audit function (exists or not).

Performance measures and compliance indicators related to enterprise governance, risk and compliance controls, may be monitored via the internal process and innovation, and the learning perspectives of BSC (*see Chapters 10 and 11*), as well as by the use of the GRC information system, as discussed in *Chapter 3*.

Conclusion

In closing, enterprise governance controls are controls that enable, facilitate, and drive strategy. Enterprise governance controls also enable, and facilitate, the operation of the other controls. Strategic controls execute, and monitor, strategy. Operational controls are controls that monitor the operational performance of all business functions, at a very detailed and practical level. These are supported by compliance and performance measures accordingly, which are monitored by the management of the organisation, for the purposes of improvement, and provision, of better products and services to customers. All of these enterprise governance controls, and compliance and performance measures, may be designed and implemented by the BSC model, as discussed in this book, and by internal control frameworks, such as COSO framework, The Sarbanes-Oxley Act, and BIS framework, etc. These corporate governance rules, policies and procedures, are accompanied by potential pitfalls that must be managed if the organisation is to avoid strategic problems. Top management must be careful to monitor and evaluate the usefulness of these controls over time. Rules, policies and procedures, constrain your people, and lead to standardised, predictable behaviour. However, rules, policies and procedures, are always easier to establish than to get rid of, and over time, the number of rules an organisation uses, tends to increase. As new developments lead to additional rules, often the old rules are not discarded, and the company becomes overly bureaucratised.[33] Also, all enterprise governance activities should be monitored by an enterprise governance monitoring action plan (*see Chapter 11 for details*).

Relating enterprise governance controls to the BMC framework

The enterprise governance controls identified in this chapter that can be deployed to enable the function of other controls, and to protect your company against fraud, asset abuse, reputational damage and other risks they may be

---

[33] For more information see: *www.icgn.org* and *www.corpgov.deloitte.com*.

faced with, while improving its performance and compliance objectives and targets, are considered to be part of various levels of business operational controls of the BMC framework (*see Figure 1: Business Management Controls Framework, Chapter 1*).

1 **First level (Organise level) of business operation**: Enterprise governance controls (EGOV Controls 1 to 5, 8 to 11, 13 and 16).

2 **Second level (Envision level) of business operation**: Enterprise performance management and reporting controls (EPMR Controls 1 to 3), EGRC performance measures (EGRP Control 1.1 and 1.2) and management philosophy and operating style controls (EGOV Control 12).

3 **Third level (Govern level) of business operation**: Business operational manuals (EGOV Control 16.1), business forms manuals (EGOV Control 16.2), business raw data retention procedure (EGOV Control 16.3), business records system (EGOV Control 16.4) and administration controls (EGOV Control 17), segregation of duties and functions (SEGD Control 1), human resource management (HRM) controls (EGOV Control 14) and personnel administration procedures (EGOV Control 15).

4 **Fourth level (Audit) of business operation**: Internal auditors (EGOV Control 6) and external auditors (EGOV Control 7).

Enterprise governance controls recommendation

Recommendation 2: Establish enough, and current, governance policies and procedures to satisfy your needs

The key points to consider in assessing this recommendation for your business environment are:

1 The design and implementation of enterprise governance controls, and corresponding compliance and performance measures with the balanced scorecard (BSC) framework, and other performance and compliance management systems (e.g. GRC information system), requires thinking, planning, discipline, and full analysis of your requirements.

2 Extraordinarily, many policies and procedures may make your company too bureaucratic and inflexible, especially if these are not accessible online, and are not reviewed and improved periodically.

CHAPTER 3: RISK AND COMPLIANCE CONTROLS

'Often the difference between a successful person and a failure is not one has better abilities or ideas, but the courage that one has to bet on one's ideas, to take a calculated risk – and to act.'

André Malraux, French Historian, Novelist and Statesman (1901–1976)

Chapter overview: This chapter, the third chapter of Part A: Establishing the Internal Controls Environment, deals with risk and compliance controls which make your company more resilient to risks and potential compliance breaches. Also, several risk and compliance controls are noted, and two recommendations (Recommendation 3: Establish strong and effective risk and compliance controls and Recommendation 4: Acquire and deploy a GRC information system and a dashboard) are offered for your consideration.

Introduction

'It's a major milestone. The settlement puts new responsibilities on Microsoft® and we accept them. I am personally committed to full compliance. We are committed to being a responsible industry leader,' is a famous quote by Bill Gates, the American founder of Microsoft®. Both of these quotes provide the motivation for managers to manage the potential risks facing their company, and to be compliant with all rules and regulations affecting their business operations.

You can manage your risks, and be compliant with rules and regulations, by using the risk and compliance controls discussed in this chapter.

Purpose and types of risk and compliance controls

The purpose of risk and compliance controls is to provide an integrated set of specific controls and performance measures and compliance indicators, to support and facilitate the operation of the primary (inbound logistics, production operations, etc.), the support (administration, finance, etc.) and the external parties' (vendors, distributors, etc.) activities of the organisation, and enable the prosperity and longevity of your company.

The usual types of risk controls for any type or size of company, include: risk management action plan, risk register, chief risk officer, risk evaluation methodology and risk response plan. The typical compliance controls, such as compliance programme, compliance action plan, corporate compliance officer, business ethics policy, compliance records system, and governance, risk and compliance (GRC) information system, are described in the next section of this chapter.

Enterprise risk controls

Uncertainty within a business, firm, or functional unit, is a fact of life. The major risks to any organisational entity pertain to the following (as an example): incorrect management monitoring and reporting, operational problems, statutory breaches, loss of income, misuse of resources, bad debts, business interruption, threats and other attacks, inferior quality of goods or end products and services delivered, and incorrect information resulting in wrong services.

For firms and functional units to be more successful in carrying out business activities, they must manage risks most effectively,[34] by specific risk controls, such as:

The risk management action plan

You manage your company risks by a risk management action plan. This plan (RISK Control 1) defines the process of risk management[35] and usually consists of several steps, as follows.

Step 1: Establishing the context. Establishing the context involves:

1 Identification of risk in a selected domain of interest.
2 Planning the remainder of the process.
3 Mapping out the social scope of risk management, the identity and objectives of stakeholders, and the basis upon which risks will be evaluated.
4 Defining a framework for the activity, and an agenda for identification.
5 Developing an analysis of risks involved in the process.
6 Mitigation of risks using available technological, human and organisational resources.

---

[34] See also: ISO Risk Standard, *ISO 31000:2009, Risk management – Principles and guidelines*, available at: www.iso.org and *Risk Governance, Towards an Integrative Approach*, 2006, International Risk Governance Council: www.irgc.org.
[35] See also: ISO/DIS 31000 'Risk management – Principles and guidelines on implementation', www.iso.org/.

Step 2: Create a risk-management plan. The risk-management plan should document the appropriate controls, or countermeasures, to measure each risk. Risk mitigation needs to be approved by the appropriate level of management. A good risk management plan should contain a schedule for control implementation, and responsible persons for those actions.

Step 3: Set up the risk register (RISK Control 2), described next.

Step 4: Execute the risk-management plan. This involves analysing, and taking appropriate actions on resolving all the identified (actual and potential) risks affecting your company, and monitoring all the taken actions to ensure that all the risks have been handled with the least possible effect.

Risk register

A good tool to record and manage your risks is the risk register. The risk register (RISK Control 2) is usually maintained for all identified risks of your company. This is a central register of your company's key risks and their resolution (*see example in Table 2*). This register could either be a manual file, a small spreadsheet application on a personal computer, or a full-fledged risk management computerised information system.

Table 2: Example of data contained in a risk register

Data of risk register
1 Risk sequence number
2 Date
3 Priority
4 Risk description
5 Probability of occurrence
6 Impact
7 Expected value
8 Final status (resolved or not)
9 Link to risk response plan
10 Reference to other document

The chief risk officer

The duties of a chief risk officer (RISK Control 3) are discussed in *Chapter 14*, in which the roles of all participants in business management controls are described.

Risk evaluation methodology

A typical risk evaluation methodology (RISK Control 4), that can assist you in managing your risks, contains steps for risk identification, risk analysis and evaluation of risk impacts, risk response action plans to resolve each risk, risk monitoring, risk control and risk reporting.[36]

---

[36] For more on risks, see also: 'IT Risk Evaluation', Kyriazoglou, John, *Intelligent Risk Journal*, Vol. 1:Issue 3, pp 14-19 (October 2011), *www.prmia.org/irisk*, and *How to Strengthen Risk Management*, Kyriazoglou, John, *http://businessmanagementcontrols.blogspot.com*.

Risk response plan

The risk response plan (RISK Control 5) expands on the risks contained in your risk register, by documenting the actual procedures to be undertaken to accept, avoid, remove, defer, prevent, transfer, exploit, or mitigate, all identified risks, depending on whether they are assessed as positive, or negative, in your given business environment. This plan:

1 Records the risks by a sequential number, as per the risk register, date occurred, classification area, impact and likelihood of occurrence.
2 Lists the applicable rules, legislation, standards, budget, company procedures and detailed risk response controls and actions (accept, avoid, remove, prevent, exploit, defer, transfer or mitigate risks) that may be used to resolve each identified risk.
3 Names the managers that have responsibility for managing each identified risk.
4 Identifies the potential triggers and indicators of each risk.
5 Records the status of resolution of each risk (by date reported, date completed, or to be completed in the future, final status: open or closed, etc.).

More on risks and how these may be mitigated is provided in *Chapter 15*.

Risk performance measures and compliance indicators

Performance measures and compliance indicators (RISK Control 6) to complement all these risk controls are noted next.

Risk performance measures (RISK Control 6.1): Number of risk assessments per time period, number of training hours on risk issues, number of risks resolved per time-period, number of audits not executed, and number of audit issues not resolved.

Risk compliance indicators (RISK Control 6.2): Risk management action plan not implemented, risk register not established, chief risk officer not appointed, risk evaluation methodology not used, and risk response plan not functioning.

Performance measures and compliance indicators related to enterprise governance, risk and compliance controls, may be monitored via the internal process, and innovation and learning perspectives of BSC (*see Chapters 10 and 11*), as well as by the use of the GRC information system, as discussed in this chapter.

Corporate compliance controls

Compliance controls protect the organisation from legal and regulatory breaches in the best possible way. Risks are a fact of our personal and business life. In many ways, they may be considered to be the 'salt' and 'pepper' that give our life an added meaning. In the world of private and public organisations which operate within legal and regulatory frameworks and standards, we need to find effective ways to deal with the risks of breaching these rules and regulations, and protect both ourselves, as managers and professionals, as well as our organisations in general.

Corporate compliance controls, such as:

1 Compliance programme (COMP Control 1).

2 Compliance action plan (COMP Control 2).
3 Corporate compliance officer (COMP Control 3).
4 Compliance committee (COMP Control 4).
5 Business ethics policy (COMP Control 5).
6 Compliance records system (COMP Control 6) and the complementing privacy and information sensitivity policies are presently considered (all of these), by most experts, one of the most effective ways to achieve compliance.

The compliance programme, compliance action plan and compliance records system, are described next. The privacy and information sensitivity policies, and the business ethics policy, are described in the *Business Management Controls Toolkit*. The role of the compliance committee and the responsibilities of a compliance officer are discussed in *Chapter 13*.

Compliance programme

A compliance programme refers to an organisation's management plan for conducting all of its activities within the frameworks of the law, rules and regulations. The contents of an effective compliance programme[37] (COMP Control 1) include, as an example: executive summary, rules and regulations, action plans, control points, codes, governance committee, ethics office and certification, communication and training, documentation and improvement.

---

[37] See also US Federal Sentencing Guidelines for an effective compliance, *https://oig.hhs.gov/*, *www.un.org*, *www.ifac.org*, *www.phrma.org*, *www.bis.org*, etc.

This compliance programme could be implemented by a compliance action plan and compliance records system (described next), and a compliance officer (COMP Control 3, described in *Chapter 14*. Other similar controls that complement compliance are:

1 Corporate policies and procedures manual (described in *Chapter 2*).
2 Business ethics policy .
3 Business operational manuals (EGOV Control 16.1).
4 Business forms manuals (EGOV Control 16.2).
5 Business raw data retention procedure (EGOV Control 16.3).
6 Business records system (EGOV Control 16.4), described in *Chapter 6*.

Compliance action plan

This plan (Compliance Mechanism 1: COMP Control 2) may be used to effectively design and implement compliance to your company. It is made up of five phases (and several actions of each phase):

Phase 1: Analysis of compliance requirements and needs.

Phase 2: Design of the compliance function of the organisation.

Phase 3: Development of compliance policies and procedures – Compliance mechanism 3.

Phase 4: Implementation of compliance programme.

Phase 5: Evaluation and improvement of compliance programme.

The data to be collected, and the corresponding performance tracking procedures for collection and processing, are maintained in the BSC, and other performance and compliance monitoring systems.

Business ethics policy

A typical business ethics policy would define the framework, and the boundaries, of conducting your business in any cultural, social, industrial, national, economic and religious environment. This policy, as an example, would contain 'rules', 'instructions' and guidance, to all participants in the operations and activities of your specific company. This policy (COMP Control 5) is usually made up of the following parts: objectives of the business ethics policy, confidentiality of company information, disclosure, protection of internal data, protection of external data, signed agreement, conflict of interest, private interests, no solicitations, taking advantage, etc.

Compliance records system

In addition to the business records system, described in *Chapter 7*, you need a dedicated compliance records system (COMP Control 6), which serves all compliance-related issues of your company. This system is normally maintained, and managed, by your compliance officer, and would contain, as an example:

1 Copies of all national laws, legal and industrial regulations and rulings, relevant to compliance.

2 Copies of all corporate compliance-related policies and procedures, such as: ethics code, employee manual, conflict of interest statements, compliance policy statement, compliance programme, compliance officer job appointment and description, documentation of the organisation's compliance process that demonstrates its integrity and effectiveness, etc.

3 Communications, such as correspondence, FAX messages, e-mail messages, minutes of the Board regarding compliance issues, etc.

4 Compliance-related education, training, incidents and resolution actions.

5 Billing and claims records per healthcare programme, if not maintained by the business records system.

6 Audit data in support, and explanation of cost reports, other financial activity, and compliance monitoring, both internal and external.

7 Monitoring actions and compliance reports.

Governance, risk and compliance (GRC) information system

A GRC information system (EPMR Control 6) is deemed necessary, as recent large, corporate scandals, frauds, and instances of improper accounting records and systems, and investment practices in the US, China, Australia, and other parts of the world, have alerted investors, the general public, regulatory authorities, and professionals, about the lack of systematic control over the governance and control of information. Governance, risk and compliance, or 'GRC', is an increasingly recognised term that reflects a new way in which organisations are adopting an integrated approach to the governance, risk and compliance aspects of their business.

Governance refers to setting the policies, structure and objectives for an organisation, and overseeing progress towards those objectives.

Risk management means managing the risks (operational, financial, strategic and regulatory risk, etc.) and taking appropriate actions to mitigate their impact.

Compliance involves the management and monitoring of an organisation's own required policies and procedures that enable management of the risks endangering the organisation. It includes reporting of regulatory and policy breaches, management of their remediation, and communications between the organisation and the regulator.

GRC encompasses very different activities, comprising corporate governance, enterprise risk management (ERM) and corporate compliance, with applicable laws and regulations. There are many ready-made software packages that can be purchased to perform these, and other compliance and audit-related functions, such as: internal audit management, financial controls management, IT policy management, compliance management, risk management, report generation, etc.

Compliance performance measures and compliance indicators

Performance measures and compliance indicators (COMP Control 7) to complement all these compliance controls are noted next .

Compliance performance measures (COMP Control 7.1): Number of corporate governance violations, number of ethics code violations and number of ethics decisions made by higher-level management.

Compliance indicators (COMP Control 7.2): Compliance programme not implemented, compliance action plan not implemented and corporate compliance officer not appointed.

Performance measures and compliance indicators related to enterprise governance, risk and compliance controls may be monitored via the internal process, and innovation and learning perspectives of BSC (*see Chapters 10 and 11*), as well as by the use of the GRC information system, as discussed in this chapter.

Relating risk and compliance controls to the BMC framework

The risk and compliance controls identified in this chapter, that can be deployed to protect organisations against fraud, asset abuse, reputational damage and other risks they may be faced with, while improving their performance and compliance objectives and targets, are considered to be part of the third level (govern level) of business operation of the BMC framework (*see Figure 1: Business Management Controls Framework, Chapter 1*).

Conclusion

All companies, regardless of their type (private, public, etc.) and their size (small, medium, large, multinationals, etc.), are expected to do everything possible to manage and maintain their corporate integrity. Pressure, and demands coming from international organisations, governments (national, federal, state, provincial, territorial, local, etc.), professional associations, standards bodies, think tanks, academic institutions, investors, the general public, business partners, and customers, require your company to have defined corporate values and ethics practices that are monitored and adapted to the demands and expectations of a changing social, economic, business and regulatory environment.

You have to monitor the risk and regulatory environment on a continuous basis. New risks and regulations appear all the time, all over the world. They impact your company, even if you operate on a local scale. Both content and information on changes to risks and regulatory environments is crucial. New laws, regulations, court rulings and standards of practice, impact and change what is required of your company.

Most large companies and public organisations at least try to address external legal requirements and compliance obligations. The expectations, demands and needs of the 21st Century are changing the role of the Board, senior executives and stakeholders of any company, and are ensuring that organisations actively manage and monitor risks and compliance issues.

Your company cannot survive for a long time if you ignore existing and potential risks, and do not resolve them by planning, assessing and resolving them effectively, and your business cannot afford to pay heavy fines that are increasingly imposed by authorities, on regulatory breaches by your management and staff.

Risk and compliance recommendations

Recommendation 3: Establish strong and effective risk and compliance controls

The key points to consider in assessing this recommendation for your business environment are:

1 Establish a valid approach to manage your risks.
2 Use a risk-based approach to manage your compliance and ethics issues.
3 Monitor your risk and regulatory environments.
4 Ensure full support of your board and senior executives for risk, compliance and ethics.
5 Know who you do business with.
6 Perform due diligence and risk assessment on your partners on a continuous basis.
7 Manage changes in your business effectively, and adapt as required.

Recommendation 4: Acquire, and deploy, a GRC information system and a dashboard

The key points to consider in assessing this recommendation for your business environment are:

1 Managing governance, risk and compliance issues can be accomplished by a GRC system.
2 Coupling the GRC system with a business dashboard system, will give you added advantage, in having instant and accurate information in an integrated visual manner, about the performance issues that are relevant to you, and usually concern you the most.

CHAPTER 4: STRATEGIC MANAGEMENT CONTROLS

'You've got to think about big things while you're doing small things, so that all the small things go in the right direction.'

Alvin Toffler, American writer and futurist (born 1928)

Chapter overview: This chapter, the first chapter of Part B: Main Types of Business Strategic and Operational Controls, deals with strategic management controls which provide the necessary motivation and drive for your company to exist and survive in the long-run. Also, several controls are noted and one recommendation (Recommendation 5: Communicate a vision for your company and involve all your staff in implementing your strategy) is offered for your consideration.

Introduction

'However beautiful the strategy, you should occasionally look at the results,' is a famous quote by political leader, Winston Churchill. But how are results to be achieved by organisations (private and public, small, medium and large, etc.) in the most effective way? These, I think, may be facilitated and achieved by control frameworks, governance, risk, compliance, strategic and operational management controls, performance measures and compliance indicators, etc, for all business activities of organisations. Strategic management controls and measures are discussed in this chapter. Operational controls and measures which complement the execution of the strategy of the organisation are discussed in the next chapters. The other types of controls are depicted in other chapters.

Strategic management process

Strategy shows which way forward your business should try to go. Regardless of your company size (small, medium, large, etc.) or type (private, public, etc.), you will need a strategy. Either 'formal', conducted according to a formal methodology and by the analysis and study of several factors and data, etc; or 'semi-formal', carried out by following an unknown method with partial data, etc; or 'informal', discussed and agreed by the management team, or owner of the business. The purpose of instituting strategic management controls is to establish, motivate and reward achievement of general business goals, specific targets and time-bound objectives of the organisation, by its board, management and employees. Also, strategy stimulates success, learning, growth and development of new ideas and strategies by all your managers and employees.

A strategic management process is the art, science and craft of formulating, implementing and evaluating cross-functional decisions that will enable your company to achieve its long-term objectives. It is the process of specifying your company's mission, vision and objectives, developing policies and plans, often in terms of projects and programmes, which are designed to achieve these objectives, and then allocating resources to implement the policies and plans, projects and programmes.

The objectives of your strategic management process should be:

1 To assist and support your management, your corporate officers and your staff, to execute the predetermined strategy, and all the associated tasks and activities, on the most proper and effective way, and within a creative and ethical corporate governance framework.

2 To improve and strengthen good governance (enterprise governance, risk governance, information technology governance, human capital governance) and the effective operation and integration of all corporate functions, transactions, and activities of your business entity (private: small-size, medium-size, large-size, conglomerate, international, and public sector organisations: central ministries, regional government authorities, local government, non-profit state-financed institutions, etc.).

3 To improve the performance (economy of resources, efficiency, effectiveness) of your company, and the audit and review process, by all its stakeholders (social, institutional, regulatory, external and internal auditors, auditing committees, shareholders, suppliers, collaborators, banks and other financing mechanisms, etc.).

4 To improve and strengthen your productive and worth-while use of the most effective and successful performance measurement systems and approaches used in your company, with the interchange of practical experiences, from different business, social, political, geographical and economical environments.

The strategic management process is made up of three major components: strategic planning, strategic and operational controls, and a strategic plan. Examples of other strategic management controls that complement this process (but not discussed within the scope of this book) are: corporate strategic planning committee, strategic budgets, strategy implementation action plans, corporate strategic execution process, and functional strategic plans (e.g. sales, production, marketing, etc.).

Component 1: Strategic planning

Strategic planning is the first part of your management process. According to Professor Anthony[38] it has three layers:

1 **Strategic planning**: The process of deciding on your company's objectives, on changes in these objectives, on the resources used to attain these objectives, and the policies to govern their acquisition and use.
2 **Management control**: The process by which you, as a manager, ensure that resources are obtained and used, efficiently and effectively, in accomplishing your company's objectives.
3 **Operational control**: The process of ensuring that specific tasks are carried out efficiently and effectively.

The strategic process just outlined, to a smaller or larger extent, applies to small business firms, large national companies, large multinational corporations, professional partnerships, charities and religious organisations, the public sector, the manufacturing sector, the services sector,

---

[38] For more, see: *Planning and Control Systems: A Framework for Analysis*, Anthony, Robert, Graduate School of Business, Harvard University (1965).

the agricultural sector, privatised utilities, and non-government voluntary organisations,[39] etc.

Component 2: Strategic and operational control process

Strategic and operational control is the process by which your managers monitor the ongoing activities of your company, and evaluate whether activities are being performed efficiently and effectively, and take corrective action to improve performance if they are not.[40]

First, strategic and operational managers choose the business strategy and structure they hope will allow their company to use its resources most effectively to create value for its customers.

Second, strategic and operational managers create control systems to monitor and evaluate whether, in fact, their company's strategy and structure are working as they, as managers, intended; how strategy and structure could be improved, and how these should be changed if they are not working.

Strategic and operational control does not just mean that you, as a manager, should react to events after they have occurred; it also means keeping your company on track, anticipating events that might occur, and responding swiftly to new opportunities that might present themselves.

---

[39] For more information, see: *The Strategy Process. Concepts, Contexts and Cases,* Mintzberg, H. et al (editors) (1998) in bibliography Mintzberg, H et al (editors) Prentice-Hall (1998).

[40] Some thinkers add a middle level, the so called tactical level. There is, however, a great deal of confusion, as tactical deals with short term (e.g. one year), while operational deals with day to day. So, to make things easier, many organisations have only two levels: strategic (two–five years or longer), and operational (day by day, month by month, one year).

Thus, strategic and operational control is not just about monitoring how well a business entity is achieving current goals, or about how well your company is utilising its existing resources. It is also about keeping your employees motivated, focused on the important problems confronting your company now and in the future, and working together to find solutions that can help your company perform better over time.[41]

Strategic and operational control is of vital importance to you, considering how it helps you to obtain superior: efficiency, quality, innovation, and responsiveness to customers; the four basic building blocks of competitive advantage.

Competitive advantage: Competitive advantage theory, as proposed by Professor Michael Porter,[42] suggests that national states and businesses should pursue policies that create high-quality goods to sell at high prices in the market. Professor Porter emphasises productivity growth as the focus of national strategies. Competitive advantage rests on the notion that cheap labour is ubiquitous, and natural resources are not necessary for a good economy.

Competitive advantage occurs when an organisation acquires, or develops, an attribute, or combination of attributes, that allow it to outperform its competitors. These attributes can include access to natural resources, such as high grade ores or inexpensive power, or access to highly trained and skilled personnel human resources, as well as

---

[41] For more information, see: *Levers of Control. How Managers use Innovative Control Systems to Drive Strategic Renewal,* Simons, Robert, Harvard Business School Press (1994).
[42] For more, see: *Competitive Advantage, Creating and Sustaining Superior Performance,* Porter, Michael, Free Press (1985).

new technologies, such as robotics and information technology (either to be included as a part of the product, or to assist making it).

Competitive advantage is defined as the strategic advantage one business entity has over its rival entities, within its competitive industry. Achieving competitive advantage strengthens and positions a business better within the business environment. The way competitive advantage may be achieved by business management controls, in relation to efficiency, quality, innovation and customer service, is outlined next.

Business management controls and efficiency: Efficiency means 'power to accomplish something'.[43] Efficiency in business describes the extent to which time, or effort, is well used for the intended task or purpose. It is often used with the specific purpose of relaying the capability of a specific application of effort to produce a specific outcome effectively, with a minimum amount or quantity of waste, expense, or unnecessary effort.

To determine how efficiently you are using company resources, you must be able to measure accurately, by the use of business management controls, how many units of inputs (raw materials, human resources, etc.) are being used to produce a unit of output. You must also be able to measure the number of units of outputs (goods and services) your company produces.

A system of business management controls, as described in *Chapters 5 and 6* (Financial and production controls), and *7* (IT and information governance controls), contains the

---

[43] From Latin *efficientia.*

measures of yardsticks that allow you, as a manager, to assess how efficiently, as well as productively and profitably, your company is producing goods and services. Moreover, if you experiment with changing the way your company is producing goods and services, to find a more efficient, productive and profitable way of producing them, these measures tell you how successful you have been. One practical way of measuring efficiency, quality, innovation and customer service, by the use of BSC, is outlined in *Table 3* (later in this chapter).

Business management controls and quality: The common element of the business definitions of quality is that the quality of a product or service refers to the perception of the degree to which your product or service meets your customer's expectations. Quality has no specific meaning unless related to a specific function and/or object. Quality is a perceptual, conditional, and somewhat subjective, attribute.[44] In the current business environment, most, if not all of the competition between companies, revolves around increasing the quality of goods and services they offer. In the car industry, for example, within each price range, cars compete against one another in terms of their features, design and reliability over time. So which car a customer will buy depends significantly on the quality of each company's product.

Business management controls, as described in *Chapters 5 and 6* (Financial and production controls), *7* (IT and information governance controls) and *8* (Business data management controls), are important in determining the

---

[44] For more see: *Out of the Crisis*, Edwards Deming, W, Cambridge, Mass: Massachusetts Institute of Technology, Centre for Advanced Engineering Study (1986).

quality of goods and services, because it gives you, as a manager, feedback on your product and service quality. Measuring the number of customers' complaints, and the number of new products returned for repairs to your company, will give you a good indication of how much quality your processes have built into your product and services offered to customers. One practical way of measuring efficiency, quality, innovation and customer service, by the use of BSC, is outlined in *Table 3* (later in this chapter).

Business management controls and innovation: Although the term 'innovation' is broadly used, innovation, in business terms, generally refers to the creation of better, or more effective, companies, products, processes, management methods and technologies, that are eventually accepted by people, markets, governments and society.[45] Innovation is different from invention ('finding or discovering of something'), or renovation ('renewing or restoring'), in that innovation generally signifies a substantial positive change compared to incremental changes[46] pertaining to renovation. To lead or sustain with innovations, you, as a corporate manager, must concentrate heavily on the innovation network and tools you can use.[47] These will show you the way, as they help you get a deep understanding of the complexity of innovation. Recently, innovations are increasingly brought to the market by

---

[45] From the Latin word *innovatus*, which is the noun form of *innovare* 'to renew or change', stemming from in — 'into' + *novus* — 'new', from Greek *neos*.

[46] For more see: *Innovation and entrepreneurship,* Drucker, Peter, Harper and Row (1985).

[47] For example: brainstorming, prototyping, project management, etc. For more, see also: *Stoking Your Innovation Bonfire: A Roadmap to a Sustainable Culture of Ingenuity and Purpose,* Kelley, Braden, John Wiley and Sons (2010) and *www.ideaconnection.com/thinking-tools/.*

networks of companies, selected according to their comparative advantages, and operating in a co-ordinated fashion.

A system of business management controls, as described in *Chapters 5 and 6* (Financial and production controls), *7* (IT and information governance controls), *8* (Business data management controls) and *13* (Human aspects of controls), contains the performance measures that allow you, as a manager, to assess how efficiently, as well as productively and profitably, you are producing goods and services. Successful innovation takes place when you create an organisational setting in which your employees feel empowered to be creative, and in which authority is decentralised to employees, so that they feel free, under certain conditions, to experiment and take risks. One practical way of measuring efficiency, quality, innovation and customer service, by the use of BSC, is outlined in *Table 3* (later in this chapter).

Business management controls and responsiveness to customers: The concept of 'customer'[48] applies to the private sector firms and, in some cases, to government provided services to citizens. The customer concept has useful application in government, but it will be helpful only if it does not undermine the principle that public administration is grounded in public law, rather than in entrepreneurial market concepts. Customer service, in the current business environment, is the provision of service to customers before, during, and after a purchase of products

---

[48] The word customer comes from Latin *custumarius*, meaning 'a person with whom one has dealings'.

or services.[49] You, as a business manager, can help make your company more responsive to your customers, if you develop a set of business management controls, including financial, production, strategic and other operational controls, that allow you to evaluate how well your employees that have customer contact are performing their jobs. This may be done by reviewing the measures in *Table 3* and by employee monitoring.

Table 3: Measuring efficiency, quality, innovation and customer service

Measuring efficiency, quality, innovation and customer service with BSC
1. Financial Perspective
1.1. Strategic objective: Increase business efficiency
1.2. Performance measures: Return on capital employed, cash flow
2. Customer Perspective
2.1. Strategic objective: Add new customers
2.2. Performance measures: Customer satisfaction index
3. Internal Process Perspective
3.1. Strategic objective: Manufacturing quality excellence
3.2. Performance measures: Quality errors, safety incident index

---

[49] For more, see: *Service This: Winning the War Against Customer Disservice*, Dall, Michael and Bailine, Adam, Last Chapter First (2004).

> **4. Innovation Perspective**
>
> 4.1.   Strategic objective: Add new innovative services
>
> 4.2.   Performance measures: percentage revenue from new services

Monitoring the behaviour of your employees can help you find ways to increase their performance level, perhaps by revealing areas in which skill training can help them, or by finding new procedures that allow them to perform their jobs better.

Employee monitoring refers to any method of tracking what an employee does whilst at work. This may include the use of video cameras, e-mail filters, or even just watching or listening to the employee. As a result of increased technology, this has become a very important issue in the workplace. Employers have many options at their disposal when it comes to monitoring their employees, but the effectiveness and legality of each technique varies depending on the situation. Some of the reasons companies monitor employee activities[50] are:

1 **Legal compliance**. In regulated industries, taping telemarketing activities gives both the company, and the consumer, some degree of legal protection. Also, electronic recording and storage may be considered part of a company's 'due diligence' in keeping adequate records and files.

2 **Performance review**. Customer service and consumer relations personnel are frequently taped as they field

---

[50] For more, see: *Vetting And Monitoring Employees: A Guide for HR Practitioners*, Howard, Gillian, Ashgate Publishing Co. (2006).

calls, and tapes are reviewed with supervisors to evaluate and improve job performance.

3 **Security concerns**. Protecting the value of proprietary corporate information is a primary concern in an age when e-mail and Internet connections continue to expand.

From a business management controls viewpoint, when your employees know their behaviours are being monitored, they may have more incentive to be helpful and consistent in the way they act towards your customers. Also, other aspects of human controls, described in *Chapter 13*, such as trust, integrity, values and beliefs, ethical climate, awards, recognition, leadership, etc, are quite important in defining your actions that will enable and improve the behaviour of your employees, especially as regards serving your customers in a better way.

Component 3: Business strategic plan

As we mentioned previously, the strategic management process is made up of three components: strategic planning, strategic and operational controls, and a strategic plan. The first two were described before. Also, operational controls and measures are described in more detail in the next chapter(s). The concept of strategy and the strategic plan, the product of strategy, are described next. Strategy means 'art of a general'.[51]

---

[51] From Greek *strategia* 'office or command of a general', from *strategos* 'general', from *stratos* 'multitude, army, expedition', lit. 'that which is spread out' + *agos* 'leader', from *agein* 'to lead'.

To successfully formulate and implement strategy for your company, you must confront four broad classes of issues:[52]

1 Boundaries of the company (size of the company, what it should do, what business it should be in, etc.).
2 Market and competitive analysis (nature of the markets, competitive forces, size of the market, etc.).
3 Position and dynamics (company's position and basis of competitive advantage, adjustments required, etc.).
4 Internal organisation (organising the structure and systems of the company, implementing systems and controls, etc.).

Formulating the strategy of your company, including your business model, overall strategic priorities, objectives, targets and measures, etc, is clearly your task as a manager, even though in many cases you may obtain the assistance of specialised external experts. The outcome of this work is your company's strategic plan,[53] as outlined next.

The contents of a business strategic plan (STRP Control 1) (as an example) are:

1 Executive summary.
2 Business model, mission, vision and values statements.
3 Critical success factors for the accomplishment of the plan.
4 Product/service idea.
5 Business goals, strategies and specific objectives.
6 Break-even analysis and market analysis.
7 Action plans.
8 Management team.

---

[52] For more, see: *Economics of Strategy,* Besanko, D et al, John Wiley and Sons (2000).
[53] For more details see: *Foundations for Corporate Success. How Business Strategies Add Value*, Kay, John, Oxford University Press (1993).

9 Analysis of risks.
10 Financing and cash-flow projections.
11 Strategic initiatives and resources plan, etc.

Examples of corporate strategies are: business strategy, organisational strategy, operational strategy, technological strategy, performance strategy, information technology strategy, risk management strategy, financial strategy, sales strategy, product marketing strategy, services marketing strategy, research and development strategy, etc.

Strategic management is the highest level of your managerial activity. Strategies are typically planned, crafted or guided by you, either a business manager of a small business entity, or a chief executive officer of a larger company, approved or authorised by your board or owner, and then implemented under your direct supervision, with the use of a performance model, like BSC.

BSC and strategy

A balanced scorecard (BSC) model is used by many public organisations and medium and large companies, to evaluate the overall performance of their business and its progress towards their objectives,[54] on the basis of strategic plans (corporate, business unit, etc.).

Your corporate strategic plan (also often known as 'business plan', as described above) may be complemented,

---

[54] For more details, see: 'The Balanced Scorecard – Measures That Drive Performance', Kaplan, RS and Norton, DP, *Harvard Business Review*, January–February 1992, pp. 71–79 (1992) and *The Balanced Scorecard: Translating Strategy into Action,* Kaplan, RS and Norton, DP, Harvard Business School Press (1996).

especially if you manage a large organisation, with the strategic business unit (SBU) plan, and with functional or support (IT, sales, marketing, production, etc.) plans. You may link all of these into an integrated whole system, by the use of the BSC framework, including overall strategic objectives and performance measures per each perspective: financial, customer, internal process, innovation and learning, as discussed in *Chapters 10 and 11*.

You may also check, and help yourself in crafting and implementing strategy, by using the following audit questionnaires and checklists: strategic management process questionnaire (STQC Control 1), strategic plan contents audit programme (STQC Control 2), strategic alignment checklist (STQC Control 3) and human resources questionnaire (STQC Control 4). These are contained in the *Business Management Controls Toolkit*.

You can use all of these to review and revisit, as required, and re-craft, if needed, your strategy, before you make changes and improvements, and change the strategic direction of your business entity. In addition to all of the above, you may improve the design and implementation of your strategy by using, and monitoring, the performance measures noted next.

Performance measures and compliance indicators

Consulting practice, in a large variety of business environments and cultures, have shown to us that it is one thing for you as a business manager to craft a strategy, and another, usually, a difficult thing, to implement it successfully, and have the results you have planned or hoped for.

Performance measures and compliance indicators (STRP Control 2) provide a means for you to track your progress and results in this regard. Examples of strategic performance measures (STRP Control 2.1) and strategic compliance indicators (STRP Control 2.2) that could be used to support and monitor your strategic management controls are noted next

Strategic performance measures: Number of improvements after budget and performance reviews, number of hours on strategic reviews, percentage of strategic investments that have surpassed targets, and number of hours of meetings with management on strategy.

Strategic compliance indicators: Clear business strategic objectives for all departments (exist or not), and corporate strategy followed (or not).

You can monitor your performance in strategic issues, in your medium or large company, by monitoring the performance measures and compliance indicators noted above via all perspectives of BSC (*see Chapters 10 and 11*), as well as by the use of the GRC information system (EPRM Control 3), as discussed in *Chapter 3*. You can monitor your performance for your small company by setting up a small manual or automated system (e.g. by using a spreadsheet application based on BSC).

Conclusion

The controls identified in this chapter (Strategic Plan (STRP Control 1), Strategic Performance Measures (STRP Control 2.1) and Strategic Compliance Indicators (STRI

Control 2.2)) that can be deployed to protect organisations against fraud, asset abuse, reputational damage and other risks they may be faced with, while achieving and improving their performance and compliance objectives and targets, are considered to be part of the second level (envision level) of business operation of the BMC framework (*see Figure 1: Business Management Controls Framework, Chapter 1*).

In conclusion, practice has shown that even a great corporate strategic plan can be destroyed by ineffective or faulty implementation. As an example of the reasons why strategic plans fail, are the following:

1 Inadequate resources and/or inability of resources to be employed.
2 No motivation of staff and management to implement strategy.
3 No staff, board or senior management sponsorship and commitment.
4 Failure to understand the market, industry, competition, regulations, laws and customer.
5 Incorrect business needs, product, services and marketing research.
6 Failure to co-ordinate between all participants.
7 Management reporting and control relationships not adequate.
8 Organisational structure not flexible enough.
9 Strategy not well-communicated.
10 Inadequate monitoring by all participants.

Your successful strategy implementation requires a complete envisioning and understanding of where your business should go, as well as the active involvement of all parties (managers and employees) that enable and execute it.

Business strategy recommendation

Recommendation 5: Communicate a vision for your company and involve all your staff in implementing your strategy

The key points to consider in assessing this recommendation for your business environment are:

1 The strategic process and its outcome (strategy, strategic plan execution), as consulting practice and various international studies have shown, are absolutely necessary for the effective management and direction of any organisation.
2 The BSC framework, when implemented successfully, has proven a very valuable tool in bringing all these to full fruition, for all stakeholders of an organisation.
3 A strategy, whether formal or informal, is required for all companies, small, medium and large. You cannot survive without it.

CHAPTER 5: FINANCIAL MANAGEMENT AND ACCOUNTING CONTROLS

'Pleasure in the job puts perfection in the work.'

Aristotle, Ancient Greek Philosopher (384–322 BC)

Chapter overview: This chapter, the second chapter of Part B: Main Types of Business Strategic and Operational Controls, deals with financial management and accounting controls which provide the necessary mechanisms for your company to control funds and ensure its long-term profitability. Also, several financial and accounting controls are noted and a recommendation (Recommendation 6: Protect your finances (cash, assets, payments, records, bank accounts) with the utmost care) is offered for your consideration.

Introduction

'The only man I know who behaves sensibly is my tailor; he takes my measurements anew each time he sees me. The rest go on with their old measurements and expect me to fit them,' is a famous quote by George Bernard Shaw. This provides the inspiration for managers to be on top of things:

1 To establish the governance, administration, strategic, operational and compliance mechanisms and controls, so that they can drive strategic and operational performance for better results.

2 To measure properly, with specific types of compliance and performance measures at each business function level, to ensure that targets are met, if not surpassed.

3 To ensure that rules and regulations are complied with, so that they make their organisations more effective and more beneficial to society.

To this effect, governance, risk, administration and compliance controls were discussed in *Chapters 2 and 3*. Strategic controls were described in *Chapter 4*. Financial management controls are described in this chapter. Production controls, IT governance controls and business data management controls, the other parts of operational controls, are presented in the following chapters.

Financial management and accounting controls

Controls at this level establish the good financial operating environment, and ensure the successful execution of the daily activities and operational transactions, as well as the long-term survival of the organisation. Financial management controls (or financial controls) are the written rules, guidelines, standards, policies, procedures and practices, as well as the relevant organisational structures and supportive management positions for achieving financial management and accounting that all organisations (private, public, etc.) are required to have in order to direct, monitor and measure, from a financial perspective, the resources of an organisation. Financial controls play a very critical and important role in ensuring the accuracy of financial reporting, eliminating, if not minimising, fraud and abuse, and protecting the organisation's resources and assets, both physical and intangible, from potential harm, wilful or accidental damage, or complete destruction.

The most important financial management controls described next, within the scope of this book, are:

1 Financial management responsibility controls
2 Financial standards, systems, policies and procedures
3 The budget.

Financial management responsibility controls

These controls relate to setting up, and organising, the finance function of your company (FINM Control 1), including setting up the function itself, appointing accounting management and operating staff, defining their job descriptions and responsibilities, and segregating financial duties of finance personnel, as required.

Chief financial officer (CFO)

If you have a medium or large company, you probably need a chief financial officer (CFO). The chief financial officer (FINM Control 1.1) provides both strategic and operational support to your company on financial issues. The CFO supervises the finance function (department, unit, etc.) and is the chief financial spokesperson for the company. The CFO reports directly to the chief executive officer (CEO) and the Board of Directors, depending on various demands and organisational aspects, and assists the chief operating officer, as well as other chief officers (chief technology officer, chief information officer, chief risk officer, etc.) on all strategic and tactical issues as they relate to finance (e.g. budget management, cost benefit analysis, forecasting financial needs, project financing, securing of new funds, etc.).

The most critical duties and responsibilities of a CFO include:[55]

1 Develop, implement, ensure, and maintain, systems of internal controls, including financial policies, procedures and practices, to safeguard all financial assets of the company.
2 Ensure that effective internal controls are in place and are executed effectively, to ensure compliance with professional financial standards[56] and applicable national (federal, state or provincial and local) regulatory laws and rules for financial and tax reporting.
3 Oversee the management and co-ordination of all fiscal reporting activities for the company.
4 Oversee the timely and accurate preparation of the annual financial statements, in accordance with relevant standards, rules and regulations.
5 Ensure adequate cash flow to meet the company's needs.
6 Oversee banking, payroll, purchasing, and other investment activities of the company.
7 Oversee the co-ordination and activities of independent auditors, ensuring that all audit issues are resolved, and all compliance issues are met satisfactorily.

Other financial management positions

Other typical financial management positions include: financial manager (FINM Control 1.2) for your accounting department, treasury manager (FINM Control 1.3) for your

---

[55] See also: *www.accountingjobstoday.com/cm/Job-Descriptions/CFO.html*.
[56] For example, GAAP, etc. See: *www.fasb.org*, *www.iasb.org*, *www.ifrs.org*, etc.

investments, and cost accountant (FINM Control 1.4) for your product or project costing activities.

Depending on the type and size of the company, the geographical location and socio-economic environment where the organisation exists and functions, the duties of financial managers may vary with their specific titles, which may include controller, treasury manager, treasurer or finance officer, credit manager, cash manager, risk and insurance manager, and manager of international banking[57] etc.

Segregation of finance duties

Once you establish, and appoint, the selected persons to manage your finance function, you would need, besides selecting and appointing your accounting personnel, to segregate their duties (FINM Control 4.5), so that you can protect both yourself, and your company, against potential abuse and fraud. This involves assigning responsibilities to accounting staff on the basis of segregation of duties rules, such that no finance employee should be responsible for two or more of the following four activities in each business process: record keeping, authorisation, asset custody and reconciliation, for posting and updating accounts, handling cash, cheques and payments, reporting, etc. *(See detailed examples in Chapter 15.)*

---

[57] See also: Bureau of Labour Statistics, US Department of Labour, *Occupational Outlook Handbook*, 2010–11 Edition, Financial Managers, at *www.bls.gov/oco/ocos010.htm* (visited 13 February 2012) and *www.humanresources.hrvinet.com/finance-manager-job-description/*.

Financial standards, systems, policies and procedures

These controls provide the principles, glossary, terms of reference, interpretations, and the framework for managing the financial activities, updating the financial accounts, and for reporting the financial results of your company[58] in terms of:

1 Developing the necessary financial policies and procedures (FINM Control 2) for your company.
2 Obtaining and deploying computerised financial systems (FINM Control 3) to suit your needs.
3 Posting and reporting of all financial transactions of your company (see Basic Accounting and Bookkeeping Controls – FINM Control 4).
4 Setting up your budget (FINM Control 5) as described next.

Financial policies and procedures manual

Once you select which financial standards apply to your business environment, you must design and develop financial management policies and procedures, educate your staff, and deploy them effectively to manage, as well as you can, the financial investments and accounts of your company. These standards, and the specific financial policies and procedures for your company, are usually included in a financial policies and procedures manual (FINM Control 2) tailored to your needs. This manual will include, as an example: executive summary, scope, legislative and company requirements, financial policy

---

[58] For more, see the standards issued by the internationally well-accepted standards, as issued by: *www.fasb.org*, *www.ifrs.org* and other national accounting associations.

statement, chart of accounts (list of accounts), basic accounting procedures, financial reporting procedures, etc.

These procedures should be based on a set of national and international (UN, EU, OECD, etc.) government standards and guidelines, such as:

1 Financial accounting standards
2 Audit standards
3 Bad cheque laws
4 Civil code
5 Tax and customs code
6 Electronic Fund Transfer Act,[59] etc.

Financial forms

Regardless of the size of your company, you will need a set of specific forms (FINM Control 2.1) that must be designed, and used, by your finance and accounting staff, to execute your financial accounting procedures, and provide the right kind of evidence and audit trail for all your financial transactions, such as:

---

[59] See also: *www.fasb.org*, *www.fasab.gov/*, *www.ifrs.org*, *www.ifac.org*, *www.consumerbadcreditguide.com/badchecklaws.html*, *www.fdic.gov/regulations/laws/rules/6500-1350.html*, etc.

1 Journal entry
2 Description of accounts
3 Daily cash report
4 Deposit log
5 Bad cheque notice
6 Bank wire instructions
7 Wire transfer form
8 Cheque signing authority log
9 Cheque request
10 Bank and book balances reconciliation
11 Invoices
12 Accounts receivable write-off authorisation
13 Account collection control form
14 Travel arrangements form
15 Travel and miscellaneous expense report
16 Entertainment and business gift expense report
17 Tax and insurance payments, etc.

Implementing computerised financial systems

The basic bookkeeping, accounting and financial reporting functions of a company, may be achieved by obtaining and deploying standard, computerised, financial systems[60] (FINM Control 3). These usually:

1 Manage the financial accounts of your company.
2 Post the accounting journal entries in the official accounting books of the company.
3 Manage the chart of accounts.

---

[60] Also known as ready-made software packages, provided by a large variety of software vendors, as per *Financial Packages Software Evaluation Report*: *http://rfp.technologyevaluation.com/rfi.asp?modelid=98&catid=FSC&km=264&kmt=ser* .

4   Execute period-end closing.
5   Manage cash receipts and deposits.
6   Produce financial reports.
7   Manage your accounts payable and accounts receivable.
8   Maintain sales in the sales ledger.
9   Maintain purchases in the purchase ledger, etc.

Basic accounting and bookkeeping procedures

The basic accounting and bookkeeping procedures (FINM Control 4) related to managing the financial accounts of your company,[61] are included in the financial policies and procedures manual (FINM Control 2), described previously.

The most critical procedures, for the purposes of this book, are detailed next.

Chart of accounts procedure

The chart of accounts (FINM Control 4.1) is a list of the accounts you can use to record all the financial transactions of your company.[62] These can be numerical, alphabetic, or alpha-numeric. Each nominal ledger account is unique, to allow its ledger to be located. The list is typically arranged in the order of the customary appearance of accounts in the financial statements, profit and loss accounts, followed by balance sheet accounts.

---

[61] For more, see: *Accounting and Bookkeeping Procedures for Internal Control,* Bizmanualz Inc. (2008).
[62] See also: *How to Implement a Standard Chart of Accounts Effectively*, Tayyebi, Aziz, www.qfinance.com/accountancy-best-practice/how-to-implement-a-standard-chart-of-accounts-effectively?page=1.

General ledger procedure

The general ledger (FINM Control 4.2), manual or computerised, is the main accounting record of your company which uses double-entry bookkeeping. It will usually include accounts for such items as assets, liabilities, owner's equity, revenues, expenses, gains, and losses. The general ledger is a collection of the group of accounts that supports the items shown in the major financial statements. It is built up by posting the transactions of the organisation (sales, purchases, cash, etc.) and general journals. The general ledger can be supported by one or more subsidiary ledgers (accounts receivable, accounts payable, etc.) that provide details for accounts in the general ledger. The balance sheet, and the income statement, are both derived from the general ledger. The listing of the account names is called the chart of accounts. The extraction of account balances is called a trial balance. The purpose of the trial balance is at a preliminary stage of the financial statement preparation process, to ensure the equality of the total debits and credits.

Trial balance procedure

The trial balance (FINM Control 4.3) is a listing of the balance at a certain date, of each ledger account (such as assets, liabilities, owner's equity, revenues, expenses, etc.) of your accounting system, in two columns, namely debit and credit. Under the double-entry system, in any transaction the total of any debits must equal the total of any credits. This means that the total of the debit side should always be equal to the total of the credit side. The trial balance thus serves as a tool to detect errors, which can result in the totals not being equal. Often credits will be represented as a negative, in which case the total of the trial balance should be 0.

Financial statements or reports procedure

Financial statements (or financial reports, FINM Control 4.4) are formal records of the financial activities of an organisation. Financial statements provide an overview of an organisation's financial condition in both the short and long term. The financial reporting aspects for all organisations (private and public) usually follow accepted international standards.

There are four basic financial statements:

1 **Balance sheet (FINM Control 4.4.1)**: also referred to as a statement of financial position or condition. Reports on the organisation's assets, liabilities, and net equity, as of a given point in time.
2 **Income statement (FINM Control 4.4.2)**: also referred to as a profit and loss statement (or a 'P&L'). Reports on the organisation's income, expenses and profits, over a period of time.
3 **Statement of retained earnings (FINM Control 4.4.3)**: explains the changes in the retained earnings of an organisation over the reporting period.
4 **Statement of cash flows (FINM Control 4.4.4)**: reports the organisation's cash flow activities, particularly its operating, investing and financing activities.

Locked safe procedure

Regardless of the size of your company (small, medium, large), it is good practice to get a locked safe (FINM Control 4.6). You can use this locked safe to keep cash, cheques and other critical documents, reports, contracts, bonds, shares, etc. Also, you must establish, and assign, responsibilities to specific staff for controlling this safe.

Detailed accounting procedures

The usual accounting procedures that your accounting staff need to record all your daily financial transactions and activities, as an example, include: post transactions and update books controls procedure, manage petty cash controls procedure, manage cheques controls procedure, manage accounts receivable controls procedure, manage accounts payable controls procedure, and manage payroll controls procedure.

In addition to all these financial accounting procedures described above, you will need a procedure (Manage Performance Controls Procedure: FINM Control 4.13) to review, improve, and manage the performance of your finance function, by carrying out the following:

1 Ensure that your finance executives (CFO, financial manager, etc.) review all budget items, and report the budget status to higher levels of management, on a weekly or monthly basis.
2 Ensure that your senior managers review periodic activity reports, to evaluate whether objectives are being achieved.
3 Ensure that financial systems, policies and procedures provide timely, accurate, and sufficient information for all levels of your management.
4 Ensure that the finance department uses ethics, benchmarking, and other measures, to evaluate

effectiveness and satisfaction by all their internal and external customers.

The budget

Regardless of the size of your company (small, medium, large) it is good practice to have a budget.[63]

The budget (FINM Control 5) is an itemised listing of the amount of all estimated revenues which your company anticipates receiving, along with a listing of the amounts of all estimated costs and expenses that will be incurred in obtaining the above mentioned income, during a given period of time. A budget is typically for one business cycle, such as a year, or for several cycles (such as a five year capital budget).

An operating budget (FINM Control 5.1) is a blueprint that states how managers intend to use organisational resources to achieve organisational goals most efficiently. Most commonly, managers at one level allocate to managers at a lower level, a specific amount of resources to use to produce goods and services.

A cash budget (FINM Control 5.2) depicts the cash you expect to receive and pay over the near term, for example a month.

A capital budget (FINM Control 5.3) depicts expenses to obtain or develop, and operate or maintain, major systems or pieces of equipment, for example, information systems,

---

[63] There are, however, examples of several conglomerates using a new approach called 'Beyond Budgeting', *www.juergendaum.com/bb.htm*, where they operate without budgets. Their example, although successful for them, is not the normal business case you find across the world.

buildings, automobiles, computer hardware systems, furniture, etc. The budget, as a control tool, is used to evaluate financial performance for all managers and business functions, in reaching their pre-determined business goals. Through the use of a budget as a standard, an organisation ensures that managers are implementing its plans and objectives. Their actual performance is measured against budgeted performance.[64]

Financial performance controls

You may monitor the good execution of all these financial management controls, besides monitoring the financial controls themselves, by reviewing the set of specialised financial performance controls (FINM Control 6) made up of performance measures (FINM Control 6.1) and compliance indicators (FINM Control 6.2), as shown next.

Financial performance measures: Stock market price, return on investment, return on assets, ROCE (return on capital employed), net results/revenue, and dividends per share.

Financial compliance indicators: Clear business objectives for finance department (exists or not), financial strategy followed (or not), and financial management procedures exist (or not).

You can monitor your performance in financial management issues, in your medium or large company, by monitoring the performance measures and compliance indicators noted above via the financial perspective of BSC

---

[64] For more, see: *Budgeting Basics and Beyond*, Shim, Jae K, Siegel, Joel G and Shim, Allison I, Wiley Corporate F&A (2011).

(*see Chapters 10 and 11*), as well as by the use of the GRC information system (EPRM Control 3), as discussed in *Chapter 3*. You can monitor your performance for your small company by setting up a small manual or automated system (e.g. by using a spreadsheet application based on BSC).

Conclusion

The financial management controls identified in this chapter that can be deployed to protect your company against fraud, asset abuse, reputational damage and other risks that your company may be faced with, while achieving and improving your performance and compliance objectives and targets, are considered to be part of the third level (govern level) of business operation of the BMC framework (*see Figure 1: Business Management Controls Framework, Chapter 1*).

Financial management controls recommendation

Recommendation 6: Protect your finances (cash, assets, payments, records, bank accounts, etc.) with the utmost care

The key points to consider in assessing this recommendation for your business environment are:

1 Financial controls, financial performance, compliance measures and indicators support, enable the strategic process and its outcome (strategy, strategic plan execution), as practice and various consulting assignments have shown.
2 These types of operational controls, as well as production, IT and business data management controls (described in other chapters), go hand-in-hand with

strategic management controls for the effective management and direction of any organisation.

3 The BSC framework, when implemented effectively, supports the financial aspects of managing an organisation very well.

CHAPTER 6: CUSTOMER SALES AND PRODUCTION MANAGEMENT CONTROLS

'Consumption is the sole end and purpose of all production; and the interest of the producer ought to be attended to, only so far as it may be necessary for promoting that of the consumer.'

Adam Smith, Scottish Philosopher (1723–1790)

Chapter overview: This chapter, the third chapter of Part B: Main Types of Business Strategic and Operational Controls, describes customer sales and production management controls which provide the necessary mechanisms for your company to control revenue creation and production of goods and services. Also, several customer sales and production management controls are noted and three recommendations (Recommendation 7: Make your customer your number one priority, Recommendation 8: Execute excellent production policies and procedures to satisfy the needs and expectations of your customers and Recommendation 9: Establish effective purchasing procedures to avoid fraud) are offered for your consideration.

Introduction

'Being busy does not always mean real work. The object of all work is production or accomplishment, and to either of these ends there must be forethought, system, planning, intelligence, and honest purpose, as well as perspiration.

Seeming to do is not doing,' is a famous quote by Thomas Edison, the American inventor (1847–1931). This provides the motivation for managers to:

1 Establish the customer sales and production management functions, so that they can drive, and achieve, strategic and operational targets, and for better results.
2 Measure properly, with specific types of compliance and performance measures, the performance of both of these critical business functions, so that they make their companies more effective and beneficial to society.

These customer sales and production management controls are described in this chapter. Financial, IT controls and business data management controls, the other parts of operational controls, are presented in other chapters.

Customer sales management controls

Controls at this level establish the good customer sales operating environment, and ensure the successful execution of the daily sales activities, and complementing operational transactions of your company. If you want your business to survive, prosper and grow in the long run, you must have constant inflows of revenues and profits. These are only possible if you either produce and sell your own quality products, or obtain them from the market and sell them, and provide, either way, excellent service, at all times, to your customers. You can achieve all these, in the best way possible, by a variety of sales management controls,[65] such as: customer sales manager, customer support manager,

---

[65] For more on customer sales, see: *Sales Management Best Practices: Six Essential Processes*, Jordan, Jason, Manage Smart (2009).

customer service policy, sales management procedure, and sales ledger, as noted next.

Other customer sales management controls, beyond the scope of this book, are: customer relationship management system, marketing strategy, marketing plan, marketing policy, marketing procedures, sales force management system, sales management system, sales training and coaching programme, and sales order management application software.

Customer sales manager

You will need a customer sales manager (CUST Control 1) regardless of the size of your company (small, medium, large). The usual role and specific responsibilities of a sales manager, as an example, include:

1 To develop a business sales strategy, policy and procedures, advertising campaign, etc, considering the products and services your company is selling and providing to the market, your existing and potential customers, and the overall socio-economic conditions your company is facing.
2 To prepare, review, promote and improve the sales documentation (product brochures, sales catalogue, services handbooks, etc.), ensuring the highest quality of presentation and printing production.
3 To manage, train and coach sales staff, as required, ensuring achievement of your company's sales goals and specific targets.
4 To manage the complete process of sales proposals, presentations and RFP responses.
5 To control expenses to meet corporate budget guidelines.

6 To adhere to all corporate policies, procedures and business ethics codes, and ensure that they are communicated and implemented effectively within the sales team.
7 To produce customer sales reports to upper levels of management, and manage the performance and development of all sales staff.

Customer service manager

The main objective of a customer service manager (CUST Control 2) is to provide excellent service and support to your customers. Depending on the type and size of your company, usual activities, as an example, are likely to include some or all of the following:

1 To provide assistance, support and advice to customers using your company's products or services.
2 To investigate and resolve, satisfactorily, all problems, incidents, events, etc, reported by your customers.
3 To communicate, in a gentle manner, with all your customers, regardless of the means of communication (telephone, person to person, letter, fax, electronic mail, etc.).
4 To determine new, and improve existing, customer service and support requirements, by maintaining contact with customers in a variety of ways (surveys, seminars, visits, benchmarking, etc.).
5 To establish, measure, monitor, report and improve customer service performance.

Customer service policy

You need a customer service policy (CUST Control 3) to inform your customers about how your sales and support staff will carry out sales and support them (your customers), regardless of the size of your business operation (small, medium or large company), and your selling activities (one or more products).

You will need to communicate this to all your customer support staff, and ensure that this policy is adhered to, in practice, in everyday dealings with your customers. You will also have to train your staff to act according to this policy.

Sales management procedure

You need a sales management procedure (CUST Control 4) regardless of the size of your business operation (small, medium or large company), so that you are more effective and efficient in selling your products and services to the world, are more responsive to your customer needs, and can ensure that all sales result in accurate sales figures and collected revenues.

A typical example of such a procedure would contain the following steps:

Step 1: Develop, and implement, written procedures for handling sales transactions (cash, cheque and credit sales, as well as consulting or services sales), approving sales orders (price, terms and conditions, credit, account balance, etc.), and reporting sales, and train your staff, as required.

Step 2: Establish a file and recordkeeping system for all sales transactions.

Step 3: Ship goods to your customers only when they are accompanied by a correct invoice (regarding customer details, unit and total prices, agreed terms of credit, etc.).

Step 4: Deliver partial invoices and a final (correct) invoice regarding services provided by your staff.

Step 5: Post sales immediately, or forward the sales transaction data to the accounting function, to be posted in the sales register, or other computerised system of your company.

Step 6: Ensure your staff know how to handle customer returns and deal with customer complaints.

Step 7: Reconcile your sales data with customer returns, invoices issued, payments received, etc.

Sales ledger

Every time you make a sale for goods or services and invoice a customer, record it in the sales ledger (CUST Control 5). This must be done immediately after the specific event (the sale) is concluded. Your total amount of sales invoiced by you at any point in time is your business turnover (or business sales income). By recording the amounts paid by customers in the sales ledger, you will also be able to identify the money owed to your business, and chase slow payers, as required. A sales ledger normally records the sales your business has made, the amount of money received for your goods or services, and money owed to your company at the end of each month, or other point of time.

Customer sales performance controls

All these customer sales controls may be monitored as to whether they operate, well or not, by a set of customer sales performance measures (CUST Control 6) and customer sales compliance indicators (CUST Control 7), as presented next.

Customer sales performance measures: Sales per person per period, percentage of sales force achieving quota, average years of sales experience by sales person and percentage of new product introductions.

Customer sales compliance indicators: Sales strategy communicated (or not), sales strategy linked to corporate policy (or not) and sales policy exists (or not).

You can monitor your performance in sales, in your medium or large company, by monitoring the performance measures and compliance indicators noted above, via the customer perspective of BSC (*see Chapters 10 and 11*), as well as by the use of the GRC information system (EPRM Control 3), as discussed in *Chapter 3*. You can monitor your performance for your small company by setting up a small manual or automated system (e.g. by using a spreadsheet application based on BSC).

Relating sales controls to the BMC framework

The sales controls identified in this chapter that can be deployed to enable and facilitate your sales, and protect your company against potential fraud, while improving your performance and compliance objectives and targets, are considered to be part of the third level (govern level) of business operation of the BMC framework (*see Figure 1: Business Management Controls Framework, Chapter 1*).

Customer sales management controls recommendation

Recommendation 7: Make your customer your number one priority.

The key points to consider in assessing this recommendation for your business environment are:

1 Providing only excellent products and services (in terms of production processes, quality and customer satisfaction) to the world will not be enough for your company to survive and prosper in the long run.
2 You need to look after all your customers like they are a unique customer, and as such, treat them like they are the only one that matters to you at that point in time – the rest will fall into place.
3 Couple this with effective risk, compliance and production policies and procedures, including training your sales staff, and you will have a financial success in your hands (as regards revenue, cost, profit, share price and growth).

Production management controls

Production management enables, and facilitates, the business operational activities of any organisation. Selling to customers is one side of the business coin. Production management and the provision of services, is the other side of the same business coin. The purpose of production management controls is to establish the good operating environment, and ensure the successful execution of the daily production activities and operational transactions (manufacturing and service) of your company, in terms of: purchasing, inventory control, production, quality management, services provision, etc.

The most critical production management controls are:

1 Production operations policies and procedures manual
2 Purchasing management controls
3 Warehouse management controls
4 Project management controls
5 Manufacturing/services management controls
6 Quality management controls, as presented next.

It is worth noting that these controls relate more to a production related corporation, even though some of these (e.g. purchasing, quality, warehouse management and project management) are also applicable to service-oriented organisations (public administration entity, bank, construction building company, etc.). In the case of a service organisation, for example, the 'production operations policies and procedures manual' will be termed 'services policies and procedures manual', and will contain all your service policies and procedures. The 'manufacturing/services management controls' will be directly related to the service you provide (e.g. specific building you are constructing, bank customer accounts function, provision of consulting services, etc.), etc, depending on your company's business, operating model, and the market in which you do your business.

Production operations policies and procedures manual

The activities of production management are carried out by appropriate policies and procedures, usually documented in a production operations policies and procedures manual (PROD Control 1). These policies and procedures should cover (as an example) the following functions:

1 Purchasing

2 Supply chain management
3 Logistics support
4 Freight management (incoming/outgoing and customer)
5 Inventory management
6 Manufacturing assembly
7 Standardisation procedures
8 Provision of services
9 Returns (return to stock, return to vendor
10 Repairs
11 Receiving
12 Quality management
13 Customer support
14 Project management, etc.

These policies and procedures are also complemented by a set of methods, work practices and techniques, to ensure that these (policies and procedures) are executed in the most effective and efficient way.[66]

Purchasing management controls

These relate to carrying out the main purchasing activities of your company (PROD Control 2), and include:

1 **Purchasing management responsibilities** (see next).
2 **Purchasing action plan and procedures (PROD Control 3)** containing, as an example, all the actions needed to establish, and operate, a purchasing function for your business, such as: issuing purchase orders, selecting and managing vendors, order placement, goods receiving, inspection, etc, stocking, product returns,

---

[66] For policies and procedures manual templates, see: *www.bizmanualz.com/*, *www.ebc.com.au/policies_manual/*.

vendor payment, etc, and purchasing files management procedure

3 **Forms for executing purchasing (PROD Control 4)**, such as: new vendor notification, vendor survey form, purchase requisition, purchase order, purchase order log, purchase order follow up, daily sundry payable log, order and arrival log, receiving log, receiving and inspection report, and inventory inspection levels,[67] etc.

Purchasing manager

The typical **purchasing manager** (PROD Control 2.1), in general terms:

1 Manages the operational activities of the purchasing function (department, unit, etc.) of your company, including planning and developing purchasing systems and procedures to improve the operating quality of purchase transactions, and the efficiency of the department.
2 Supervising purchasing staff in accordance with company policies and procedures.
3 Hiring, training, supporting and coaching the employees of the purchasing function.[68]

Depending on the size and type of your business operation, the purchasing manager may be involved in procuring only the strategic raw materials and other resources necessary for the production of goods and the provision of services to your customers, while he or she may not be involved in purchasing parts and services from external vendors related

---

[67] For more, see: *Purchasing* (Barron's Business Library), Harding, Michael and Harding,, Mary Lu, Barron's Educational Series (2001), and more resources, at: *www.cips.org/*.
[68] For more, see: *http://job-descriptions.careerplanner.com/Purchasing-Managers.cfm*.

to maintenance, repairs, as well as obtaining capital goods and services, etc.

Other purchasing controls

Detailed examples of other purchasing controls that complete your purchasing management controls (included in *Chapter 12* 'Case Studies'), are:

1 PROD Control 2.2 Purchasing Standards, Systems, Policies and Procedures
2 PROD Control 2.3 Computerised Purchasing System
3 PROD Control 2.4 Purchasing Responsibilities
4 PROD Control 2.5 Locked Safe
5 PROD Control 2.6 Manage Performance
6 PROD Control 2.7 Improve Performance.

Warehouse management controls

These controls relate to managing the asset inventory of the organisation and the related records (PROD Control 3), and include:

1 Inventory management responsibilities (see next).
2 Inventory procedures (PROD Control 3.2) for inventory stocking and storage, inventory usage, inventory protection, inventory obsolescence, inventory disposal, inventory counting, period end cut-off, asset acquisitions, capitalisation, depreciation and dispositions, etc.
3 Inventory records (PROD Control 3.3), such as inventory master records (IMR) file and inventory transactions file.

Also, specific forms (PROD Control 3.4) that must be designed and used by each organisation to execute these procedures, may be:

1 Asset and inventory entry forms
2 Inventory requisition
3 Inventory count sheet
4 Inventory tag
5 Capital asset requisition
6 Asset disposition form
7 Bill of sale
8 Material return notice.[69]

Only the inventory management responsibilities are briefly noted here, as the other controls are beyond the scope of this book.

Warehouse inventory manager

The typical warehouse inventory manager (PROD Control 3.1), in general terms:

1 Manages the operational activities of the warehouse inventory function (department, unit, etc.) of your company, including planning and developing inventory control systems and procedures, to improve the operating quality of inventory and the efficiency of the department.
2 Supervises warehouse staff in accordance with company policies and procedures.
3 Hires, trains, supports and coaches the employees of the warehouse function.[70]

---

[69] For more, see: *Warehouse Management: A Complete Guide to Improving Efficiency and Minimising Costs in the Modern Warehouse*, Richards, Gwynne, Kogan Page Limited (2011).
[70] See also: *www.bestjobdescriptions.com/restaurant/inventory-manager-job-description*.

Project management controls

The most crucial project management controls (PROD Control 4) include, as an example: project manager, project cost accountant, project management methodology and project cost report, as described next.

Project manager

The typical project manager (PROD Control 4.1), in general terms:

1 Manages the operational activities of a project of your company, including planning and developing project management systems and procedures, to improve the operating quality of implementing projects.
2 Supervises project staff in accordance with company policies and procedures.
3 Acquires, deploys, trains, supports and coaches the employees of the specific project.[71]

Project cost accountant

If you manage a small, medium, large or joint project, and you want, or have an obligation to manage the projects and improve profits to all parties, you may want to appoint a project cost accountant (PROD Control 4.2).

Project management methodology

A project management methodology (PROD Control 4.3) will be more than useful to use if you want to execute your project as well as possible, and meet the project's

---

[71] For more details on what a project manager does, see: *www.best-job-interview.com/project-manager-job-description.html*.

objectives. Such a methodology will, as an example, contain all phases of managing your projects,[72] such as:

1 Defining and organising your project.
2 Managing your project's risks and quality.
3 Assigning the project manager and forming the project team.
4 Planning and executing your project.
5 Tracking the progress of your project.
6 Reviewing the performance of your project.
7 Closing out your project.

Project cost report

The usual project management reports you may employ to manage and monitor the progress of your project include:

1 Project control charts, project budget, project progress report, project problems log, project plan (beyond the scope of this book).
2 A project cost report (noted next).

A typical project cost report (PROD Control 4.4), contains the following information:

1 Project title and period of reporting (from xx/xx/xxxx to yy/yy/yyyy).
2 Progress of each major activity.
3 Budget costs (original, revised, projected amounts).
4 Committed costs (original, revised, projected amounts).
5 Actual costs (original, revised, projected amounts).
6 Variance costs (original, revised, projected amounts).
7 Approved changes.

---

[72] For more, see: *A Guide to the Project Management Body of Knowledge: (Pmbok Guide)*, Project Management Institute (2008): *www.pmi.org/*.

Manufacturing/services management controls

These controls relate to:

1 Manufacturing/services management responsibilities (see next).
2 Procedures to support the design and implementation of the manufacturing process controls for your specific needs, such as: standardisation procedures and quality policy and procedures (described next).
3 Other manufacturing/services controls, not within the scope of this book, such as: environmental policy and production process, new product development strategy, setting up and maintaining manufacturing and production files (e.g. bill of materials (BOM) file, master production schedule (MPS), materials and vendors contingency list, and equipment operational description file), and implementing computerised systems (e.g. material requirements planning system (MRP), cost accounting system, enterprise resource planning (ERP) system and preventive maintenance system,[73] etc.).

Manufacturing/production manager

The typical manufacturing/production manager (PROD Control 5.1), in general terms:

1 Manages, controls and co-ordinates the operational activities of the production function (manufacturing plant, department, unit, etc.) of the organisation, including planning and developing production systems and procedures to improve the operating quality of

---

[73] For more, see: *Fundamentals of Modern Manufacturing: Materials, Processes and Systems,* Groover, Mikell P, John Wiley and Sons (2002).

production activities and the efficiency of the department.

2 Supervises production staff in accordance with company policies and procedures.

3 Hires, trains, supports and coaches the employees of the production function.[74]

Standardisation controls

Standardisation controls (PROD Control 6) refers to the degree to which your company specifies how decisions are to be made, so that your employees' behaviour becomes predictable.[75]

In practice, there are three things you can standardise: inputs, conversion activities and outputs.

Standardisation of inputs (PROD Control 6.1). One way in which your company can control the behaviour of both people and resources is to standardise the inputs into your production process. This means that your managers screen inputs according to pre-established criteria or standards, and then decide which inputs to allow into your process. If employees are the input in question, for example, then one way of standardising them is to specify which education, training, qualities, dexterities and practical skills they must possess, and then to select only those applicants who possess them.

Standardisation of conversion activities (PROD Control 6.2). The aim of standardising conversion activities is to programme production activities so that they are executed

---

[74] For more see: *www.prospects.ac.uk/production_manager_job_description.htm*.
[75] For more see also: *Standardization Essentials: Principles and Practice,* Spivak, Steven M and Brenner, F Cecil, Marcel Dekker Inc.(2001) and *www.ticsi.org/*.

the same way, time and time again. The definite goal is predictability. Fast-food restaurant chains, such as McDonald's, for example, standardise all aspects (resources, preparation, production and service) of their restaurant operations, with the result being, standardised fast food of certain quality dimensions in all their service locations.

Standardisation of outputs (PROD Control 6.3). The goal of standardising outputs is to specify what the performance characteristics of the final product or service should be – what dimensions or tolerances the product should conform to, for example. To ensure that your products are standardised, you must apply quality control and use various criteria to measure this standardisation.

Quality management controls

'Quality in business, engineering and manufacturing[76] has a pragmatic interpretation as the non-inferiority or superiority of something; it is also defined as fitness for purpose.' Quality controls (PROD Control 7) are implemented, at a practical level, by a quality management policy, according to international standards,[77] and by quality inspection procedures and practices.

Production performance controls (PROD 8)

All these production controls (operations policies and procedures, purchasing, warehouse inventory, project

---

[76] As per: *http://en.wikipedia.org/wiki/Quality_(business)*.
[77] Such as: Service Standards: *http://servicestrategies.com/scp-standards/*, *www.serviceinstitute.com/customer_service_certification.html*, and ISO9004:2009 Quality Standard: *www.iso.org*.

management, manufacturing, standardisation, quality) are monitored as to their operation, and are complemented and supported by a set of performance measures (PROD Control 8.1) and compliance indicators (PROD Control 8.2), as noted next .

Production performance measures: Number of new products, inventory on hand, production rate, and production cycle time controls (set-up time, processing time, queue time, wait time, idle time).

Production compliance indicators: Operations policies and procedures established (or not), purchasing procedures followed (or not), and quality management system established and used (or not).

You can monitor your performance in producing goods and providing services in your medium or large company, by monitoring the performance measures and compliance indicators noted above, via the internal process perspective of BSC (*see Chapters 10 and 11*), as well as by the use of the GRC information system, as discussed in *Chapter 3*. You can monitor your performance for your small company, by setting up a small manual or automated system (e.g. by using a spreadsheet application based on BSC).

Relating production controls to the BMC framework

The production controls identified in this chapter that can be deployed to enable and facilitate your sales, and protect your company against potential fraud, while improving your performance and compliance objectives and targets, are considered to be part of the third level (govern level) of business operation of the BMC framework (*see Figure 1: Business Management Controls Framework, Chapter 1*).

Conclusion

While financial goals and controls are an important part of the balanced scorecard (BSC) approach, it is also necessary to develop goals and controls that tell managers how well their strategies are creating a competitive advantage, and building distinctive competences and capabilities that will lead to future success.

When strategic managers implement the balanced scorecard approach, and establish goals and measures to evaluate efficiency, quality, innovation and responsiveness to customers, they are using production or output control.

Customer sales ensure your revenue and long-term survival. Production management controls (or production controls), along with other operational controls (IT, data management, etc.), facilitate your customer process.

Production management controls recommendations

Recommendation 8: Execute excellent production policies and procedures to satisfy the needs and expectations of your customers

The key points to consider in assessing this recommendation for your business environment are:

1 Effective production controls and production performance measures, and compliance indicators, support and enable the strategic process and its outcome (strategy, strategic plan execution), as practice and various consulting assignments have shown.
2 Complement these with efficient quality and other operational controls, such as finance, customer sales, IT and business data management controls, and a visionary

strategy, and you will be more than effective in managing and directing your company.

Recommendation 9: Establish effective purchasing procedures to avoid fraud

The key points to consider in assessing this recommendation for your business environment are:

1 Establish purchasing procedures to handle, as an example, issues, such as: request for proposal, vendor selection process, vendor inspection, vendor management, goods receiving, inspection, rejection, discrepancies and disposition, stocking, product returns, shipping, receiving, claims, order placement, vendor payment, and purchasing files management.
2 Implement segregation of purchasing duties.
3 Complement these by a set of forms, such as: new vendor notification, vendor survey form, purchase requisition, purchase order, purchase order log, purchase order follow up, daily sundry payable log, order and arrival log, receiving log, receiving and inspection report, inventory inspection levels, etc.

CHAPTER 7: IT GOVERNANCE CONTROLS

'Consult and deliberate before you act, that you may
not commit foolish actions.'

Pythagoras of Samos (Ancient Greek Philosopher and
Mathematician, c. 570–c. 495 BC).

*Chapter overview: This chapter, the fourth chapter of Part
B: Main Types of Business Strategic and Operational
Controls, deals with IT governance controls which provide
the necessary mechanisms for your company to control the
creation and execution of IT systems, and the provision of
information to all your stakeholders. Also, several IT
governance controls are noted and one recommendation
(Recommendation 10: Be vigilant and proactive with all
your IT resources, systems and networks) is offered for
your consideration.*

Introduction

'It is important that organisations recognise the differences
in the types of employees who commit each type of crime,
as well as how each type of incident evolves over time:
theft or modification for financial gain, theft for business
advantage, IT sabotage, and miscellaneous (incidents that
do not fall into any of the three above categories),' was

quoted in a recent Carnegie-Mellon study.[78] This provides the motivation and inspiration for IT managers to be more proactive, effective, and efficient, in protecting the IT assets and the information systems, resources and processes of the modern enterprise (private or public organisation). IT governance controls are an integral part of the operational controls of your company, small, medium or large, much like financial, customer sales and production controls, described in previous chapters.

IT governance controls

IT governance controls enable, and facilitate, the running of information systems, and the provision of information services of the organisation. The purpose of IT governance controls is to establish a good operating environment, and to ensure the successful execution of the daily activities and operational transactions of the information systems and services of the computerised organisation. IT governance controls are made up of three major types: general IT controls, application systems controls and information governance controls.

The general IT controls relate to: IT procurement, IT personnel management, systems development and maintenance, enterprise architecture, IT applications operation, IT standards, IT security, IT disaster recovery planning, computer insurance, physical protection policies and procedures, access policies and procedures (data, software, files, forms, reports, facilities, firewalls,

---

[78] For more, see: *Common Sense Guide to Prevention and Detection of Insider Threats,* 3rd Edition – Version 3.1, Cappelli, Dawn and others (January 2009): *www.cylab.cmu.edu.*

encryption, electronic mail, etc.), health and safety policies and procedures, security and safety controls for personal computers, and audit tools and methods.

The application systems controls relate to: protection of specific systems, processing accuracy and timely maintenance of the data of these systems, completeness and validation of input, back-up and recovery of data, and application software,[79] etc.

Information governance controls relate to managing and controlling the specific compliance, security, integrity and privacy aspects of personal information and personal data, and information processes related to these, and ensuring that the organisation (private company, public agency, hospital, other healthcare institution, pharmacy, etc.) provides a confidential service to all its stakeholders (customers, patients, vendors, etc.), and its staff, will be continued to be trusted to look after all information entrusted to them, and maintained by the systems of the organisation.

The most important IT governance controls are described next. These are complemented by the business data management controls and business intelligence and espionage controls, presented in *Chapters 8 and 9*.

---

[79] . For more on IT and Application Controls, see: *IT Strategic and Operational Controls*, Kyriazoglou, John, IT Governance Ltd (2010): *www.itgovernance.co.uk*, *www.isaca.org*, and *www.itpi.org*.

IT general controls

The IT general controls, considered as the most critical within the scope of this book, are described in the paragraphs that follow.

IT management responsibility controls

These controls relate to setting up and organising the IT function of your company, including the definition of the operational terms of reference for the IT function, designing job responsibilities and segregation of duties for IT personnel, and appointing the required management and staff positions to run the IT function and develop systems. A brief job description of an IT executive is described next. Segregation of duties for IT personnel, as a case study, is depicted in *Chapter 15*. Other IT management responsibility controls and IT job descriptions, such as: systems development manager, information systems analyst, computer programmer, system programmer, computer operations manager, web developer, computer operator, etc, are described in another book of the author.[80]

CIO/IT manager job description

Depending on the size of your company, you may appoint a CIO, who will have IT managers reporting to him or her; or an IT manager, with only some staff to handle all IT issues.

The duties of this person (ITOR Control 1), however, will be to:

---

[80] For more on IT positions and detailed job descriptions, see: *IT Strategic and Operational Controls*, Kyriazoglou, John, IT Governance Ltd (2010): www.itgovernance.co.uk.

1 Provide technology, vision, strategy and leadership, in the development and implementation of the information technology (IT) investments of the organisation.
2 Lead the organisation in planning and implementing enterprise information systems, to support both distributed and centralised business operations.
3 Facilitate communication between staff, management, vendors, and other technology resources, within the organisation.
4 Oversee the back office computer operations of the affiliate management information system, including local area networks and wide-area networks.
5 Design, implement, and evaluate the systems that support end-users in the productive use of computer hardware and software, etc.

IT administration controls

These controls relate to setting up and organising the administration aspects of the IT function of the organisation. The most important controls in this area are described next.

Information technology (IT) policy

This policy establishes computer usage guidelines for your company. Depending on the size of your business operation (small, medium, large, etc.), the development of this IT policy (ITAD Control 1) may be carried out by the IT committee and ratified by your board (large and medium companies), or by your most senior executive and the IT manager (small company).

IT budget

You set up an IT budget (ITAD Control 2) to reflect all your IT management decisions, IT activities, IT actions, system development projects, application maintenance, IT solutions procurement and deployment, computer system support, outsourcing and offsourcing activities, and in general, anything involving your IT assets and investment.

The typical IT budget of your company will contain annual amounts for:

1 Main computer hardware
2 Software (operating system, database, networking, application systems, security, etc.)
3 Personnel payroll
4 Data centre administration
5 Personal computers
6 Office equipment
7 Smart devices
8 Security administration
9 Education and training
10 Computer insurance, etc.

IT procurement process controls

In order to avoid any potential cases of IT fraud, and to increase effectiveness, efficiency, transparency, accountability, and the best use of your corporate and societal resources, IT procurement controls (ITAD Control 3) are necessary. These controls are usually the same controls which apply for all purchases of your company, but with specific emphasis on IT. In some large organisations, an IT procurement function is set up.

This procurement process for information technology (IT) solutions and services, for any large or medium corporate or organisational environment (e.g. public sector), is usually made up of the following actions:

Action 1: Establishment of the whole IT procurement process.

Action 2: Setting up an IT budget for procurement.

Action 3: Executing the IT procurement procedure.

Action 4: Considering infrastructural issues.

Action 5: IT vendor management.

Action 6: Undertaking effective project scoping.

Action 7: Reviewing and improving the whole process.

Small companies will probably do all of these by one purchasing officer. Ways to segregate purchasing duties, and establish compensating controls to protect you against potential IT purchase fraud, are described in *Chapter 15*.

IT asset controls

The usual IT asset controls (ITAD Control 4) you need to set up to manage your specific IT assets, include:

1 A hardware and software inventory.
2 An information asset register, describing the types of information existing, and maintained, in all files.
3 An IT consumables inventory.
4 Maintenance registers for systems and application software, and hardware.
5 Visitor's logs, for both offices and computer rooms.
6 Hardware locks, and hardware tagging with property labels, serial numbers, etc.
7 IT safe storage (ITAD Control 6, described in *Chapter 15*).

IT management reporting controls

Your IT department manager (CIO, etc.) must report (ITAD Control 5) on some predetermined period, as well as on an ad hoc basis, to upper levels of management (CEO, board, etc.), the IT related issues of your company, such as:

1 Progress of your IT projects
2 Changes, problems, and backlog of requests
3 Help desk related issues
4 Development issues of new applications
5 Project actual costs (against budgets)
6 IT security incidents and resolutions
7 Post-implementation review issues.

IT governance standards, policies and procedures

IT governance standards, policies and procedures (ITGO Control 1) should be identified and formally established, especially if you manage a large or medium company.

These should cover:

1 Analysis, development, design, implementation and evaluation of computerised information systems.
2 Enterprise architecture and IT strategy.
3 IT security.
4 Back-up and disaster recovery for critical computerised applications.
5 Documentation.
6 Data centre operations.
7 Computer availability management, etc.

They should follow well-accepted international standards.[81] These are usually contained in an IT policies, procedures and practices manual.

IT strategic controls

It is good practice to have:

1 An IT vision, mission and values (ITST Control 1).
2 An IT strategic process (ITST Control 2).
3 An IT strategy methodology (ITST Control 3).
4 An IT strategic plan (ITST Control 4).
5 An IT strategic projects budget (ITST Control 5).
6 Enterprise architecture controls (ITST Control 6), especially if you manage a large or medium company.

Out of all of these, you definitely need an IT strategic plan, formal or informal, even if you manage a small company. For a more detailed description of this, see 'IT Strategic Plan' in the *Business Management Controls Toolkit*. The other strategic controls are not within the scope of this book.

Data and information security practices and controls

According to the Institute of Internal Auditors (*www.theiia.org*), 'Effective security is not only a technology problem, it is a business issue. It must address people's awareness and actions, training, and especially the corporate culture, influenced by management's security

---

[81] Such as: COBIT®, ITIL®, ISO/IEC 38500, The Calder-Moir IT Governance Framework, etc, as per: *www.isaca.org*, *www.itgovernance.co.uk/calder_moir.aspx*, *www.iso.org*, *www.38500.org*, and *www.itil-officialsite.com*.

consciousness and the tone at the top'. This is more than true for your business data. You must therefore protect them as much as possible, against harm, damage and potential abuse.

The usual tools, practices and techniques that you may employ to reach this protection, are:

1 Security policy, password controls and computer security incident controls, described next.
2 Social engineering controls, described in paragraph '7.5 Information Governance Controls'.
3 The vital records package, described in *Chapter 14.*

IT security policy

A usual IT security policy (ITSE Control 1) contains high-level statements, describing the general objectives of your company as regarding the control, protection and security, over critical information assets, such as, your information systems, information technology and application software, operating systems and database management system software, buildings, computer rooms, cabling, network and computer facilities, other related installations and technical infrastructures, data, back-up media and archived files, and information resources in general.[82] Reference will also be made to a security incident monitoring and resolution[83] mechanism.

---

[82] For more, see: *ISO27001 and Information Security Resources*: *www.itgovernance.co.uk/iso27001.aspx*.
[83] See also: *ISO17799 Checklist*, SANS Institute: *www.sans.org*.

Password controls

A password policy (ITSE Control 2) and associated compliance procedures, should be established and put into operation for your company to handle the specific password control requirements. This password policy should relate to the following: structure of password, storing of passwords, password display, default passwords, password disabling, etc.

Computer security incident controls

A computer security incident can result from a computer virus, other malicious code, or a system intruder, either an insider, or an outsider.

A computer security incident handling capability[84] (ITSE Control 3) may be viewed as a component of contingency planning, because it provides the ability to react quickly and efficiently to disruptions in normal processing. This system should include, for all incidents (potential and actual), the following stages: preparation, detection, containment, eradication, recovery, follow-up, reporting, and feedback and review.

IT systems development controls

The typical system development controls that will ensure better development of your systems are:

1 IT systems development methodology (ITSD Control 1, noted later).

---

[84] For more on computer security incident, see: *Incident Response*, Berkley Ca, Mandia, Kevin and Prosise, Chris, Osborne/McGraw-Hill (2001), *Computer Forensics*, Heiser, Jay and Kruse, Warren, Addison-Wesley (2002).

2 System development products (ITSD Control 2).
3 IT project management (ITSD Control 3).
4 System development security plan (ITSD Control 4).
5 IT system test plan (ITSD Control 5, noted later).

Out of all of these, and within the purpose of this book, only the following two are described next.[85]

IT systems development methodology

All your IT application systems should be developed on the basis of a system development life cycle methodology (ITSD Control 1). This methodology is usually made up of the following phases:

1 System feasibility
2 System definition
3 System analysis
4 System design
5 System construction
6 System implementation
7 Post-implementation review.

IT system test plan

The contents of a typical IT system test plan (ITSD Control 5) are the following:

1 Testing strategy.
2 Detailed testing design plan for each unit (programme, sub-system, etc.).
3 Definition of testing responsibilities and organisation.
4 Components to be tested (function, load stress, volume, hardware configuration and portability, database loading

---

[85] For more on these controls, see: *IT Strategic and Operational Controls*, Kyriazoglou, John, IT Governance Ltd (2010): *www.itgovernance.co.uk*.

and data conversion, security, performance, availability, out of sequence transactions, recovery, hardware maintainability, interfaces, documentation, and human factors).
5   Expected results of tests.
6   Formalised test procedures, including test scenarios, forms, and test data.
7   Post implementation review.

IT operational controls

To run efficient IT systems you need IT operational controls, such as:

1   Data centre controls (ITOP Control 1).
2   IT back-up and disaster recovery plan (ITOP Control 2).
3   Hardware controls (ITOP Control 3).
4   Personal computers controls (ITOP Control 4).
5   Audit trails (ITOP Control 5).
6   IT technical controls (ITOP Control 6, controls to ensure that the operating system, applications software, and database and data communications software, can remain in good operational status, etc.).

The second control, IT back-up and disaster recovery plan, is briefly presented next. The other controls are not discussed, as they are deemed to be outside the scope of this book.[86]

---

[86] For more on these controls, see: *IT Strategic and Operational Controls*, Kyriazoglou, John, IT Governance Ltd (2010): *www.itgovernance.co.uk*.

IT back-up and disaster recovery plan

You need an IT back-up and disaster recovery plan document (ITOP Control 2), regardless of the size of your company. This plan describes what must be done in order to recover from a pre-defined failure, and resume operating your information system or your data centre, after a failure of some kind. The plan must, at least, contain (as an example): back-up procedure, recovery invocation process, and recovery procedures, organisation and personnel.

This plan may be complemented, depending on your situation, by a wider-scope 'IT continuity plan', as described in *Chapter 11*.

Application systems controls

Application systems controls (ITAP Control 1) ensure that the computer programs of a particular computerised application (e.g. financial system, inventory system, payroll system, etc.), process the business transactions according to a set of predefined rules, and store the processed data in computerised files and databases, in a safe and secure way.

The main application systems controls are:

1 Input controls
2 Processing controls
3 Output controls
4 Database controls (file updated report, critical transactions report, application-specific access authorisation, database health checks, etc.)
5 Change controls
6 Testing controls
7 Spreadsheet controls.

Out of all these, controls 1 to 6 (of above) are deemed to be outside the scope of this book, and are not described any further.[87] Control 7 (spreadsheet controls) is described next.

Spreadsheet controls (ITAP Control 2). As computerised spreadsheet applications proliferate, you must be very careful to implement controls that will preclude potential wrong decisions, and fraud, from using data produced by undocumented and untested spreadsheet applications. As these are usually outside the realm and control of IT, and as they are mostly not properly documented, tested, etc, they present a major risk in any company, even yours.[88]

The usual controls that may be applied to mitigate these risks are:

1 **Inventory control**: Record all the spreadsheets used in all departments of your company and how they function, what decisions are made in the basis of their data, etc. This spreadsheet inventory should be assigned to a manager (e.g. IT systems development manager), and should be updated continuously as users add, or delete, spreadsheets in their departments.

2 **Standards**: Ensure that a standard spreadsheet design template is developed and employed for all spreadsheets in your company.

3 **Testing**: Confirm that all spreadsheets are tested, and that testing documentation is kept.

4 **Documentation**: Ensure that the data input sources, rules, calculations, formulas, and other instructions, are

---

[87] For more on these controls, see: *IT Strategic and Operational Controls*, Kyriazoglou, John, IT Governance Ltd (2010): *www.itgovernance.co.uk*.
[88] See also my article: 'IT Risk Evaluation', Kyriazoglou, John, *Intelligent Risk Magazine*, Page 14 (October 2011): *www.prmia.org*.

recorded in the documentation of all spreadsheets. This documentation should also have a printed copy of the spreadsheet, and it should always be kept current.

5 **Back-up**: Instruct all users to back-up their work. Copies of all spreadsheet applications should be kept at a central location (IT, administration, etc.).

Controlling the development and use of spreadsheets should be the task of all managers of your business entity.[89] It is better to inventory, examine, and take control of the department's spreadsheets, before a problem comes to light, or a crisis develops. For example, if a key person leaves the organisation and nobody knows how his or her spreadsheets are used in the management decision process, etc.

Information governance controls

Information governance is a 'framework for handling information in a confidential and secure manner to appropriate ethical and quality standards in a modern health[90] service'.

These controls are especially critical and important in:

1 Health-related organisations (primary public and private hospitals, healthcare provision units, pharmacies, patient examination laboratories, pharmacies, etc.).

---

[89] For more on controlling spreadsheets, see: 'Preventing Errors in Spreadsheets', Kee, Robert C and Mason Jr, John O, *Internal Auditor Magazine*, Feb. 1988, pg. 42-47 (1988), 'Building Structured Spreadsheets', Stone, Dan N and Black, Robert L, *Journal of Accountancy*, Oct. 1989, pg. 131 (1989).
[90] As per *Information Governance*, (14 January 2011), www.igt.connectingforhealth.nhs.uk/

2 National, regional and local authorities (social care federal and provincial/state entities, city and regional councils, etc.).

3 Companies (small, medium, large, etc.), in which patient, customer and other personal detailed information of a very sensitive nature, is kept.[91]

These controls are complemented and supported by other IT governance and business management controls (as discussed in this chapter and other chapters of this book).

The most important information governance controls, within the scope of this book, are:

1 Information governance officer (may be exercised by the CIO described in this chapter).
2 Compliance officer (*see Chapter 12*).
3 Information sensitivity and data privacy policies.
4 Personnel administration procedures (*see Chapter 2*).
5 Data privacy officer (*see Chapter 12*).
6 Social media governance management plan.
7 Laptops and smart devices controls.
8 Confidentiality policy.
9 Social engineering controls
10 Internet and e-mail policy, presented next.

Other information governance controls, outside the scope of this book, are: health data coding policy, health records management policy, electronic patients handling policy, medical records archiving, etc.

---

[91] As per specific IT laws, health protection and data privacy laws of US, Australia, UK, Canada, The EU Data Privacy Directive, etc, such as: *www.ico.gov.uk*, *http://privacyruleandresearch.nih.gov/*, *www.privacy.org.au*, *http://ec.europa.eu/justice/data-protection/index_en.htm*, *www.opsi.gov.uk/Acts/Acts1998/ukpga_19980029_en_1*, *www.priv.gc.ca/legislation/02_06_02a_e.cfm*, etc.

Social engineering controls

'Social engineering' is a euphemism for non-technical or low-technology means (such as lies, persuasion, influence, friendly behaviour, impersonation, tricks, fax messages, e-mail messages, mobile telephone messages, bribes, blackmail, and threats, etc.), used to gain illegal access to your sensitive assets, offices, information systems, etc, with intent to gain, damage or abuse them.[92]

The respective controls (IGOV Control 1) that could defend your company, when implemented effectively, against 'social engineering' tactics, are described next:

1 **Risk assessment**: Regardless of the type (bank, e-money courier service, e-trading company, etc.) and size (small, medium, large) of your company, if you are involved in electronic activities, you should undertake, and execute, a full risk assessment study, before you develop and deploy specific protective measures against 'social engineering' tactics and threats.

2 **Data classification**: All your business data (printed reports, typed reports, manuals, digital media, tape copies of computerised information, etc.) should be classified according to your data classification policy (confidential, private, internal, etc.).

3 **Data off-site storage**: Your valuable, sensitive or critical business data, should be encrypted and stored off-site (see also Vital Records Package in *Chapter 14*).

4 **Data release**: All your business data (e.g. printed reports, typed reports, manuals, digital media, taped copies of computerised information, etc.) should be

---

[92] For more, see: *Social Engineering: The Art of Human Hacking,* Hadnagy, Christopher, Wiley Publishing (2010).

released according to the information release authorisation policy you will need to develop, or according to specific release instructions, at the time of the event. All releases should be logged, reported and monitored by you accordingly.

5 **Disclosing information over the phone**: Sensitive information should not be disclosed over the phone to anyone. Verbal security codes should be used to identify persons authorised, and allowed, to obtain sensitive codes, passwords, financial information, details of IT systems, software, networks, etc, of your company. Internal directory information should not be released over the phone. These requests should be recorded and handled, either by the customer service function, or the requested department. When disclosure takes place to authorised persons only, this should be logged and reported.

6 **Documenting suspicious calls**: All suspicious calls should be documented by the person receiving the call, and reported accordingly.

7 **Sending passwords to remote users**: All passwords to remote users should be delivered by person, and released upon the signature of the authorised users themselves. All these actions should also be logged and reported.

8 **Personal identification**: All employees should have badges, with a large photo, worn at all times. All visitors should also have badges worn at all times while in the offices, or premises of the organisation. The personal data of visitors should be recorded in a visitor's log and reported.

9 **E-mail handling**: All electronic mail attachments should be handled and checked by your central administration function, and only released to the particular person when

a security check has been performed. Generic e-mail addresses should be set up for business functions of your company communicating with external parties.

10 **Fax relaying**: Relaying of fax messages should not be allowed.

11 **Domain registrations**: When registering Internet domain names of your company, no personal contact details should be given. Only generic functional data (department name, address, etc, should be recorded as contact data).

12 **Personnel roaming**: Unauthorised company employees, visitors, and external maintenance personnel, should never be allowed to roam unescorted within any business areas containing sensitive information.

13 **External contractor handling**: The credentials and work orders of anyone performing technical work in or around any offices of your company should be checked. A responsible officer should double-check, and verify, that the work being executed was actually requested and necessary. Have someone representing your interests accompany these visitors while on your property. Have them complete their work during normal business hours. Outside contractors should never be allowed to roam unescorted within any business areas.

14 **Items left for pick up**: Before releasing any item to be picked up by anyone (e.g. external messenger, or another company employee), the person giving the item should record all personal and business details of the recipient.

15 **Garbage handling**: All garbage items (printed reports, work notes, company documentation of any kind, management reports, performance data, digital media, manuals, policies, procedures, printer cartridges, unused forms, etc.) should be destroyed completely, either by

using a paper shredder (for paper garbage), or a degaussing device (for digital media).

16 **Audit review**: All these controls should be reviewed by auditors and external experts as to their effectiveness and suitability, and improved on a cost-benefit basis, given the existence of new threats, regulations, and business risks.

Internet and e-mail policy

It is good practice, regardless of the size of your company, to institute and have all your staff use an Internet and e-mail policy (IGOV Control 2) when they communicate with both your known, and prospective, customers. .

IT governance performance controls

The IT governance controls may be monitored, as to their good operation, by performance measures (ITPM Control 1) and compliance indicators (ITCM Control 1) noted next.

IT governance performance measures: Percentage computer and network availability, number of lines coded/tested/changed, number of applications supporting critical business functions, average response time and average availability time.

IT governance compliance indicators: IT policies and procedures exist (or not), IT strategy plan exists (or not), IT security policy and procedures exist (or not).

You can monitor your performance in IT in your medium or large company by monitoring the performance measures and compliance indicators noted above, via the internal process and innovation and learning perspectives of a corporate BSC, or by an IT-specific BSC (*see Chapters 10 and 11*), as well as by the use of the GRC information system, as discussed in *Chapter 3*. You can monitor your performance for your small company by setting up a small manual or automated system (e.g. by using a spreadsheet application based on BSC).

Relating IT governance controls to the BMC framework

The controls identified in this chapter that can be deployed to protect your IT assets and information against potential fraud, while improving your business and IT performance and compliance objectives and targets, are considered to be part of the third level (govern level) of business operation of the BMC framework (*see Figure 1: Business Management Controls Framework, Chapter 1*).

IT governance controls recommendation

Recommendation 10: Be vigilant and proactive with all your IT resources, systems and networks

The key points to consider in assessing this recommendation for your business environment are:

1 Implement IT governance controls and complement them by performance measures, and compliance indicators, to support and enable your information processes and outcomes in the modern network-driven enterprise.

2 Monitor your data volumes, e-mail traffic, and other network transactions, and ensure that their growth is accommodated by relevant controls.

3 Ensure that your CEO, CIO and board directors are vigilant and proactive, and implement the required IT and information governance controls to ensure that your business operations are safe and secure in the new Web-based environment.

CHAPTER 8: BUSINESS DATA MANAGEMENT CONTROLS

'The common idea that success spoils people by making them vain, egotistic, and self-complacent, is erroneous; on the contrary, it makes them, for the most part, humble, tolerant, and kind. Failure makes people cruel and bitter.'

W. Somerset Maugham, English Playwright and Writer (1874–1965)

Chapter overview: This chapter, the fifth chapter of Part B: Main Types of Business Strategic and Operational Controls, deals with business data management controls which provide the necessary mechanisms to protect your company's data, so that all your business functions and systems perform better. Also, several business data management controls are noted and one recommendation (Recommendation 11: Establish effective policies and procedures to manage your business data) is offered for your consideration.

Introduction

Business data are at the nucleus of your business activities, and the main source of your business information systems. Business data from your business records (paper or digital), are expressed in paper or digital documents, and are processed and maintained by recordkeeping systems.

A record, in business terms, is an item or collection of data, which may contain: a set of fields in a database related to one entity, data about business transactions, medical history and treatments of persons, personal data of people, minutes of meetings, music, video, pictures, other forms of digital information, etc.

A document is 'any concrete or symbolic indication, preserved or recorded, for reconstructing, or for proving a phenomenon, whether physical or mental'.[93] Documents in business environments may contain: invoices, purchase order data, contracts, packing slips, reports, spreadsheets, bills of lading, vendor quotations, customs manifests, licences, certificates, transaction forms, computerised text files, etc.

Documents and records may be organised, and stored, in either paper or computerised files, or in some cases, where all paper documents and records have been digitised, in only computerised files. Paper and digital records will only have value for your organisation if they are accessible, and if you can preserve their authenticity and integrity over time.

A record-keeping system is a system that captures, protects and provides access to records over time. Record-keeping systems therefore make records accessible, and also employ the necessary controls that can ensure record authenticity and integrity. They are necessary business tools for the use and preservation of both your paper and digital records. No business, regardless of its type or size, can survive and flourish without high-quality business data. As business

---

[93] See *Information and Information Systems*, Buckland, M, New York: Greenwood Press (1991).

data are deemed to be critical assets of the modern enterprise, you must protect them, as their loss would be catastrophic to your company.

This protection is achieved, at the level of your company, by developing specific procedures and controls, such as:

1 Business record-keeping systems
2 Files, documents and records (FDR) management procedures
3 Business data register
4 Business data librarian, etc.

These should be implemented by an action plan, such as the one noted in this chapter, and supported by data quality procedures and controls, as described later in this chapter.

Business record-keeping systems

Regardless of the type and size of your company, you will have to organise, and maintain, all your business paper and digital records, and complementary management procedures, in a set of business record-keeping systems, such as:

1 **A corporate policies and procedures manual (EGOV Control 16**, *see also Chapter 2 for more details*) would usually contain your general corporate policies and procedures, for the following issues of your company: board operation, management procedures, personnel administration, business strategy, financial accounting, expense management, revenue control, regulatory compliance, risk management, purchasing, payroll, etc.
2 **Business operational manuals.** The corporate policies and procedures manual, in most companies, would be complemented with business operational manuals

(EGOV Control 16.1), detailing how operational staff, in all business functional departments (finance, IT, sales, production, quality, customer service, etc.), are required to carry out their detailed tasks.

In most organisations, this would involve multiple manuals, or sets of manuals. For example, a manufacturing company would likely have detailed procedures manuals for each product that they produce. They might even have a separate procedures manual for the operation of each piece of equipment. Also, in finance there would be a financial policies and procedures manual, in IT there would be a manual containing IT procedures, as well as several IT application systems manuals, one for each computerised application, etc.

3 **Business forms manual**. All your policies and procedures will need to be enabled and executed better with the use of specific forms, usually maintained in a business forms manual (EGOV Control 16.2).

This manual must be designed and used by your company to execute all your corporate policies and procedures, and may contain examples of forms and instructions on the use of the following forms: purchase order, invoice, journal entry, expense approval, vacation approval, overtime approval, master file inventory log, records inventory log, reports inventory log, documents inventory log, files, documents and records transfer form, files, documents and records deletion form, document distribution form, document revision form, etc.

4 **Business records system**. Regardless of the type and size of your company, you need a business records

system (EGOV Control 16.4), which would contain, as an example:

a. Employee personnel records, all employee accidents and illnesses, copies of monthly safety meetings, with the date and signatures of all employees in attendance, employee training records, including health, safety, payroll, and payments to pensioners (permanent retention).

b. Employment applications (five years' retention).

c. Expense reports (to be retained as many years as specified in the tax system of each country).

d. Insurance policies and claims, accounting and posting journal entries, financial statements and general ledgers (permanent retention).

e. Payments, cheques, bank statement, cash slips, invoices from vendors and to customers (to be retained as many years as specified in the tax system of each country).

f. Correspondence, electronic mail and fax messages, security logs and incidents, visitor's logs, audit reports, tax returns, contracts, and minutes of Board of Directors, including bylaws and articles of incorporation (permanent retention).

g. Purchase orders, sales records, inventory records, asset disposition records, etc. (as specified in the tax system of each country), etc.

5 **Compliance records system.** In addition to the business records system, described in the previous paragraph, you need a dedicated compliance records system (COMP Control 6), which serves all compliance-related issues of your company. This system is normally maintained and managed by your compliance officer. *(See Chapter 3 for details of its contents.)*

Files, documents and records (FDR) management procedures

You need, for a variety of purposes and reasons (e.g. corporate performance, auditing, compliance, legal, etc.), a set of FDR management procedures (BUSD Control 1) to manage the filing system of your company, the safe storage of these records, documents, normal correspondence, electronic messages, and company books for the predefined statutory time, and the legal destruction of old and not needed records, messages, documents and files, as per well-accepted standards.[94]

These procedures should be based on a set of national and international (UN, EU, OECD, etc.) government standards and guidelines, such as: Health Insurance Regulations, Age Discrimination Guidelines In Employment, Disabilities Act, Civil Rights Act, Employee Retirement Income Security Act, Labour Standards Act, Family and Medical Leave Act, Immigration Reform and Control Act, Occupational Safety and Health Act, Rehabilitation Act, Data Privacy Legal Frameworks and Regulations, Tax and Pension Records Retention Requirements, Tax and Customs Code, Health Acts, etc.

Special care must be paid to electronic health records and their management and protection aspects.[95]

---

[94] Also see: US Laws: DoD Standard 5015.2 and Federal Records Act (44 USC 3301), ISO15489 International Standard for Records Management (*www.iso.org*), and The Generally Accepted Record-keeping Principles® of Accountability, Integrity, Protection, Compliance, Availability, Retention, Disposition and Transparency, at: *www.arma.org/GARP/*.

[95] See: Relevant Acts and E-Health Standards: The UK Consumer Credit Act, The US Health Insurance Portability and Accountability Act, Health related standards (Health Level Seven, ISO/TS 21547:2010 and ISO/TR 21548:2010, ANSI X12(EDI), EN13606, EN13940, EN12967, ASTM International Continuity of Care Record standard, DICOM.

The specific forms that must be designed and used by your company to execute these procedures, are included in the business forms manual described before.

Files, documents and records (FDR) management action plan

Implementing protection for your business critical data by the FDR procedures identified above may be carried out by the files, documents and records management action plan (BUSD Control 2). You may use this plan to organise, establish, and manage the context, acquire resources, manage risks, etc, of your records.[96] This plan may be executed according to the approach for implementing business management controls described in *Chapter 11*.

This plan is made up of the following steps:

Step 1. Establish the context

Step 2. Manage risks

Step 3. Execute a disaster plan

Step 4. Monitor technology developments

Step 5. Manage metadata

Step 6. Keep source ('raw') records for a long period

Step 7. Limit the number of file formats used

Step 8. Use standard templates and creation rules

The European Institute for Health Records, etc, DIRECTIVE 2011/24/EU of the European Parliament and of the Council, etc.
[96] See: *Document Management for the Enterprise: Principles, Techniques, and Applications*, Sutton, Michael JD, John Wiley and Sons (1996).

Step 9. Manage the process

Step 10. Monitor, review and improve the process.

Business data administration controls

Business data are usually managed and controlled by the following mechanisms:

Business raw data retention procedure (EGOV Control 16.3). All incoming, processed and outgoing data and transactions of your company, will need to be kept in the original ('raw') format, in a well-protected, safe (from fire, etc.) and secure (access restriction rules) location, for as long as required by government regulations (tax, health, safety, etc.), and in accordance to industrial and other practices (stock exchange, banks, etc.) applicable to your business operation.

Business data register. The purpose of this register (BUSD Control 3.1), usually a computerised file, is to record the attributes (data element description, type, format, validating and editing instructions, business processing rules, etc.) of the business data of all your business documents, records and files used and maintained by the record-keeping systems, files and databases of your company. For more effective control, this should be a central repository of all business data, and may take the form of a classical data dictionary or enterprise architecture repository, or data directory or data repository[97] which should include all data

---

[97] Related to this is 'the knowledge warehouse' tool offered by several software vendors. For more on this, see: *Why use a Data Dictionary – Directory*, Kyriazoglou, John, European GUIDE Computer Conference Proceedings, England (June 1984) and

elements (paper, computerised, digitised, etc.), their sources and collection mechanisms for both internal business data (such as paper files, computerised application systems and databases, etc.), and external business data (such as libraries, industry reports, electronic repositories, etc.), and their editing and processing business rules, in accordance to various internal and external compliance rules and regulations.

Business data librarian. The business data librarian (BUSD Control 3.2):

1 Manages, develops and implements services related to the use of all data (paper, digital, etc.) for the business functions of the organisation.
2 Works closely with corporate management to determine needs, and support the use of business data.
3 Provides technical assistance and data custodian services for the business data created by all systems.
4 Monitors emerging trends and technologies in data governance technologies.
5 Participates in the needs identification, evaluation, design, and implementation of new business data.

Business data steward and custodian. In data governance groups, especially in large companies, responsibilities for data management are increasingly divided between the business process owners and information technology (IT) departments. Two functional titles commonly used for these roles are business data steward (BUSD Control 3.3) and

Enterprise Architecture and Metadata Modelling: A Guide to Conceptual Data Model, Metadata Repository, Business and Systems Re-engineering, Turco, Carl, Infinity Publishing (2009).

business data custodian, or sometimes database administrator (BUSD Control 3.4).

Business data stewards are commonly responsible for what is stored in data fields and the data content, context, and associated business rules.

Business data custodians are responsible for the safe custody, transport, storage of the data and implementation of business rules, and for the technical environment and database structure.[98]

Data and information quality monitoring and improvement process

Data[99] are typically the lowest level of abstraction of unprocessed ('raw') data, like characters, images, numbers and representations of physical quantities and facts, results of measurements, etc, from which information and knowledge are derived.

In business terms, these are processed by computerised systems, stored in computer-based devices and digital storage media, and transmitted to all authorised users, networks, computer programs, systems, stakeholders, etc, for further processing, decisions, actions, etc.

Information[100] represents knowledge communicated to all interested parties. In business terms, knowledge puts shape

---

[98] For more, see: *Database Administration: The Complete Guide to Practices and Procedures,* Mullins, Craig S, Addison-Wesley Professional (2002).
[99] Plural of *datum,* Latin for 'given' from Greek *dido* = to give, *didomi,* ancient Greek.
[100] From Latin *in + formare* denotes a concept, outline, or idea. Ultimately *formare* comes from the ancient Greek term *morphe* = form, from the ancient Greek god Morpheus, the god of shapes.

and meaning to 'raw' data, and it is the result of processing these data with a set of rules.

Knowledge is familiarity or acquaintance with data, facts, information, principles, concepts, ideas, values, descriptions, skills, dexterities, etc, obtained through study, investigation, education, training, experience, and other methods.

For the purposes of all types and forms of enterprises, business data and related information, represent the ever-changing world in which private, not-for-profit, and public organisations operate and survive. People, such as employees, customers, vendors and stakeholders, move, die and change, and therefore their data recorded in various digital resources and information systems and databases becomes obsolete and out of date. Vendors change their products and supplies. Standards change. Regulations change. Rules of doing business change. Market and economic forces require new types, and different data, which impact organisations. And as information, according to Deming, the noted US quality guru, is the second-most important resource to the organisation, next to its people resources,[101] it needs special and concentrated attention, so that it remains relevant and valid, both at the data level from which information is derived, as well as at the quality level which manifests its impacting and dynamic force.

This special attention, quality and protection of your business data, can be effected by a process of standards and best practices, and the use of the following procedures (data

---

[101] As quoted at: *www.infoimpact.com*.

quality monitoring procedure, data quality improvement procedure) and security controls, as noted next.

Data quality monitoring and improvement procedure

Without a strategic commitment to continuous business data quality, your business data quickly becomes incorrect or invalid, as incorrect or contaminated data reach your mission-critical business applications. The quality of your information may be monitored by:

1 A quality monitoring procedure
2 A data quality officer
3 A data quality improvement procedure
4 Data cleansing controls, outlined next.

Data quality monitoring procedure (BUSD Control 5.1): The quality of information can be measured, according to various studies and standards,[102] on the basis of about 20 attributes such as:

1 Accuracy
2 Consistency
3 Timeliness
4 Availability
5 Accessibility
6 Understanding, etc.

Data monitoring has become a key component of a complete data quality process, giving you the tools you

---

[102] Such as: US Government Departments: *www.nist.gov*, ISO/IEC 15939, 25012 and 15426, ISO/TR 22221:2006, ISO/TS 8000, ISO9001:2008 and ISO9004:2009, and article by Knight and Burn in *Information Science Journal*, Vol.8. 2005, at: *inform.nu*, article by Pipino, Lee and Wang, 'Data Quality Assessment', in *Communications of the ACM*, April 2002, Vol. 45, No. 4, etc.

need to understand how, and when, your data strays from its intended purpose.

Monitoring supports ongoing data governance efforts to ensure that all incoming and existing data meets pre-set business rules. With a data quality monitoring procedure in place, you, as a manager, can recognise data problems, inspect data sources and data processes, and implement the data corrections to get the problems fixed.

These may be achieved by:

1 A data quality officer
2 A data quality improvement procedure
3 Data cleansing controls, outlined next.

Data quality improvement (BUSD Control 5.2): You must also understand that the outcome of monitoring routines (reports, exception items, etc.) can provide important insight into the processes that create bad data. By studying this information, you can do more than correct the data. You can begin to improve the overall efficiency of the organisation. Data quality can be improved by a data improvement methodology and a data monitoring tool.

One such typical data quality improvement procedure is made up of seven steps:[103]

Step 1: Discover problem causes

Step 2: Measure data quality aspects

Step 3: Measure business rule integrity

Step 4: Complete problem analysis

---

[103] For other tools and methods see: *iaidq.org* and *www.infoimpact.com*.

Step 5: Plan the data improvement process

Step 6: Execute the data improvement process

Step 7: Improve the data quality improvement process.

Data cleansing controls

Data cleansing (BUSD Control 5.3), or data cleaning, or data scrubbing, is the process of detecting, removing, correcting and deleting (in certain cases), incorrect, incomplete, irrelevant, corrupt, out of date, formatted incorrectly, duplicated, etc, data or records from a computerised file, database table, database, or record set, etc. Data cleansing differs from data validation, in that data validation is applicable to checking input data for errors when these data are entered in an online (or batch) computerised application, for example general ledger system, payroll system, inventory control system,[104] etc. Data quality problems are present in single data collections, such as files and databases, for example, due to misspellings during data entry, missing information, or other invalid data. When multiple data sources need to be integrated, for example, in data warehouses, federated database systems, or global Web-based information systems, the need for data cleaning increases significantly. This is because the sources often contain redundant data in different representations.

Data cleansing may be achieved by an automated data cleansing process, using computer software programs with reference to rules, algorithms, statistical methods, logical

---

[104] For more on data validation methods, see Chapter 9 of *Strategic and Operational Controls*, Kyriazoglou, John, IT Governance Ltd (2010): *www.itgovernance.co.uk*.

checks, specialised look-up tables, etc, as described next. Data quality problems are also noted later in this section.

Automated data cleansing process: This process (BUSD Control 4) includes generalised (for all computerised applications), or specific, computer software for the specific application (general ledger, payroll, personnel management, order processing, inventory control, etc.) that is executed to perform data cleansing functions, and report the errors found and the additional actions to be undertaken, to correct the erroneous data found.

This software includes (as an example):

1 **Format checks**, such as: character validation tests that check data fields to see if they contain alphanumeric characters, when they are supposed to have only numeric characters, etc.

2 **Reasonableness checks**: These checks compare input data to expected values, by testing logical relationships, or checking whether an upper limit has not been exceeded. For example, employee weekly hours should not be automatically processed if the sum of regular and overtime hours per individual exceeds 80.

3 **Code checks**: The system can compare one code with other valid codes existing in the corporate, or other, database.

4 **Balancing checks**: Balancing checks confirm that output figures balance back to inputs from which they are derived.

5 **Database health checks**: These checks involve writing and executing software code to read all records in application classical files and databases, and navigating all the paths of the tree, or other structure of the databases, and printing a summary report with details of

what records, data and figures exist in the files and the databases.

Data quality officer

A data quality officer, or manager, or analyst, etc (BUSD Control 5.4), helps your company maintain high-quality data. The duties and responsibilities of a data quality officer, in general terms, are the following:

1 Establish a data quality monitoring and improving methodology, documenting a set of steps for determining, investigating and resolving data quality issues, and maintaining quality data, by defining data quality audit procedures.

2 Analyse, develop, document and maintain data quality goals, standards, and processes.

3 Work with all business users, and the software development team of your company, to identify, document and correct data quality issues.

4 Utilise data profiling, statistical, and other data quality tools, to detect, uncover, and determine root causes and anomalies of data quality in all your corporate systems.

5 Recommend amendments and corrections to your business data, and enhancements to the data acquisition processes, to improve accuracy of the business data maintained in corporate databases and data warehouses.

6 Work with the software development team to ensure that data rules are being supported and properly maintained.

7 Design, create, implement, and maintain test plans, use cases, scenarios, and scripts, to assure high quality in your business data.

8 Execute data test cases according to the defined data test methodology.

9 Prepare a weekly, or as required, status report, highlighting accomplishments and progress on all issues and concerns that may relate to business data.

10 Communicate and keep all data users aware of the needs and benefits of maintaining high data quality in all systems of your company.

Data mart and data warehouse controls

A data mart is a collection of data related to subject areas of a business, and organised for decision support, based on the needs of a given department or business function. The finance function has their data mart, the marketing function has theirs, the sales function has theirs, and so on. Data warehouses are significantly different from data marts. Data warehouses are arranged around the corporate subject data areas found in the corporate data model. Usually, the data warehouse is built and owned by centrally co-ordinated organisations, in large companies, such as the classic IT organisation.[105]

Consulting practice, across a variety of companies and industries, has shown that there are various issues related to both data marts and data warehouses (BUSD Control 6), such as: large numbers of redundant data, erroneous codes and other irrelevant content, inconsistent and illogical data, etc. This is because, many times, the data in a data mart and a data warehouse are not cross-checked back to their legacy application that generated these data, and therefore errors creep in the data marts and data warehouses, etc. The major

---

[105] For more, see: *Data Warehousing Fundamentals for IT Professionals*, Ponniah, Paulraj, John Wiley and Sons (2010).

controls that may apply to resolving these data error issues, besides the usual data warehouse construction and security controls (e.g. identify data, classify data, risk assessment, security access, etc.), are the data cleansing controls, described in this chapter.

Business data management performance controls

All of the above-mentioned controls may be monitored as to their operation, and complemented by a set of performance measures (BUSD Control 7.1) and compliance indicators (BUSD Control 7.2) noted next.

Business data management performance measures: Percentage of errors in data fields, internal quality failure costs, external quality failure costs and consistency errors.

Business data management compliance indicators: Data quality monitoring policies and procedures established (or not), data quality improvement policies and procedures established (or not) and data cleansing controls followed (or not).

You can monitor your performance in business data management in your medium or large company by monitoring the performance measures and compliance indicators noted above, via the internal process and innovation and learning perspectives of a corporate BSC (*Chapters 10 and 11*), as well as by the use of the GRC information system, as discussed in *Chapter 3*. You can monitor your performance for your small company by setting up a small manual or automated system (e.g. by using a spreadsheet application based on BSC).

Relating business data management controls to the BMC framework

The controls identified in this chapter that can be deployed to protect your business data, records and files against potential fraud, asset abuse, reputational damage and other risks that your company may be faced with, while achieving and improving your performance and compliance objectives and targets, are considered to be part of the following levels of controls of the BMC framework (*see Figure 1: Business Management Controls Framework, Chapter 1*), as noted next.

1 **First level (organize level) of business operation**: business data management controls (BUSD Control 3.2 to 5.4).

2 **Third level (govern level) of business operation**: files, documents and records (FDR) management procedures (BUSD Controls 1 and 2), enterprise governance controls (EGOV Controls 16.1 to 16.4), compliance records system (COMP Control 6), and business data administration controls (BUSD Controls 3 to 6).

3 **Fourth level (audit level) of business operation**: data quality monitoring and improvement controls (BUSD Control 5.1 to 5.3).

Conclusion

Not adequately addressing your business data protection, data quality, and data management issues, could have serious consequences to your business operations, including:

1 Complete or partial loss of business, as your customers and suppliers are unable to conduct business when the

business data and/or computerised applications become unavailable.

2 Loss of productivity while your business data are being recovered.

3 Legal liability, especially due to the requirements of the various national data privacy and security laws and regulations, and the fines given to organisations on compliance and security breaches.

4 Damaged reputation, as loss of business data can lead to a loss of credibility.

The Data Warehousing Institute (TDWI) reported in its study of 647 companies on data quality, that 40% of the companies surveyed have suffered losses, problems, or costs, due to poor data quality,[106] such as:

1 Lack of validation routines in data entry systems, or in system loading.

2 Mismatched syntax (first name, last name, versus last name, first name).

3 Data formats (6-byte versus 4-byte data fields) and code structures (male/female versus m/f).

4 Unexpected changes in source systems.

5 The number and complexity of system integration interfaces.

6 Poor system design.

7 Data conversion errors.

---

[106] See: *Data Quality and The Bottom Line,* Eckerson, Wayne W, The Data Warehouse Institute (2002).

Business data management controls recommendation

Recommendation 11: Establish effective policies and procedures to manage your business data

The key points to consider in assessing this recommendation for your business environment are:

1 Establish a data custodian role and assign it to a specific person.
2 Copy critical business data via the tool of the vital records package.
3 Test the recovery process on a pre-determined basis.
4 Establish security and data classification procedures.
5 Train your personnel on protecting your business data.
6 Monitor your data quality and correct any errors.
7 Finally, ensure that you have a comprehensive business continuity plan (*see also Chapter 14*).

CHAPTER 9: BUSINESS INTELLIGENCE AND ESPIONAGE CONTROLS

'Speak softly and carry a big stick; you will go far.'

Theodore Roosevelt, American President (1858–1919)

Chapter overview: This chapter, the sixth chapter of Part B: Main Types of Business Strategic and Operational Controls, deals with business intelligence and espionage controls which provide the necessary methods and tactics for your company to improve your position against your competition, and protect your business from all forms of crime control. Also, several business intelligence and espionage controls are noted and one recommendation (Recommendation 12: Establish efficient mechanisms to give you excellent business information and protect your intangible and property assets) is offered for your consideration.

Introduction

The most critical assets in the 21st Century for private and public enterprises, for business entities and organisations in general, for the global society, and for the economy (local, regional, national, international), are not of physical nature (equipment, machines, installations, plants), or of financial nature (money, credit or other financing instruments), or of computer software nature. The most critical assets are the knowledge and ideas (concepts) that exist in the brains of people, which are stored in classical paper files, computerised systems (personal and corporate), multimedia devices, electronic messages, network servers, back-up devices, digital records, CAD, and other office automation files, web records, etc, in the modern business environment.

The computer technology and related infrastructure, the information systems, the network backbone (intranet, extranet, metropolitan, Internet, etc.), and related media technologies, give everyone within a given organisational environment, direct access to what is going on: within the given organisation, in the industrial sector to which it belongs, and in the general economy and market in which it operates. A question is relevant here. Are all of these protected?

According to various global data, surveys and studies,[107] many large companies (North America, Europe, and Australia) have BCP and disaster recovery plans for their IT systems and their data networks, while this is not the case in smaller companies. Most large companies in Asia, Latin America and Africa, do not have any such plans. But even where these plans exist, in the majority of the cases reported, they are not comprehensive, as they do not include all critical elements of operating an organisation, such as people, processes, property, infrastructure and data, etc. All these critical assets of the modern enterprise must be protected, as their loss would be catastrophic to the organisation concerned. Various protection measures and controls have been discussed in previous chapters.

---

[107] See *www.thebci.org*, *www.drj.com*, *www.iwar.org.uk*, etc.

This chapter expands on these by:

1 Adding a set of controls related to business intelligence, most relevant to the long-term protection and survival of any company, regardless of its type and size.
2 Presenting specific measures to protect a company from potential, corporate espionage and sabotage, the latest major threats to companies all over the world.

Business intelligence controls

The successful existence and long-term, social and economic survival of your company, presupposes effective and accurate decision-making by its management. This survival needs continuous, accurate and up-to-date business information and 'raw' data, from both internal and external sources, as well as a set of methods of applying all this business intelligence to the specifics of your business entity. Business intelligence,[108] within the scope of this book, refers to a variety of techniques, technologies and software applications used to identify, analyse and process both the 'raw' business data of your company, as well as data from external sources, for decision-making purposes, on several business issues, such as:

1 Identification of all aspects of current and future competition.
2 The impact of these factors on the strategy and operations of your business enterprise.

---

[108] For more on business intelligence, see: *Business Intelligence: Making Better Decisions Faster,* Vitt, Elizabeth, Luckevich, Michael and Misner, Stacia, Microsoft Press (2002), *Strategic and Competitive Analysis: Methods and Techniques for Analysing Business Competition,* Fleisher, Craig S and Bensoussan, Babette, Prentice Hall (2002), *www.businessintelligencetoolsx.com/, www.globalintelligence.com/,* and *www.scip.org.*

3 Development of new products and services,[109] etc.

Achieving the benefits of business intelligence for your company requires the following controls, as a minimum:

1 The appointment of a business intelligence data manager.
2 Business intelligence policy.
3 The full execution of a business intelligence system management plan, described next.

Business intelligence data manager

The duties and responsibilities of a business intelligence data manager (BUSI Control 1) include, as an example:

1 To manage, develop and implement, collection mechanisms, strategy, policies and procedures, for all business intelligence data (internal and external) for the business functions of the organisation.
2 To processes, analyse and report to all authorised levels of management, business intelligence reports containing relevant internal and external data related to: industry, competition, market, regulatory environment, corporate performance, employee issues, business transactions processed, etc.
3 To work closely with corporate management to determine needs, and support the use of business intelligence data.
4 To provide technical assistance and business intelligence services for the business data created by all systems, and collected from external sources.

---

[109] For more definitions, see: *www.cio.com*, and *www.businessdictionary.com*.

5   To monitor emerging trends and technologies in business intelligence and data governance technologies.

6   To participate in the needs identification, evaluation, design, and implementation of new business intelligence sources and data.

Business intelligence system management plan

The business intelligence system management plan (BUSI Control 2) is made up of the following steps, as an example:

Step 1: Define the business intelligence mission, strategy, policy (see example next) and performance targets.

Step 2: Select and appoint a business intelligence data manager, and establish the organisational structure for business intelligence, by assigning detailed responsibilities and reporting mechanisms.

Step 3: Draft a budget, obtain board approval, and acquire the necessary resources, personnel, funds, systems, office space, equipment, subscriptions to external databases, etc.

Step 4: Identify the business intelligence internal and external sources, and define the data and related quality checking and correction procedures that will make up the business intelligence data repository.

Step 5: Organise, and install, the process and the business data collection mechanisms from internal corporate sources, internal computerised application systems, and business transaction data, as well as the other corporate warehouse data which will feed the business data repository.

Step 6: Organise, and set up, the collection mechanisms for obtaining external data which will feed the business intelligence data repository.

Step 7: Test the business data collection mechanisms.

Step 8: Develop a disaster recovery plan.

Step 9: Operate the business intelligence function, and provide the required reports and analyses to approved management levels.

Step 10: Review, and evaluate, the results of the business intelligence function, and improve the structure, operation, staff, systems and reports of the business intelligence process.

Business intelligence policy

The guidelines included in this policy (BUSI Control 3) should be used in instructing your company personnel in their gathering activities of competitive intelligence information from various external sources. A business intelligence policy will include guidelines to company personnel, on issues, such as: use only public information, be ethical guideline, use legitimate social engineering practices, use consulting services, and use information from third sources.

Corporate espionage and sabotage controls

We presently live in 'knowledge-based[110]economies', where an economy is dependent, to a very large extent, on service and technology provision companies.

In the current century of globally-interconnected economies and companies, scientific research and technological advances and developments can, and probably will, have very powerful effects on how private and public organisations provide goods and services to improve the lives of all people.[111]

The most valuable business assets of these companies are not, in fact, the land and buildings they own, the capital invested, or shares and other investments they utilise, the heavy equipment or sophisticated machinery and production lines in their manufacturing plants, but their intangible and proprietary assets.

Intangible and proprietary assets are assets that are not physical in nature, such as: intellectual property, patents, trademarks, trade secrets, product designs, production formulas, calculations, prototypes, procedures, software algorithms, production methods, processing techniques, copyrights, pricing formulas, customer lists and accounts, business plans, business methodologies, recipes, research results, information systems, goodwill, brand names, reputation, business data, personnel and health records, maintenance contracts, etc.

---

[110] For more on this, see: *The Knowledge-Based Economy. Modelled, Measured, Simulated*, Lydesdorff, Loet, Universal-Publishers (2006): www.oecd.org/dataoecd/51/8/1913021.pdf.
[111] See also. *The Future of Technology and its Impact on Our Lives*, www.wpp.com/wpp/marketing/digital/the-future-of-technology.htm.

These are typically documented, and maintained, in various policies, procedures, practices, manuals, systems, files, media and locations of your company.

These intangible and property assets are usually fundamental to your company's survival and long-term profitability, and distinguish them from their legitimate or copycat competitors.

It is, therefore, up to you, the responsible business manager, and the Board, to ensure that these valuable assets are protected in the best possible way, by a set of controls, as described next.

Corporate anti-espionage and anti-sabotage manager

The duties and responsibilities of a corporate anti-espionage and anti-sabotage manager (BUSI Control 4) include, as an example:

1 To manage, develop and implement strategy, policies and procedures for the protection of the company from all internal and external espionage and sabotage threats.
2 To process, analyse and report to all authorised levels of management, espionage and sabotage incidents.
3 To work closely with senior corporate management to determine anti-espionage and anti-sabotage tactics.
4 To provide technical assistance to all corporate management, as regards anti-espionage and anti-sabotage measures.
5 To monitor emerging trends and technologies in anti-espionage and anti-sabotage technologies.
6 To participate in the needs identification, evaluation, design, and implementation of new anti-espionage and anti-sabotage sources and data.

Corporate espionage and sabotage controls action plan

In addition to the governance controls described in *Chapter 2*, and the soft controls in *Chapter 13*, consider improving (if they exist), or instituting (if they do not exist), the following corporate espionage and sabotage controls, as described in the following action plan (BUSI Control 5), containing 12 components, as noted next.

Component 1: Improve internal controls

Action 1: Carry out a risk assessment (in terms of business intelligence and corporate espionage/sabotage aspects) and a due diligence on the major aspects of controlling your business data, by using the audit programmes and checklists described in *Chapter 15*, and by going through the following list and making the necessary control improvements when specific gaps in control practices and procedures are identified:

Action 2: Describe your company's major governance, risk, compliance, operational, production and financial controls, and compare them with your industry standards, and with the similar-type controls established by other similar companies, and identify any obvious gaps and required improvements.

Action 3: Describe the protection mechanisms of the business data, patents, trademarks and information systems used by your company, and compare them with your industry standards, and with the protection controls established by other similar companies, and identify any obvious gaps and required improvements.

Action 4: Quantify, in terms of money, the total investments (data, systems, patents, buildings, plants, other assets, etc.) owned and managed by your company at this point in time.

Action 5: Describe your company's major physical (buildings, offices, plants, etc.), IT and web-enabled applications security controls, and identify any obvious gaps and required improvements.

Action 6: Improve your protection mechanisms of the business data, patents, trademarks and information systems, and other assets of your company, according to the gaps identified above.

Action 7: Implement an internal controls system to your needs, and ensure your board's and audit committee's oversight.

Action 8: Ensure that the management of your company has the skills and expertise, as well as the intelligence, background, and experience specific to designing, introducing, and testing internal controls for protecting all corporate assets against industrial espionage threats, frauds and other risks.[112]

Action 9: Improve your internal audit system, and ensure execution of both periodic and ad hoc audits of all your business operations and internal controls.

Action 10: Ensure certification of financial, and other corporate information, by senior management (CEO, CFO, etc.) and other corporate personnel.

---

[112] See also articles and other data in various sites, such as: *www.csis-scrs.gc.ca/prrts/spng/xmpls-eng.asp*, *www.becca-online.org*, *www.sans.org*.

Component 2: Register patents, copyrights and trademarks (BUSI Control 5.1)

In addition to the governance controls described in *Chapter 2*, consider improving (if they exist), or instituting (if they do not exist), the following controls.

Action 1: Record all your patents, copyrights and trademarks, etc, in your 'business intangible assets register', described later.

Action 2: Submit all the documentation required to register your patents, copyrights, intellectual property, inventions, and trademarks with the proper authorities.[113]

Action 3: Carry out a risk assessment (in terms of business intelligence and corporate espionage/sabotage aspects) and review your international partners adequately before you establish any working relationships with them involving your patents, and other intellectual property items.

Component 3: Business data classification (BUSI Control 5.2)

In addition to the governance controls described in *Chapter 7*, consider improving (if they exist), or instituting (if they do not exist), the following controls.

Action 1: Carry out a risk assessment (in terms of business intelligence and corporate espionage/sabotage aspects) of the risks related to your business data.

Action 2: Identify the types of your business data and information (R&D processes, product innovations, new

---

[113] For US patents, at: *www.uspto.gov/*, for Canada, at: *www.patentregister.ca/*, for European patents, at: *www.epo.org*, for UK at: *www.ipo.gov.uk* and for Australia, at: *www.ipaustralia.gov.au/*.

market strategies, personnel files, pricing structure, and customer data, customer files, etc.) your company holds that must protected.

Action 3: Classify your business data according to sensitivity criteria, etc.

Action 4: Implement procedures for de-classifying business data and information when they do not need protection, etc.

Component 4: Business intangible assets register (BUSI Control 5.3)

In addition to the business data management controls described in *Chapter 7*, consider improving (if they exist), or instituting (if they do not exist), the following controls.

Action 1: Maintain a register of your critical business intangible assets (patents, copyrights, intellectual property, inventions and trademarks, product designs, processes, formulas, as described above), data, documents and files, and their physical (office) or logical location (network, information system, etc.).

Action 2: Review this register, at least annually, and add or remove items, as required, and improve the process as needed.

Component 5: Security controls (BUSI Control 5.4)

In addition to the IT governance controls described in *Chapter 6*, consider improving (if they exist), or instituting (if they do not exist), the following controls.

Action 1: Design, develop and implement adequate security controls on the basis of a company-wide risk assessment of the threats and risks facing your specific company.

Action 2: Implement physical access and improve procedures for accessing protected information, and recording all business transactional activities.

Action 3: Escort your visitors to all areas.

Action 4: Use computer passwords, safes, and locked file cabinets, to restrict access to proprietary information, etc.

Action 5: Implement surveillance and eavesdropping detection controls, by specialised task forces.

Action 6: Establish, and enforce, tactics to protect your company from outsiders, especially when they are using social engineering controls to access your sensitive assets (*see also Chapter 7 for more details*).

Action 7: Train all your users, managers, and IT staff, in protecting and safeguarding your business data and information against social engineering techniques that can be used to gain access to sensitive data, and what procedures they should execute to report compromises or suspected attempts to solicit sensitive information.

Component 6: Business information distribution (BUSI Control 5.5)

In addition to the business data management controls described in *Chapter 7*, consider improving (if they exist), or instituting (if they do not exist), the following controls.

Action 1: Carry out a risk assessment (in terms of business intelligence and corporate espionage/sabotage aspects) of the risks facing your business information distribution specifics.

Action 2: Implement procedures for the safe transmission, communication and transfer of protected business data and information, both internally and externally, by any means and methods.

Action 3: Maintain a register for recording any such transfers of protected information and data.

Component 7: Production process controls (BUSI Control 5.6)

In addition to the production controls described in *Chapter 5*, consider improving (if they exist), or instituting (if they do not exist), the following controls.

Action 1: Risk assessment: Assess the risks of failure, espionage or sabotage, in your product design and development, process design and implementation, people (non-active) involvement, (non-availability of) strategic resources and partner reliability, and protect your company with specific measures.

Action 2: Product liability: Implement production processes that ensure your products are not defective, support these products after they are sold, fix them if they are found defective, and inform your customers if your products are found problematic.

Action 3: Supply chain: Ensure continuous flow of your goods and the services you provide, have extra critical inventory, learn the various customs regulations in the regions you operate and comply with them, and ensure availability of strategic input resources.

Component 8: Personnel administration controls (BUSI Control 5.7)

In addition to the governance controls described in *Chapter 2* and the soft controls in *Chapter 13*, consider improving (if they exist), or instituting (if they do not exist), the following controls.

Action 1: Carry out a risk assessment (in terms of business intelligence and corporate espionage/sabotage aspects) of the personnel administration risks facing your company.

Action 2: Establish, and enforce, personnel administration controls, such as: perform background checks on all your staff, valid employment agreements, employee non-disclosure agreements, human resource exit interview process, etc.

Action 3: Treat everybody fairly and ensure that no violence takes place in your workplace (*see also Chapter 9 for more ideas*).

Action 4: Ensure that all your staff are professionally qualified and certified.

Action 5: Ensure that all your personnel sign a confidentiality agreement.

Component 9: Business continuity (BUSI Control 5.8)

In addition to the business continuity controls described in *Chapter 12*, consider improving (if they exist), or instituting (if they do not exist), the following controls.

Action 1: Carry out a risk analysis of the threats (insider and outsider) relevant to your company, and obtain the necessary funds to develop a suitable programme and plan for your operating conditions.

Action 2: Establish, and test, your business and IT continuity programme and plan, organisation and procedures.

Action 3: Perform due diligence to all your business continuity partners.

Action 4: Back-up everything that is important, and take copies to an off-site safe, storage location.

Component 10: Corporate administration (BUSI Control 5.9)

In addition to the governance controls described in *Chapter 2*, consider improving (if they exist), or instituting (if they do not exist), the following controls.

Action 1: Carry out a risk assessment (in terms of business intelligence and corporate espionage/sabotage aspects) of the corporate administration risks facing your company.

Action 2: Implement vendor and other contractors' maintenance agreements.

Action 3: Perform due diligence on all of your contractors, before assigning work to them, and annually thereafter.

Action 4: Have all your external partners sign confidentiality agreements with your company, and keep them in a safe place.

Action 5: Establish, and execute, trash and other rubbish handling and disposal procedures, such as: shred paper documents, destroy digital media by the use of special 'crunching' equipment, etc.

Action 6: Implement policies for copying and duplicating protected information.

Component 11: Ethics and compliance (BUSI Control 5.10)

In addition to the governance controls described in *Chapter 2*, consider improving (if they exist), or instituting (if they do not exist), the following controls.

Action 1: Carry out a risk assessment (in terms of business intelligence and corporate espionage/sabotage aspects) of your ethics and compliance risks facing your company.

Action 2: Establish an ethics and compliance programme for your company.

Action 3: Develop an employee training and awareness programme, including orientation presentations, for all your staff.

Action 4: Implement procedures for internal reporting of resource abuse or fraud suspicions, and any other breaches, etc.

Action 5: Research, and resolve, all espionage or sabotage cases or incidents, in your business operation.

Action 6: Ensure legal prosecution of all corporate criminals, and inform appropriate authorities, and request assistance if you need any.

Component 12: Continuous business management monitoring (BUSI Control 6)

In addition to the governance controls described in *Chapter 2*, consider improving (if they exist), or instituting (if they do not exist), the following controls.

Action 1: Carry out a risk assessment (in terms of business intelligence and corporate espionage/sabotage aspects) of your risks related to monitoring business intelligence controls.

Action 2: Establish a corporate intelligence and espionage/sabotage monitoring system.

Action 3: Collaborate and connect to other partners, members of industrial associations, companies you do business with, etc, and interchange non-privileged information related to the actual, or potential, crime committed, or other suspicious event, as needed.

Action 4: Report all cases, formally and informally, to the proper state authorities.

Action 5: Be vigilant and proactive, to protect both yourself and your company.

Business intelligence and espionage performance controls (BUSI Control 7)

All of the above-mentioned controls may be monitored, as to their operation, by a set of performance measures (BUSI Control 7.1) and compliance indicators (BUSI Control 7.2) noted next .

Business intelligence and espionage performance measures: Security violations per time-period, number of security assessments carried out by management per time-period, percentage of documents classified incorrectly, security violations by department, number of patents registered and number of patent violations.

Business intelligence and espionage compliance indicators: Business intelligence controls exist (or not), business intelligence data manager exists (or not), business intelligence system management plan exists (or not), and corporate espionage and sabotage controls exist (or not).

You can monitor your performance in business intelligence and espionage in your medium or large company by monitoring the performance measures and compliance indicators noted above, via the internal process and innovation and learning perspectives of a corporate BSC (*Chapters 10 and 11*), as well as by the use of the GRC information system (EPRM Control 3), as discussed in *Chapter 3*. You can monitor your performance for your small company by setting up a small manual or automated system (e.g. by using a spreadsheet application based on BSC).

Relating business intelligence and espionage controls to the BMC framework

The controls identified in this chapter that can be deployed to protect your business data, records and files against potential fraud, asset abuse, espionage, sabotage, reputational damage, and other risks that your company may be faced with, while achieving and improving your performance and compliance objectives and targets, are considered to be part of the third level (govern level) of business operation of the BMC framework (*see Figure 1: Business Management Controls Framework, Chapter 1*).

Conclusion

Business managers cannot afford to sit back and wait for a corporate espionage incident to occur, and not have adequate business intelligence to do their job. It is imperative that they are proactive, and develop an holistic approach to gathering business intelligence, and for enhancing their security, that pre-empts malicious attacks and mitigates risk. Your business assets, and the value they represent or can accrue to you, and your company, as various studies and data have shown, are threatened by industrial espionage (also known as economic or corporate espionage), white-collar crime, corporate crime, etc. These persons or organisations, besides accessing information about a company's plans, products, clients or trade secrets, can also include attempts to destroy data or prevent you, the legitimate owner, from accessing these assets.[114] It is, therefore, up to the responsible business manager and the Board, to ensure that these valuable assets are protected in the best possible way, by a set of controls, as described in this chapter.

Business intelligence and espionage controls recommendation

Recommendation 12: Establish efficient mechanisms to give you excellent business information and protect your intangible and property assets

The key points to consider in assessing this recommendation for your business environment are:

1 Collect and process business information
2 Register your patents
3 Carry out due diligence on your staff and partners
4 Enforce security control practices.

---

[114] For example, for US industrial espionage cases, see: *www.wright.edu/rsp/Security/Spystory/Industry.htm*. Also see Proctor and Gamble vs. Unilever, case of 2001: *http://news.bbc.co.uk/2/hi/business/4595745.stm*) and *Dishonest Dollars: The Dynamics of White-Collar Crime*, Leap, Terry L, Ithaca: Cornell University Press (2007).

CHAPTER 10: BUSINESS PERFORMANCE MANAGEMENT FRAMEWORKS

'Employ your time in improving yourself by other men's writings, so that you shall gain easily what others have laboured hard for.'

Socrates, Ancient Greek Philosopher (469–399 BC)

Chapter overview: This chapter, the first chapter of Part B: Implementing Business Management Controls, describes various business performance management frameworks which enable, facilitate and support the good operation of all your business management controls. Also, several business performance management framework controls are noted and one recommendation (Recommendation 13: Select and implement a performance management framework that suits your needs) is offered for your consideration.

Introduction

'Every discourse, even a poetic or oracular sentence, carries with it a system of rules for producing analogous things and thus an outline of methodology,' is a famous quote by Jacques Derrida.[115] It is, therefore, paramount that in order for organisations to be controlled and managed in the most effective way, a framework, as we concluded in *Chapter 1*, as well as an associated methodology, is required for best

---

[115] Jacques Derrida, French philosopher, 1930–2004, founder of 'deconstruction'.

results. The most used frameworks are presented next. A BSC methodology for implementing controls is discussed in *Chapter 11*.

Purpose and types of business performance management frameworks

In the current business environment, regardless of the type and size of your operation, you need an holistic approach to manage the performance of each function of the business entity, as well as the whole company. The purpose of a business performance management framework is to provide you with such an approach that allows you to look at the business as a whole, instead of at each part. A business performance management framework would include reviewing your overall business performance and determining how your business can better reach its overall strategic goals and specific operational objectives. Such a framework contains of a set of theories and standards, widely accepted, and enough to serve as the guiding principles of implementation within a particular discipline.

In the area of business management, especially in strategic and operational controls, such a framework is established by the performance management process. This includes, in a general sense, formulating and setting up the performance measurement system (e.g. BSC at the corporate level), entering the performance data, carrying out the required performance analyses, and setting up a corporate award system.

There are several types of such business performance measurement and management frameworks, models, and ready-made software systems in the market, for implementing strategic and operational controls for all types of organisations (private, public, etc.), such as:

1 Quality management frameworks
2 Government self-assessment performance frameworks
3 General-use performance frameworks, as described, in summary, next.

Quality management frameworks

The two representative examples in the quality management frameworks area are: TQM framework and EQFM framework.

TQM framework

Total quality management (TQM) (BPMF Control 1) is a management approach that originated in the 1950s and has steadily become more popular since the early 1980s. Total quality is a description of the culture, attitude and organisation of a company that strives to provide customers with products and services that satisfy their needs.[116]

Total quality management (TQM) is based on the theories[117] of Deming, Juran and Feigenbaum, since the 1980s.

---

[116] For TQM case studies, see: *www.businessballs.com/qualitymanagement.htm*.

[117] For more details see: *Quality, Productivity, and Competitive Position*, Edwards Deming, W, MIT Centre for Advanced Engineering, Cambridge Mass, US (1982), *The Management and Control of Quality*, Evans, RJ and Lindsay, MW, South-Western, US (2002), *Total Quality Control*, Feigenbaum, Armand Vallin, McGraw-Hill (1961) and *www.juran.com*.

To be successful in implementing TQM, according to Deming, an organisation must concentrate on eight key elements:

1   Ethics
2   Integrity
3   Trust
4   Training
5   Teamwork
6   Leadership
7   Communication
8   Recognition.

EFQM framework

The EFQM excellence model (BPMF Control 2) was introduced at the beginning of 1992, as the framework for assessing organisations for the European Quality Award. It is now widely used in Europe, and it has become the basis for the majority of national and regional, quality awards. The EFQM excellence model[118] is a non-prescriptive framework based on nine criteria, in two major types: enablers and results.

The 'enabler' criteria (leadership, people, strategy, partnerships and resources, processes, products and services) covers what an organisation does. The 'results' criteria (people results, customer results, society results, key results) covers what an organisation achieves.

---

[118] For more details, see: European Foundation for Quality Management: *www.efqm.org* and articles and books in the bibliography section. For EFQM case studies, see: *www.cioindex.com/it strategy/ArticleId/70589/EFQM-Business-Excellence-Model-Case-Studies.aspx*.

'Results' are caused by 'Enablers' and 'Enablers' are improved using feedback from 'Results'.

The model, which recognises there are many approaches to achieving sustainable excellence in all aspects of performance, is based on the premise that: excellent results, with respect to performance, customers, people and society, are achieved through leadership driving policy and strategy, which is delivered through people, partnerships and resources and processes.

Government self-assessment performance frameworks

Two representative examples of government self-assessment performance frameworks are: Canada's MAF and the European Union's CAF, as briefly described next.

Canada: Management accountability framework (MAF)

The Treasury Board Secretariat (TBS: part of the Federal Government of Canada: *www.tbs-sct.gc.ca*) carries out assessments of management performance of all major Canadian federal departments, and some small agencies, annually. These are carried out by the use of the management accountability framework (MAF) (BPMF Control 3) and its 10 elements, as noted next:

1 Public service values element
2 Governance and strategic directions element
3 Policy and programmes element
4 People element
5 Citizen-focused service element
6 Risk management element
7 Stewardship element

8   Accountability element
9   Results and performance element
10 Learning, innovation and change management element.

Organisations provide TBS with evidence for each of the areas of management for which they are assessed. TBS uses information submitted by organisations to prepare the assessments, which are shared mid-cycle with departments and agencies for discussion, and at the end of the cycle, with the deputy head. The results from the MAF assessments are also used as an input in the performance management programme for deputy heads. All assessments are reported to all authorised parties. The whole emphasis of implementing the MAF is to increase focus on improving managerial performance within all Canadian federal departments and organisations.

European Union: Common assessment framework (CAF)

The common assessment framework (CAF) (BPMF Control 4) provides a self-assessment framework which is conceptually similar to the major total quality models, in particular the excellence model of the European Foundation for Quality Management (EFQM), but which is especially designed for public-sector organisations, taking into account their characteristics.

The CAF has four main purposes:[119]

1 To **introduce** public administrations to the principles of TQM and gradually guide them, through the use and understanding of self-assessment, from the current 'Plan-Do' sequence of activities, to a complete 'Plan-Do-Check-Act (PCDA)' cycle.
2 To facilitate the **self-assessment** of a public organisation, in order to arrive at a diagnosis and **improvement actions**.
3 To act as a **bridge** across the various models used in quality management.
4 To facilitate **bench learning** between public-sector organisations.

The CAF model is a framework based on nine criteria, as shown in *Table 4*.

Table 4: CAF enablers and results

Enablers		Results
1 Leadership		1 People results
2 People		2 Citizen/customer results
3 Strategy and planning		3 Society results
4 Partnerships and resources management		4 Organisational performance results
5 Execution of processes		

---

[119] For more details see: *www.eipa.eu*. For case studies, see: *Five Years of CAF 2006: From Adolescence to Maturity – What Next?*, Staes, P, Thijs, N, Stoffels, A and Geldof, S, Maastricht: EIPA (2011): available at *www.eipa.eu/caf* submenu 'Publications', and on *new.eupan.eu*.

The model is based on the principle that the **results** from the operation of an organisation (people results, citizen/customer results, society results, and organisational performance results), are derived from a set of **enablers** (leadership, strategy and planning, people management, partnerships and resources management, and execution of processes).

Other government performance assessment frameworks

Other government related frameworks (BPMF Control 5) include:

1 UK's 'Capability review programme' (*www.civilservice.gov.uk*).
2 US 'President's management agenda' (*www.whitehouse.gov/sites/default/files/omb/assets/omb/budget/fy2002/mgmt.pdf*).
3 New Zealand's 'Performance improvement framework' (*www.ssc.govt.nz/pif*).
4 India's 'Performance system' (*www.performance.gov.in*), etc.

General-use performance frameworks

Numerous general-use performance management frameworks and systems are used in all types and sizes of private and public organisations across the world, to manage and improve corporate performance. The most successful, so far, is the balanced scorecard (BSC), as described next. The other frameworks and systems are briefly noted in the paragraphs that follow.

BSC framework

According to the balanced scorecard model (BPMF Control 6), strategic managers have traditionally relied on financial measures of performance, such as profit and return on investment, to evaluate organisational performance. But financial information, although important, is not enough by itself. If strategic managers are to obtain a true picture of organisation performance, financial information must be supplemented with performance measures that indicate how well an organisation has been achieving the four building blocks of competitive advantage – efficiency, quality, innovation and responsiveness to customers.

This is so because financial results simply inform strategic managers about the results of decisions they have already taken; the other measures balance this picture of performance, by informing managers about how accurately the organisation has in place the building blocks that drive the future performance and obtain a competitive advantage.[120]

The BSC (balanced scorecard) model is a performance management tool which began as a concept for measuring whether the smaller-scale operational activities of a company are aligned with its larger-scale objectives, in terms of vision and strategy. By focusing not only on financial outcomes, but also on the operational, marketing and developmental inputs to these, the balanced scorecard helps provide a more comprehensive view of a business,

---

[120] For more details see: *The Balanced Scorecard: Translating Strategy into Action,* Kaplan, RS and Norton, DP, Harvard Business School Press (1996), *What is a Modern Balanced Scorecard?, Management Case Study,* Marr, B, The Advanced Performance Institute (*www.ap-institute.com*) (2010) and *Balanced Scorecards for the Public Sector,* Marr, Bernard, Ark Group, London (2010).

which in turn helps organisations act in their best long-term interests. Organisations were encouraged to measure, in addition to financial outputs, what influenced such financial outputs. For example, process performance, market share/penetration, long-term learning and skills development, and so on. The underlying rationale is that organisations cannot directly influence financial outcomes, as these are 'lag' measures, and that the use of financial measures alone to inform the strategic control of the company, is unwise.

Organisations should instead also measure those areas where direct management intervention is possible. In so doing, the early versions of the balanced scorecard helped organisations achieve a degree of 'balance' in selection of performance measures.

BSC perspectives

Four general perspectives have been proposed by the balanced scorecard model by Kaplan and Norton, the founders of this approach: financial perspective, customer perspective, internal process perspective, and innovation and learning perspective.

The financial perspective examines if the company's implementation and execution of its strategy are contributing to the bottom-line (financial) improvement of the company. It represents the long-term strategic objectives of the organisation, and thus it incorporates the tangible outcomes of the strategy in traditional financial terms. Some of the most common financial measures that are incorporated in the financial perspective are revenue growth, costs, profit margins, cash flow, net operating income, etc.

The customer perspective defines the value proposition that the organisation will apply to satisfy customers, and thus generate more sales to the most desired (i.e. the most profitable) customer groups. The measures that are selected for the customer perspective should measure both the value that is delivered to the customer (value proposition) which may involve time, quality, performance and service and cost, and the outcomes that come as a result of this value proposition (e.g. customer satisfaction, market share). The value proposition can be centred on one of the three: operational excellence, customer intimacy, or product leadership, while maintaining threshold levels at the other two.

The internal process perspective is concerned with the processes that create, and deliver, the customer value proposition. It focuses on all the activities and key processes required in order for the company to excel at providing the value expected by the customers, both productively and efficiently. These can include both short-term and long-term objectives, as well as incorporating innovative process development in order to stimulate improvement. In order to identify the measures that correspond to the internal process perspective, Kaplan and Norton propose using certain clusters that group similar value-creating processes in an organisation.

The clusters for the internal process perspective are operations management (by improving asset utilisation, supply chain management, etc.), customer management (by expanding and deepening relations), innovation (by new products and services) and regulatory and social (by establishing good relations with the external stakeholders).

The innovation and learning perspective is the foundation of any strategy, and focuses on the intangible assets of an organisation, mainly on the internal skills and capabilities that are required to support the value-creating internal processes. The innovation and learning perspective is concerned with the jobs (human capital), the systems (information capital), and the climate (organisation capital) of the enterprise.

These three factors relate to what Kaplan and Norton claim is the infrastructure that is needed in order to enable ambitious objectives in the other three perspectives to be achieved. This, of course, will be in the long term, since an improvement in the learning and growth perspective will require certain expenditures that may decrease short-term financial results, whilst contributing to long-term success.

BSC development logic

The logic of BSC development is the following: based on an organisation's mission and goals, strategic managers develop a set of strategies to build competitive advantage to achieve these goals. They then establish an organisational structure to use resources to obtain a competitive advantage. One version of the way the balanced scorecard operates is presented next.

Step 1. Establish a company's mission and goals: This is achieved by crafting and communicating mission and vision (BPMF Control 6.1). Mission, vision, beliefs and core values, shape the culture and the philosophy of the organisation, and ultimately lead to a set of general strategic performance goals.

Step 2. Develop a strategy and structure (BPMF Control 6.2): This is achieved by:

1 Collecting, and understanding, customer demands, as customer requirements and expectations drive, and show, the way an organisation responds with products and services to local, national, and global market opportunities.

2 Formulating and implementing strategy, as the strategic process of the organisation provides the specific objectives to meet customer demands, needs and expectations, and achieve the desired performance goals.

3 Allocating resources, as identifying and obtaining resources and funds completes the addition of the new initiatives to the current operation of the organisation to improve its performance.

4 Executing initiatives, as new initiatives provide new information to successfully meet the challenges and test the strategy of the organisation. *(See also Chapter 3 'Strategic Management Controls'.)*

Step 3. Create business management control systems that measure efficiency, quality, innovation and responsiveness to customers (BPMF Control 6.3): This is achieved by:

1 Establishing specific objectives.
2 Setting desired expected levels of performance (targets).
3 Designing specific performance measures to record performance, per BSC perspective (customer, financial, internal process, and innovation and growth).

See also Chapter 1 (Business Management Controls Framework (BMCF Control 1), and Business Management Controls System Manual (BMCF Control 2)).

Step 4. Manage corporate performance (BPMF Control 6.4): This is achieved by:

1 Establishing specific performance data collection mechanisms to monitor specific performance measures, per BSC perspective (customer, financial, internal process, and innovation and growth).
2 Analysing these performance data.
3 Taking the required actions to improve performance, change strategy, amend objectives, re-set targets, etc.

See also Chapter 2 (Enterprise Performance Management and Reporting Controls: Performance Management System (EPMR Control 1), Business Management Reporting Procedure (EPMR Control 2) and Governance, Risk and Compliance (GRC) Information System (EPMR Control 3)).

BSC examples

The following examples (*see Figure 2*) are based on the balanced scorecard model, and they describe the strategic controls for a bank, for the four classical BSC perspectives, as defined by Kaplan and Norton: financial, customer, internal process, and innovation and learning.[121]

---

[121] For more on BSC case studies, related performance management white papers and other resources, see: *Balanced Scorecard Examples and Success Stories*: *www.balancedscorecard.org*, *www.ap-institute.com*, and *Strategic Performance Management*, Marr, Bernard, Butterworth Heinemann, Oxford (2006).

Figure 2: A balanced scorecard example for a bank

FINANCIAL Perspective	
Strategic objectives	*Performance measures*
Financial performance	Stock price, profit, return on investment
CUSTOMER Perspective	
Strategic objectives	*Performance measures*
Increase customer satisfaction	Customer retain ratio
INTERNAL PROCESS Perspective	
Strategic objectives	*Performance measures*
Innovative services creation	Acceptance of new services
INNOVATION AND LEARNING Perspective	
Strategic objectives	*Performance measures*
Improve employee skills	Number of specialised seminars

Various computerised software packages (BPMF Control 6.5) are available in the market to assist and support the easier implementation of BSC in an organisation and its units and functions, such as: Balanced Scorecard Designer, QPR Software, Excelsis, Cockpit Communicator, 4GHI Solutions, Actuate, Clarity, Cognos 8 Business Intelligence, CORDA, Corporater Enterprise Performance Management

Suite, Covalent, Cubus, Escendency System, Hyperion Performance Scorecard,[122] etc.

Business performance software solutions

There are several ready-made, computerised systems (packages) (BPMF Control 7) in the market, offering functions related to business performance management. The three typical examples include:[123]

1 SAP Strategic Enterprise Management System (SAP SEM): This delivers, according to the vendor,[124] end-to-end ERP software capabilities to support the entire performance management life cycle, including: consolidated financial reporting, planning, budgeting and forecasting, corporate performance management and scorecards, risk management, etc.

2 Oracle Hyperion Performance Management System: This delivers, according to the vendor,[125] performance management applications to support strategic planning and goal setting, financial and operational planning, the end-to-end financial close and reporting process, and profitability management, in a comprehensive and fully integrated suite.

3 IBM Cognos Performance Management System: This delivers, according to the vendor,[126] functions to co-

---

[122] Without any commitment by both the author and the publisher as to their suitability or effectiveness, etc.

[123] The three examples noted should be evaluated as to their suitability by each company requiring such ready-made solutions. The author and the publisher assume no responsibility whatsoever for any of these products, their functions, etc.

[124] For more details, see: *www.sap.com/solutions/business-suite/erp/sapsem.epx*.

[125] For more details, see: *www.oracle.com*.

[126] For more details, see: *www-01.ibm.com/software/analytics/cognos/performance-management/*.

ordinate financial and operational planning, and improve forecasting in diverse industries and essential functional process areas.

Other performance frameworks

Other performance management frameworks (BPMF Control 8) include the following:

1 UK Government Performance Framework (*http://alphagov.files.wordpress.com/2012/06/digitalperf ormanceframework-alpharelease-1.pdf*).
2 Six Sigma Performance Measurement Framework (*www.isixsigma.com*).
3 The Performance Prism (*www.performanceprism.com*).
4 The Seven Ss Framework (*www.12manage.com/methods_7S.html*).
5 Lean Thinking (*www.lean.org*).
6 EVA (*http://pages.stern.nyu.edu/~adamodar/New_Home_Pag e/lectures/eva.html*).
7 GRI Framework.
8 Best Value Accounting,[127] etc.

Relating business performance framework controls to the BMC framework

The controls identified in this chapter that can be deployed to manage the performance of the organisation, and enable it to achieve and improve its performance and compliance objectives and targets, are considered to be part of the second level (envision level) of business operation:

---

[127] For more details also see: *www.ge.com*, *www.performanceportal.org*, *www.valuebasedmanagement.net/methods_7S.html*.

performance management system (EPMR Control 1) of the BMC framework (*see Figure 1: Business Management Controls Framework, Chapter 1*).

Conclusion

In closing, business performance management, in general, enables, and allows, organisations and management to more efficiently and effectively collect data from their various sources, analyse it, and take appropriate action, as required. Through continuous and real-time reviews and assessments, business performance management provides the data to help private and public organisations monitor efficiency of operations, projects and employees, against strategic and operational targets. Problems and risks can be identified before they become difficult to resolve, and forecasting and business decision-making can become more reliable and predictable.

A good business performance management system, such as the BSC, must communicate strategy, measure performance in real time, offer an integrated performance project management capability, and acknowledge and enable emotional contracting with all staff, which is so vital for linking individual commitment and activity to the attainment of organisational plans and goals. It should also be noted that additional governance, risk and compliance controls must be implemented to complement the BSC approach, and enable and facilitate each other in an effective corporate setting.

Business performance management (BPM) allows companies to more efficiently collect data from their various sources, analyse it, and take appropriate action.

Through continuous and real-time reviews, BPM provides the data to help companies monitor efficiency of projects and employees against operational targets. Problems can be identified before they grow, and forecasting can become more reliable and predictable. BPM can also be used to analyse risk, and predict outcomes of various scenarios, including mergers and acquisitions.

A comparison of four frameworks (BSC, CAF, TQM and EFQM) on the basis of the criteria of:

1 Organisational planning
2 Connecting performance indicators with strategy
3 Balance of performance measures
4 Standard method for implementation
5 Management involvement at all levels
6 Implementing performance to all levels of the organisation
7 Improving accountability and responsibility
8 Change management
9 Results of implementation in a relatively short time, has shown that the BSC model is the best model to use for the design and implementation of strategic and operational controls for organisations.[128]

This is complemented by the experience of the author, and of other business performance consultants. The balanced scorecard (BSC) is the proposed strategic performance management framework that allows organisations to

---

[128] For more details, see: 'The Balanced Scorecard', Salterio, Steven and Webb, Alan, *CA Magazine*, *www.camagazine.com*(2003). See also *Business Performance Measurement Study*, Kellen, Vince: *www.kellen.net/bpm.htm*, and *Latest Trends in Corporate Performance Measurement*:
www.cimaglobal.com/Documents/Thought_leadership_docs/tech_techbrief_latest_trends_0702.pdf.

manage, and measure, the delivery of their strategy. Experience shows that the BSC, when applied properly, establishes focused channels and processes to ensure effective communication throughout the organisation. The concept was initially introduced by Robert Kaplan and David Norton in a *Harvard Business Review* article in 1992 and has since then been voted one of the most influential business ideas of the past 75 years.

Performance management framework recommendation

Recommendation 13: Select and implement a performance management framework that suits your needs.

The key points to consider in assessing this recommendation for your business environment are:

1 There are several performance management frameworks in the market for implementing strategic and operational controls for all types of organisations (private, public, etc.).
2 The BSC model is the proposed strategic performance management framework that allows you to manage, and measure, the delivery of your strategy.
3 Focus on it, apply it properly, establish and ensure effective communication, and the results are bound to be great.

CHAPTER 11: IMPLEMENTING BUSINESS MANAGEMENT CONTROLS

'Anyone who has never made a mistake, has never tried anything new.'

Albert Einstein, German–American Physicist (1879–1955)

Chapter overview: This chapter, the second chapter of Part B: Implementing Business Management Controls, describes a methodology for implementing business management controls to enable and support the good operation of all your business functions and control systems. Also, several implementation business management controls are noted and one recommendation (Recommendation 14: Implement your business management controls with due care and an open mind) is offered for your consideration.

Introduction

'Thinking is easy, acting is difficult, and to put one's thoughts into action is the most difficult thing in the world,' is a famous quote by the German poet, Johann Wolfgang von Goethe. This cautions us, and informs us of the difficulties in implementing any pre-designed actions on any issue in everyday life. We should, therefore, be aware of all difficulties, and the critical issues, in implementing controls systems with any approach, such as the BSC, noted next.

Responsibility for internal controls

In practical terms, as I explained in *Chapter 1*, the internal controls system is a system of integrated elements (people, structure, processes, policies, procedures and practices) acting together to provide reasonable assurance that your company achieves its strategic and operational goals. While all people of an organisation (private, public, etc.) are an integral part of the internal controls system, certain parties merit special mention. These include the Board of Directors, executive management, the audit committee, the internal audit function, and external auditors. Internal controls must be formally, and periodically, assessed and monitored, in order to provide executive management and stakeholders of the organisation with some assurance regarding its effectiveness. Internal control would be judged as effective if its components (policies, procedures, practices, staff, organisational structure, methods, monitoring practices, etc.) are present and function effectively for operations, financial reporting and compliance. Strategic and operational controls, and their supportive performance and compliance measures, play a critical role in the monitoring aspects of your company's performance.

The Board of Directors (or other top management committee for public organisations), the C-level executives, and the audit committee of the organisation, have responsibility for ensuring that the internal control system functions adequately for the purposes of the specific organisation. All these controls need a methodology for more effective implementation and monitoring. This is described next.

A methodology for implementing business management controls

Strategic and operational control, as we just discussed, is part of the internal controls system. Strategic and operational control systems are the formal target-setting, measurement and feedback systems that allow strategic managers to evaluate whether a company is achieving superior efficiency, quality, innovation, customer responsiveness, and implementing its strategy successfully.

An effective control system should have three characteristics:

1 It should be flexible enough to allow managers to respond as necessary to unexpected events.
2 It should provide accurate information, giving a true picture of organisational performance.
3 It should supply managers with the information in a timely manner, because making decisions on the basis of outdated information is a recipe for failure.

Strategic and operational controls also provide the controls for the primary, the support, and the external parties' activities of the organisation, such as:

1 Logistics (raw materials, materials handling, stock control, transport, etc.).
2 Operations (manufacturing of products, provision of services, assembly, testing, packaging, locating the process, facilities and plant, etc.).
3 Marketing.
4 Sales.
5 Maintenance.
6 Systems, policies and procedures (finance, planning, IT, quality control, security, HR, management, etc.).

7 External parties' management, etc.

Implementing strategic and operational controls may be done via the use of the BSC framework. Compliance controls may be implemented by a compliance action plan, discussed in *Chapter 3*.

Designing an effective business management controls system, including strategic and operational controls, via the use of the BSC framework, requires a methodology (methodology for implementing business management controls (IMPL Control 1)) which is made up of the following stages (and their processes, actions, etc.), as shown in *Table 5*, and described, in detail, next:

Table 5: A methodology for implementing business management controls

STAGES	PROCESSES
1. Organise your company	1. Set up your organisation.
	2. Establish your standards and targets.
	3. Create and execute your governance, risk and compliance systems.
	4. Develop, and implement, your risk management action plan.
	5. Implement segregation of duties.
	6. Establish compensating controls.
	7. Craft, and implement, your compliance mechanisms.
2. Craft and execute your strategy	1. Establish your vision, mission and goals (and performance management).

	2. Develop, and implement, your strategy.
	3. Execute your initiatives.
	4. Allocate needed resources and funds.
3. Monitor, review and improve your operations	1. Establish, and execute, your performance management activities.
	2. Execute your business operations monitoring action plan.
	3 Evaluate your company's performance.
	4. Ensure, correct and improve your business controls process.

Stage 1 of business management controls implementation: Organise your company

This stage is made up of the following processes (*see also Chapters 1, 2, 4 to 10 and 12, for more detailed information on the relevant controls involved in this stage*).

1 Stage 1-Process 1: Set up your organisation (IMPL Control 1.1)

You and other top managers establish an organisational structure.

This involves such things as internal control frameworks, policies, procedures, organisational chart, reporting structures, employee handbook, department descriptions and roles for all business functions, a performance management framework (such as BSC, etc.), setting up a BSC team, developing and deploying a business dashboard, establishing an FDR system (files, documents and records for all activities of the organisation, *see Chapter 8 for more details*), staff hiring and dismissal, allocation of responsibilities and duties, work processes, etc.

All these are documented, and maintained, in corporate and business function manuals, and are expressed by the activities of the specific people in each business function. Implementing protection for the business critical data may be carried out by the files, documents and records management action plan (as described in *Chapter 7*).

2 Stage 1-Process 2: Establish your standards and targets (IMPL Control 1.2)

You, and other top managers, establish the standards and targets against which your company performance is to be evaluated. The standards and targets managers select are the ways in which a company chooses to evaluate its performance. General performance standards often derive from the goal of achieving superior efficiency, quality, innovation or customer responsiveness. Specific performance targets are derived from the strategy pursued by the company. The specific targets are maintained in the BSC-related files.

3 Stage 1-Process 3: Create and execute your governance, risk and compliance systems (IMPL Control 1.3)

You, and other top managers, create the enterprise governance, risk and compliance (GRC) measuring and monitoring systems that indicate whether the standards and targets are being reached, and whether the rules are being complied with. Enterprise risks may be managed by a risk management action plan. You segregate duties, implement compensating controls, and establish performance and compliance procedures for assessing whether work goals at all levels of your company are being achieved, and whether rules and regulations are complied with.

4   Stage 1-Process 4: Develop and implement your risk management action plan (IMPL Control 1.4)

You manage your company risks by a risk management action plan, as described in *Chapter 3* (Risk Management Action Plan (RISK Control 1)), which defines the process of risk management, consisting of several steps, such as: establishing the context, create a risk-management plan, set up the risk register and execute the risk-management plan.

5   Stage 1-Process 5: Implement segregation of duties (IMPL Control 1.5)

The company segregates duties by following an action plan (Segregation of Duties (SOD) Action Plan (SEGD Control 2) as described next. A person with multiple functional roles, in many cases, has the opportunity to abuse those powers bestowed upon him or her.

Segregation of duties (*see also Chapter 2: Segregation of Duties and Functions* (SEGD Control 1)) is the tool to resolve this issue. Therefore, in the current business environment, no employee should be assigned the responsibility of two or more of the following five activities in each business process: record keeping, authorisation, asset custody, reconciliation and managerial review.

A generalised method to achieve this is:

Step 1. Analysis of business processes: Determine your business processes requiring SOD.

Step 2. Risk assessment: Perform a risk assessment of the potential fraud and other protection measures required for each of your business process, identified in Step 1.

Step 3. Corporate SOD policy and rules: Develop your overall SOD policy, rules and compensating controls, and store these data in a computerised file.

Step 4. Develop business process SOD: Determine who currently performs the five separate duties within each process. Determine who performs the duties in the absence of the primary employee. Identify those areas where the same individual performs more than one of the five duties. Determine if there are adequate compensating controls in those areas, where more than one duty is performed by the same individual.

Step 5. Test SOD for each business process: Test your SOD policy, rules and compensating controls, and revise, if needed, for each business process.

Step 6. Audit and review SOD: Perform a periodic review of all your SOD applications, to determine actual versus expected results.

Step 7. Improve SOD: Improve and document all changes to all SOD applications in the various business processes of your company.

Examples of how SOD may be applied in practical business terms for the critical business processes of purchasing, IT and cash handling, in any small, medium or large organisation, are included in *Chapter 15*.

6 Stage 1-Process 6: Establish compensating controls (IMPL Control 1.6)

When, depending on your company's size and location, duties or business functions cannot be segregated, due to various reasons (e.g. resource availability problems, resource job constraints, etc.), compensating controls should be considered.

Compensating controls are internal controls that are intended to reduce the risk of an existing, or potential, control weakness. If a single person can carry out, and conceal errors and/or irregularities in the course of performing their day-to-day business activities, they have been assigned SOD incompatible duties. Compensating controls can be preventative, detective, or monitoring controls, that are executed by independent, management-level employees who do not have custody, record-keeping authorisation, or reconciliation responsibilities for the specific business process.

Compensating controls (SEGD Control 3) are less desirable then separation of duties because they generally occur after the business transaction or activity is complete (post audit). Relying completely on compensating controls is less desirable and preferable than separation of duties. Compensating controls usually take more resources to investigate and correct errors, and recover losses, than it does to prevent them. However, in many circumstances, organisations have no choice in the matter. In these instances it is important for management to implement controls that compensate for the increased risk.

The usual types of compensating controls that can be implemented by an independent, management-level, employee to address not having adequate segregation of duties, in a business function, process or department, are to:

1 Investigate exceptions, errors, shut-downs, irregularities and discrepancies.
2 Review a random or critical sample of transactions.
3 Review actions, reports, etc, of all transactions executed by the employee who can perform all key activities of a business transaction.
4 Review all transactions executed by the staff of the specific department.
5 Compare cash, and other assets, to accounting records and other company-maintained data.
6 Monitor budget, project, and cost details.
7 Review all registers, logs and security incidents.
8 Monitor high-risk activities, payments above a certain limit, budget, project, and cost details.
9 Audit all compensation transactions.
10 Audit all computerised audit trails.
11 Perform periodic, or daily reconciliation of computerised application activities, depending on the application and the business data involved.
12 Undertake due diligence activities for critical staff.
13 Rotate critical staff on an ad hoc basis.
14 Request a review by an internal auditor or external expert.

7 Stage 1-Process 7: Craft and implement your compliance mechanisms (IMPL Control 1.7)

The usual compliance mechanisms related to your company are made up of a compliance action plan, a compliance programme, compliance policies and procedures, and a compliance officer, as described in *Chapter 3* (Risk and Compliance controls).

The data to be collected, and the corresponding performance tracking procedures for collection and processing, are maintained in the BSC and other performance and compliance monitoring systems.

Stage 2 of business management controls implementation: Craft and execute your strategy

This stage is made up of the following processes (*see also Chapter 3 for more detailed information on the relevant controls involved in this stage*):

1 Stage 2-Process 1: Establish your vision, mission and goals

You craft a vision, mission and goals for your company (IMPL Control 1.8). Mission, vision, beliefs and core values shape the culture and the philosophy of your company, and ultimately lead to a set of general strategic performance goals. Management also collects and understands customer demands. Customer requirements and expectations drive, and show, the way an organisation responds with products and services to local, national, and global market opportunities. These data are maintained in the BSC-related files.

2 Stage 2-Process 2: Develop and implement your strategy

After you craft a vision, mission and goals for your company (IMPL Control 1.9), you must develop a strategy to drive your company forward (*see also Chapter 3*). This strategic process provides your company with the specific objectives to meet customer demands, needs and expectations, and achieve the desired performance goals.

The specific strategic objectives are maintained in the BSC-related files.

3 Stage 2-Process 3: Execute your initiatives

In many cases, and to attain a better strategy, you need to execute the initiatives (IMPL Control 1.10) to provide new information, in order to successfully meet the challenges and test the strategy of your company. This effort is aligned with the BSC objectives as recorded in the BSC files.

4 Stage 2-Process 4: Allocate needed resources and funds

To implement your strategy, deploy the business management controls system (IMPL Control 1.11) and the BSC throughout the organisation; complete the addition of the new initiatives to the current operation of the organisation, and improve your company's performance. You must identify, and obtain, the required resources and funds. These resources and funds are documented in the BSC objectives, and are monitored and controlled by management.

Stage 3 of business management controls implementation: Monitor, review and improve your operations

This stage is made up of the following processes (*see also Chapter 2 for more detail information on the relevant controls involved in this stage*):

1 Stage 3-Process 1: Establish and execute your performance management activities (IMPL Control 1.12)

Your first action is to create strategic and operational control systems that measure efficiency, quality, innovation and responsiveness to customers. Your second action is to establish specific performance controls, activities and measures to monitor the strategies and their specific objectives of your company, per BSC perspective (customer, financial, internal process, and innovation and growth). Your third action in this process is to monitor all governance and business activities by executing a business operations monitoring action plan (details later in this section). The specific measures are maintained in the BSC-related files.

2 Stage 3-Process 2: Execute your business operations monitoring action plan (IMPL Control 1.13)

All your governance and business activities may be monitored by a plan (business operations monitoring action plan (EGOV Control 18)). These operations and activities must be monitored and reviewed, so that the problems and issues that surface during the everyday aspects of the specific business are resolved in the best way possible. All critical items (e.g. business strategy, management responsibilities, compliance issues and breaches, risks, budgets, corporate investments, mission support systems, business continuity plan and testing, functional and IT operational transactions and errors, corporate performance (financial, production, project, IT, etc.), asset management issues, security issues and incidents, customer satisfaction, internal and external communication, data and service quality, segregation of duties in all critical functions, innovation activities, R&D efforts and projects, human resource management issues and problems, new project implementations, and business intelligence, espionage and sabotage activities, etc. should be monitored, reviewed, evaluated and improved on a time-period (quarterly, annually, etc.), appropriate to the conditions of your company for which these controls operate.

You also may want to perform, either on a continuous basis or on an ad hoc basis, forensic testing, to complement your business monitoring activities. This forensic testing (EGOV Control 18.1) may be carried out by following the steps identified next:

Step 1: Identify business areas, policies, systems, transactions and data that may be tested.

Step 2: Perform risk assessment, prioritise high-risk issues and develop a detailed forensic test plan.

Step 3: Review current systems, availability of software and other tools (e.g. audit trails), and establish test environment.

Step 4: Monitor business transaction execution, review segregation of duties and compensating controls, review continuous auditing activities, execute forensic tests in specially-established test environment and measure results.

Step 5: Collect and analyse results, findings and data from forensic testing.

Step 6: Study, and understand, the impact of collected data, findings and results to the existing business environment.

Step 7: Make recommendations and submit report to senior management and the Board of the related company.

3 Stage 3-Process 3: Evaluate your company's performance (IMPL Control 1.14)

You, as a manager, must evaluate whether, and to what extent, your company's performance deviates from the standards and targets developed in the previous stages, and whether all your staff comply with the rules and regulations applicable to your company.

Audits can also be carried out by internal and external auditors (*see also Chapter 16*); benchmarking studies can be conducted by specialised industry experts to compare the performance of your company to other similar organisations, etc. If performance is higher, you may decide that you have set the company standards too low, and you may raise them for the next time period. On the other hand, if performance is too low, you must decide whether to take remedial action. This evaluation is based on the data to be collected and processed, as maintained in the BSC and other performance and compliance monitoring systems.

4 Stage 3-Process 4: Ensure, correct and improve your business controls process (IMPL Control 1.15)

First of all you must ensure that all components of the business management controls framework (*see Chapter 1, Figure 1*), customised to suit the purposes and demands of your company, are instituted and function to a satisfactory, if not best, level. The five levels of business operation controls proposed in the business management controls framework (*Chapter 1*), are:

(1) First level (Organise): Set up:

1 Board, management and committee roles, structure and responsibilities
2 Business functions and resources
3 Standards, policies and procedures
4 Internal controls framework and manual
5 Soft controls.

(2) Second level (Envision): Institute:

1 Corporate culture, vision, mission and values
2 Strategy, goals, objectives and targets
3 Performance framework and management.

(3) Third level (Govern): Implement:

1 Strategy
2 GRC (governance, risk and compliance) controls
3 Operational controls (purchasing, finance, IT, data, security, fraud, etc.)
4 Personnel administration, including segregation of duties, compensating controls, etc.
5 Management and compliance reporting.

(4) Fourth Level (Audit): Carry out:

1 Monitoring controls
2 Internal audits
3 Self-assessments
4 External audits
5 Regulatory audits.

(5) Fifth Level (Augment): Compare organisation to external entities:

1 Studies by external experts
2 Certify personnel
3 Certify organisational components (structure, service quality, policies and procedures)
4 Corporate social responsibility, including community involvement, etc.

Secondly, you initiate corrective action when you decide that the standards and targets are not being achieved. The final stage in the control process is to take the corrective and improvement action that will allow your company to meet its goals. Such corrective and improvement action may mean changing any aspect of your company's strategy, structure, policies, procedures, practices, management systems, etc. The point here is that a disciplined, problem resolution process must be conducted by management which will identify the performance problems, analyse their root causes, and recommend alternative actions to correct and improve the situation. The corrections and improvements decided to be carried out are maintained in the BSC and other performance and compliance monitoring systems.

Conclusion

Before you follow the above, proposed methodology strictly, and implement it to your specific purposes, you must be aware of the key issues to be handled, for the best achievement of implementing controls with the BSC. The key issues that must be considered in designing and implementing effective business management, strategic and operational control systems with the BSC framework, and compliance controls and measures, are:

1 **Management tools**: Policies, procedures and systems of corporate governance, organisation, financial management, human resource management, production, sales, IT management, etc. are very important and you must use them wisely.

2 **Performance project management**: You must ensure that the whole performance management process (BSC, other performance and compliance systems) is properly managed, during all phases of performance and compliance monitoring activities, by a project management process.

3 **Performance measurement culture**: Establishing and enhancing the role of the performance management manager, adding resources to the performance measurement teams with the appropriate skills, dexterities and talents: financial management, sales, human resource management, IT systems development and operation, production process management, customer support, etc, is paramount to the success of BSC and controls implementation.

4 **Training**: Training and educating your management staff to enable them to acquire, and enhance their skills, on the analysis of all performance data (e.g. financial, customer, internal corporate processes, employee learning and development, etc.) should not be forgotten.

5 **Professional knowledge**: Very strong knowledge of your company's processes, the industry to which your company belongs, the culture of your business and its operating model, and effective inter-personal communication skills at all levels etc, adds to the success of BSC and controls implementation.

6 **Top management commitment**: Very strong commitment to performance is required by all participants in implementing your controls (board, corporate leadership, top management, management committees, various organisational committees, operating staff, etc.).

7 **Organisational structure**: Your organisational structure does not operate effectively unless the appropriate control and incentive systems are in place to shape and motivate your employees' behaviour.

8 **Control systems at all levels**: Control takes place at all levels in your company (corporate, divisional, functional, and individual). Effective control systems are

flexible, accurate, and are able to provide quick feedback to strategic planners. Many kinds of performance standards are available to implement a company's strategy. The kinds of measures you choose affect the way your company operates.

9 **Modern reporting model**: An open and widely-distributed environment of information and know-how exchange regarding performance, and the production and support processes, and a flexible, modern and continuously kept up-to-date reporting model for the organisational performance, and for the consequences of the organisation's operations on the greater environment, society, economy, etc, adds to the success of BSC and controls implementation.

10 **Reward systems**: Your company's reward systems constitute the final form of control. You should design the company reward systems to provide employees with the incentives to make its structure work effectively, and to align their interests with your company's goals and objectives.

It should also be noted that performance measures and compliance indicators related to the implementation effort of business management controls and related issues (business strategy, management responsibilities, compliance issues and breaches, risks, budgets, etc.), are monitored by the specific business controls in each functional area (administration, finance, IT, etc.), and by BSC, as described in this and other chapters of this book, as well as by the use of the GRC information system (EPRM Control 3), as discussed in *Chapter 2*.

Implementing BM controls recommendation

Recommendation 14: Implement your business management controls with due care and an open mind

The key points to consider in assessing this recommendation for your business environment are:

1 The implementation of strategic and operational controls with the balanced scorecard (BSC) framework is quite a difficult process.

2 One of the most critical aspects is your company's culture and how it impacts the behaviour of all people. This is the product of your management team's values and attitudes, and the way all of you choose to design the company's structure and the strategic reward systems.

3 All your managers should handle cultural issues most carefully, so that the best results for controls are achieved.

4 A good number of performance measures for you to monitor your company's performance is about 20-24 at the maximum (five-six for each BSC perspective: financial, customer, internal process, and innovation and learning).

CHAPTER 12: ROLES AND RESPONSIBILITIES OF PARTICIPANTS IN BUSINESS MANAGEMENT CONTROLS

'As we express our gratitude, we must never forget that the highest appreciation is not to utter words, but to live by them.'

John F. Kennedy, American President (1917–1963)

Chapter overview: This chapter, the third chapter of Part B: Implementing Business Management Controls, deals with the roles and responsibilities of all participants (board, managers, auditors, etc.) which are heavily involved in implementing your critical business management controls, and ensures the good operation of all your business functions and control systems. Also, several roles and responsibilities controls are detailed and one recommendation (Recommendation 15: Ensure the involvement of all participants (managers, board, etc.) in implementing your business management controls) is offered for your consideration.

Introduction

'Efficiency is doing things right; effectiveness is doing the right things,' is a famous quote by management guru, Peter Drucker. But how are these to be enabled, facilitated and achieved, without losing control of the organisation, and taking into consideration the impact of the organisation to society? Corporate governance, as well as roles and responsibilities of the various participants in the affairs of the organisation, are a major contributor to the execution of corporate management controls, according to practice and various research studies.

Corporate governance mechanisms and internal control

Organisations are established, and run, by people with the support aspects, review activities, and facilitation tools of various internal and external mechanisms, such as: corporate governance, internal controls, internal auditing, external auditing, regulatory authorities, etc.

In terms of corporate governance, the five most critical mechanisms for internal control that are relevant to business management controls, as described next, are:

1 Board of Directors
2 Auditing
3 Segregation of duties and functions
4 Disclosure and accountability
5 Remuneration.[129]

1. Board of Directors: A Board of Directors is a corporate governance mechanism that protects the interests of a company's shareholders. The shareholders use the Board to bridge the gap between them and company owners, directors, managers and employees. The Board is often responsible for reviewing company management, and removing individuals who don't improve the company's

---

[129] For more details see: *Report of the Committee on the Financial Aspects of Corporate Governance*, Cadbury, Adrian, Gee. London, UK, (1992): *OECD Principles of Corporate Governance*, OECD (2004): *www.oecd.org*.

overall financial and other performance aspects.[130] More details are noted later in this chapter.

2. Auditing: Auditing is an independent review of an organisation's business and financial operations. This corporate governance mechanism ensures that organisations follow national accounting, and other relevant standards, regulations, or other external and internal guidelines. Shareholders, investors, banks and the general public, rely on this information to provide an objective assessment of an organisation. Auditing can also improve an organisation's standing in the business, industry and international environment. More details are noted later in this chapter and in *Chapter 16*.

3. Segregation of duties and functions: Segregating duties is a very critical, corporate governance mechanism. It involves assigning specific responsibilities between board members, directors, managers and other individuals, so that each individual's responsibility is well within reason, and is not conflicting for the organisation. Also, this mechanism can separate the number of functions that one division or department completes within an organisation. Creating well-defined roles also keeps the organisation flexible, ensuring that operational changes, or new hires, can be made without interrupting current operations. This mechanism is described in more detail in *Chapter 2*. Case studies are included in *Chapter 15*.

4. Disclosure and accountability: Disclosure and accountability pertain to issues of transparency in the activities and operations that the organisation (private,

---

[130] See also: *Ownership and Control: Rethinking Corporate Governance for the Twenty-First Century*, Blair Margaret M, Washington: Brookings Institute (1995).

public, etc.) is involved in, as well as being accountable for the results of its activities to its own employees, the government, and regulatory authorities that regulate its affairs, and the communities that are affected by the activities and operations of the specific organisation.

The OECD standards and other global organisational guidelines[131] encourage organisations to apply high-quality standards for disclosure, accounting and audit, and provide timely, regular, reliable and relevant information regarding their activities, operations, structure, financial situation and performance, including environmental, sustainability and social reporting issues.

5. Remuneration: This may be deemed to be a governance mechanism, as remuneration and other benefits reward performance in organisations, and in that sense, control or regulate behaviours of all people involved in the activities of the organisation, and may benefit the specific organisation in the long run. Remuneration, and other benefits, are established and managed by the personnel benefits committee described later in this chapter.

These corporate governance mechanisms are the basis, and the conceptual framework, within which all participants in the affairs of the organisation discharge their business management responsibilities, in terms of internal control.

---

[131] For example: OECD Principles of Corporate Governance: *www.oecd.org*, Global Reporting Initiative: *www.globalreporting.org*, EU strategy 2011-14 for Corporate Social Responsibility: *http://ec.europa.eu/enterprise/policies/sustainable-business/files/csr/new-csr/act_en.pdf*.

Roles and responsibilities of all participants

A role is a set of inter-connected behaviours and obligations of persons (like managers, board members, auditors, etc.) involved in a set of activities of an organisation. Responsibility means that the person is answerable, or accountable, for whatever he or she does as regards to the duties he or she has been charged with, in an organisational framework. The role and responsibility that all participants have in executing business management controls falls into three major categories:

Category 1: Main management duty

1 Managers
2 The Board of Directors, or executive committee
3 Audit committee
4 Operating staff
5 Corporate compliance officer
6 Data privacy officer
7 Chief risk officer.

Category 2: Audit duty

1 Internal auditors
2 External auditors.

Category 3: Advisory and support duty

1 Personnel benefits committee
2 Compliance committee
3 Advisory and regulatory third parties
4 Stakeholders (customers, unions, beneficiaries, suppliers, citizens, donors, etc.).

The roles and responsibilities of these participants are described next. *(See Chapter 2 for other governance controls and how they impact the execution of business management controls.)*

Category 1: Main management duty

1. Managers (EGOV Control 3): regardless of their level in the hierarchy of the organisation, managers are directly responsible for all activities of an organisation, including directing, designing, developing, implementing, supervising, monitoring, and controlling the proper functioning of, maintaining, documenting and improving the internal control system. Their specific role and responsibilities vary depending on their function in the organisation, and the given organisation's characteristics, country, culture, industry-type, and other socio-economic factors and conditions.[132]

The typical job description of a business manager, in general terms, is described next:

1 Manage the operational and business activities of the department or business entity, to include: staffing levels, budgets, strategic, financial and operational goals, etc.
2 Plan, and develop, systems and procedures to improve the operating quality and efficiency of the department or business function.
3 Analyse, and document, business processes and problems, and develop solutions to enhance efficiencies and resolve problems.
4 Co-ordinate, and implement, solutions from process analysis and general department projects.

---

[132] See also: *Managers and the Legal Environment: Strategies for the 21st Century,* Bagley, Constance E and Savage, Diane, South-Western (2010).

5 Direct and support staff in the provision of solutions to customer problems, and in development, analysis, and preparation of reports, in accordance with company policies and procedures.

6 Conduct interviews, hire new staff, provide employee orientation, coach and provide career development advice to staff.

7 Establish employee goals and conduct employee performance reviews.

8 Manage staff and issues, to include: work assignments/rotations, employee training, employee vacations, employee breaks, overtime assignment, back-up for absent employees, shift rotations, etc.

9 Assist and support staff to resolve complex, or out of policy, operational problems.

10 Co-ordinate with human resources for appropriate staffing levels.

11 Responsibility to meet department productivity and quality goals, including establishing an anti-fraud culture in the department, and transparency and accountability.

12 Respond to, and support, the Board of Directors, in the development of policies dealing with internal control and fraud.

In terms of internal controls and performance management they set up the BSC team, the compliance and performance monitoring teams, as well as the set up the BSC implementation project, and review and guide their activities.

2. Board of Directors: The role and responsibilities of the Board of Directors (EGOV Control 1), in general terms, are to:

12: Roles and Responsibilities of Participants in Business Management Controls

1 **Internal controls**: Establish the internal control framework, system, environment and process, and ensure that this control system operates effectively and efficiently. Ensure that an effective, internal controls system is established, reviewed and improved accordingly.

2 **Adequacy of board**: Ensure that an effective Board of Directors is in place, and that the Board possesses, within its membership, the appropriate skills, know-how and dexterities to enable it to fulfil its duties and responsibilities.

3 **Appointments**: Elect the chief executive officer and replace if necessary, and elect all other executive officers on the recommendation of the chief executive officer.

4 **Reviews**: Review annually. Review and evaluate, on a continuous basis, the corporate strategic plans (overall, business unit, functional, etc.), the organisation's community involvement and corporate social responsibility activities, and the annual capital and operating budgets.

5 **Decision making**: Under established policies and procedures, approve critical decisions not delegated to management, such as: major acquisitions, divestitures, capital investments, IT systems, loans, and strategic plans.

6 **Committees**: Through its committee system, provide supervision regarding certain activities of the company, such as: benefits, audit, compliance, compensation, finance, community relations, personnel management, security, etc. Establish additional committees from time to time, as may be necessary to fulfil the needs, duties and responsibilities of the Board. Monitor and perform

an evaluation, at least annually, to determine whether the Board and its committees are functioning effectively.

7 **Fraud control**: Select members to constitute an audit committee. Manage conflicts of interest. Serve as external liaison with external auditors. Direct the internal audit process. Serve as a direct internal control entity in relation to the fraud actions of senior management. Act as a spokesperson for the organisation, in relation to fraud committed by senior management. Select members to constitute an audit committee.

8 **BSC and performance**: In terms of internal controls and performance management, they guide, review and monitor all performance activities and reports, including the BSC implementation project; and sponsor all performance and compliance activities.

3. Audit Committee: The role and the responsibilities of the audit committee[133] (EGOV Control 2), in general terms, are to:

1 **Internal controls**: Discuss with management, internal and external auditors and major stakeholders, the quality and adequacy of the organisation's internal controls system and risk management process, and their effectiveness and outcomes; and meet regularly and privately with the director of internal audit.

2 **Financial statements**: Review, and discuss with management and the external auditors, and approve the audited financial statements of the organisation, and make a recommendation regarding inclusion of those

---

[133] See also Public Company Accounting Oversight Board: *http://pcaobus.org*, American Institute of Certified Public Accountants, *www.aicpa.org*, International Organisation of Supreme Audit Institutions: *www.intosai.org*.

financial statements in any public filing. Also, review with management and the independent auditor, the effect of regulatory and accounting initiatives, as well as off-balance sheet issues in the organisation's financial statements.

3 **Information disclosure**: Review and discuss with management, the types of information to be disclosed, and the types of presentations to be made, with respect to the company's earning press release and financial information and earnings guidance, provided to analysts and rating agencies.

4 **Audit activities**: Confirm the scope of audits to be performed by the external and internal auditors, monitor progress and review results, and review fees and expenses. Review significant findings or unsatisfactory internal audit reports, or audit problems, or difficulties encountered by the external independent auditor. Monitor management's response to all audit findings.

5 **Complaints**: Manage complaints concerning accounting, internal accounting controls, or auditing matters.

6 **Reporting**: Receive regular reports from the chief executive officer, chief financial officer, and the company's other control committees, regarding deficiencies in the design or operation of internal controls, and any fraud that involves management or other employees with a significant role in internal controls.

7 **Fraud control**: Support management in resolving conflicts of interest. Monitor the adequacy of the organisation's internal controls, and ensure that all fraud cases are acted upon.

8 **BSC and performance**: In terms of internal controls and performance management, they guide, sponsor,

review and monitor all performance and compliance activities and reports, including the BSC implementation project. They also ensure that auditors review the compliance and performance measures for all critical and mission-contributing functions of the organisation.

4. Operating staff: All staff members (EGOV Control 5) should be responsible for reporting problems of operations, monitoring and improving their performance; and monitoring non-compliance with the corporate policies and various professional codes, or violations of policies, standards, practices and procedures. Their particular responsibilities should be documented in their individual personnel files. In BSC and performance management activities they take part in all compliance and performance data collection and processing activities, as they are part of various organisational units, and may also be responsible for various compliance and operational-related activities of the organisation.

5. Corporate compliance officer: The role and the responsibilities of the corporate compliance officer (COMP Control 3), in general terms, are to:

1 **Compliance programme**: Develop, initiate, maintain, and revise policies and procedures for the general operation of the compliance programme and its related activities, to prevent illegal, unethical, or improper conduct. Also, run and manage the day-to-day operation of the programme.
2 **Standards**: Develop, and periodically review and update, standards of conduct, to ensure continuing currency and relevance in providing guidance to management and employees.

3 **Collaboration**: Collaborate with the corporate compliance committee and other departments of the organisation (e.g. risk management, internal audit, employee services, etc.), to direct compliance issues to appropriate existing channels for investigation and resolution. Consult with the corporate attorney, as needed, to resolve difficult legal compliance issues.

4 **Investigation**: Respond to alleged violations of rules, regulations, policies, procedures and standards of conduct, by evaluating, or recommending, the initiation of investigative procedures. Develop, and oversee, a system for uniform handling of such violations.

5 **Monitoring**: Monitor, and as necessary, co-ordinate compliance activities of other departments, to remain abreast of the status of all compliance activities, and to identify trends. Identify potential areas of compliance vulnerability and risk.

6 **Reporting**: Ensure proper reporting of violations or potential violations, to duly authorised enforcement agencies, as appropriate and/or required.

7 **BSC and performance**: Provides reports on a regular basis, and as directed or requested, to keep the Board, corporate compliance committee and senior management, informed of the operation and progress of compliance efforts, by reviewing all compliance measures of the organisation.

6. Data privacy officer: The role and the responsibilities of the data privacy officer (EGOV Control 8), in general terms,[134] are to:

---

[134] See also: *Effective Data Protection*, Webster, Mandy, ICSA Information and Training Ltd (2011).

12: Roles and Responsibilities of Participants in Business Management Controls

1 **Data privacy programme**: Develop, initiate, maintain, and revise policies and procedures for the general operation of the data privacy programme and its related activities, including educating, training and coaching all participants of the organisation to prevent illegal, unethical, or improper data privacy breaches. Run, and manage, the day-to-day operation of the programme.

2 **Data privacy standards**: Develop, and periodically review and update standards of conduct, to ensure continuing currency and relevance in providing guidance to management and employees on data privacy issues, according to the current national and local data privacy laws and practices.

3 **Collaboration**: Collaborate with corporate compliance committee and other departments of the organisation (e.g. risk management, internal audit, employee services, etc.), to direct data privacy issues to appropriate existing channels for investigation and resolution. Consult with the corporate attorney, as needed, to resolve difficult legal data privacy issues.

4 **Data privacy investigation**: Respond to alleged violations of rules, regulations, policies, procedures and standards of data privacy, by evaluating, or recommending, the initiation of investigative procedures. Develop, and oversee, a system for uniform handling of such violations.

5 **Data privacy monitoring**: Monitor, and as necessary, co-ordinate compliance activities of other departments to remain abreast of the status of all data privacy compliance activities, and to identify trends. Identify potential areas of data privacy, vulnerability and risk.

6 **Reporting**: Ensure proper reporting of violations, or potential violations, to duly authorised enforcement agencies, as appropriate and/or required.

7 **BSC and performance**: The data privacy officer could use the BSC to provide reports on a regular basis, and as directed or requested, to keep the Board, corporate compliance committee and senior management, informed of the operation and progress of data privacy, by reviewing all data privacy issues of the organisation.

7. Chief risk officer: The role and the responsibilities of the corporate chief risk officer (RISK Control 3), in general terms, are to:

1 **Risk management action plan**: Develop, initiate, maintain, and revise policies and procedures, for the general operation of the risk assessment function. Run, and manage, the day-to-day operation of the risk function, by maintaining the risk register and the company's risk plan which may also include a description of contributing factors and avoidance approaches for each risk, as well as general guidance on how to react swiftly to risk events, to help control damage.

2 **Risk policies and procedures**: Develop, implement and periodically review and update the organisation's risk management policies and procedures, to ensure continuing currency and relevance in providing risk guidance to management and employees.

3 **Risk identification and monitoring**: Identify and monitor risks that could be applicable to the organisation, and develop a set of key risk indicators to

be monitored.[135] These could be achieved by the continuous study, review and research of various sources, such as: government and industry rules and regulations; company policies, procedures, manuals, strategies, objectives, internal and external audit reports, previous losses, previous crises, security issues and other incidents, major customer financial payments, sales and production data, etc, industry events, incidents, prices of raw materials, strategic resource availability, etc.

4 **Risk reporting**: Ensure proper reporting of all actions to prevent, or avoid, actual, or potential, risks to higher levels of management, including the Board, and to duly authorised enforcement agencies, as appropriate and/or required.

5 **Collaboration**: Collaborate with the corporate compliance committee, and other departments of the organisation (e.g. legal function, internal audit, employee services, etc.), to assess, and resolve, risk issues as needed.

6 **BSC and performance**: Risks can be measured by the use of the balanced scorecard approach. The BSC can be used to provide reports on a regular basis, and as directed or requested, to keep the Board, and senior management, informed of the operation and progress of risk resolution efforts, by reviewing all key risk indicators and risk resolution actions of the organisation.

Category 2: Audit duty

1. Internal auditors: Internal auditors (EGOV Control 6) examine and evaluate internal controls, certify the financial

---

[135] See also: *Developing Key Risk Indicators to Strengthen Enterprise Risk Management,* Beasley, Mark S et al (2010): December 2010, *www.coso.org,*

statements of the organisation, and draw attention to any instances of irregularity, impropriety or poor financial control. They evaluate the organisation's internal controls and how they contribute towards its risk management. They issue a report for each audit, and provide an annual opinion on the overall system of control to the audit committee. They provide assurance to the audit committee in preparing corporate governance statements and also review and report on the corporate governance process.[136]

In BSC and performance management they review, and use, all compliance and performance data, and measure and report any discrepancies and improvements in their audit reports.

2. External auditors: An external auditor is an audit professional who performs audits in accordance with specific national laws or professional guidelines and rules, on the financial statements of an organisation (private, public, etc.), and who is independent of the corporate entity being audited.[137] External auditors (EGOV Control 7) also provide advice and recommendations on the internal controls of the entity audited. In BSC and performance management, they review, and use, all compliance and performance data and measures, and report any discrepancies and improvements in their audit reports.

Category 3: Advisory and support duty

The roles and responsibilities of advisory and support duty parties (personnel benefits committee, compliance

---

[136] See also: *Internal Auditing: Assurance and Consulting Services*, Reding, Kurt F et al, IIA Research Foundation (2009).
[137] For more information, also see: *www.theiia.org*.

committee, advisory and regulatory third parties and stakeholders) are described further in the *Business Management Controls Toolkit*.

Performance measures and compliance indicators (MGMT Control 1)

Performance measures (MGMT Control 1.1) and compliance indicators (MGMT Control 1.2) related to the management roles and responsibilities controls, are noted next.

Roles and responsibilities performance measures: Percentage of board members with finance background, amount of training budget for board members per year, number of management report reviews per year and percentage of board members active in professional societies.

Roles and responsibilities compliance indicators: Management reporting procedures exist (or not), clear internal audit function (exists or not), and corporate committees (audit, risk, business continuity, etc.) functioning (or not).

You can monitor your performance in the roles and responsibilities controls of implementing your business management controls in your medium or large company, by monitoring the performance measures and compliance indicators noted above, via the internal process and innovation and learning perspectives of a corporate BSC (*Chapters 10 and 11*), as well as by the use of the GRC information system (EPRM Control 3), as discussed in *Chapter 3*. You can monitor your performance for your small company by setting up a small manual or automated system (e.g. by using a spreadsheet application based on BSC).

Relating roles and responsibility controls to the BMC framework

The controls identified in this chapter that can be deployed to ensure effective implementation of business management controls by organisations, while achieving and improving their performance and compliance objectives and targets, are considered to be part of the first level (organise level) of business operation of the BMC framework (*see Figure 1: Business Management Controls Framework, Chapter 1*).

Roles and responsibilities controls recommendation

Recommendation 15: Ensure the involvement of all participants (managers, board, etc.) in implementing your business management controls

The key points to consider in assessing this recommendation for your business environment are:

1 The primary responsibility for the development and maintenance of internal control and compliance, and performance management systems, rests with your company's management.

2 Without forgetting good policies and procedures (hard controls) for implementing internal control, focus more on the overriding philosophy and operating style (soft controls) within your company.

3 Placing emphasis on these soft controls highlights the importance of your senior management's involvement in the internal control system, and the related performance and compliance issues.

4 Making your internal control system and its related performance management controls the first priority for management and, secondarily, of the other participants in the affairs of the organisation, will enhance your company's chance in being more effective and efficient in the long run.

CHAPTER 13: HUMAN FACTORS IN APPLYING BUSINESS MANAGEMENT CONTROLS

'Human beings, by changing the inner attitudes of their minds, can change the outer aspects of their lives.'

Williams James, American Psychologist and Philosopher (1842–1910)

Chapter overview: This chapter, the fourth chapter of Part C: Implementing Business Management Controls, describes the human factors, and their impact in applying your business management controls, to all your business functions. Also, several human factor controls are detailed and one recommendation (Recommendation 16: Design good hard controls and implement them with effective soft controls) is offered for your consideration.

Introduction

'All human actions have one or more of these seven causes: chance, nature, compulsion, habit, reason, passion, and desire,' is a famous quote by Aristotle. But how these human factors are used to implement controls by you, your managers, and your employees in your company, in the best way, is quite a difficult and tedious job. This gives us the motivation to describe the characteristics of these human factors, and what they may mean for the implementation effort of the business management controls for your company.

13: Human Factors in Applying Business Management Controls

Description of hard and soft controls

Controls, as we have discussed so far, have to do with your formal policies and procedures (hard controls), and how well, or not, they are designed and implemented, by you and your staff.

Hard controls are tangible things, usually well-defined, formalised and approved, like organisational structure, assignment of authority and responsibility, corporate standards, policies and procedures, ethics code, compliance procedures, computerised systems, company books, registers, audit trail mechanisms, personnel controls, for example, segregation of duties, taking a vacation, job descriptions, confidentiality statements, etc. These hard controls are implemented and used, in everyday business practice, to carry out the activities of your business operation by various participants, i.e. your people, such as your employees, your managers, your board members, your customers, etc. These participants usually operate with their feelings, their beliefs, their trust and confidence, their motives, etc, collectively termed soft controls.

A good example of why strategies fail, these being hard controls, is the study of Paramount Consulting.[138] It was found that around 65% of strategic plans fail, and as much as 97% of plans are ineffectively implemented. This is mainly due to human factors (soft controls).

Soft controls are intangible things that have to do with behavioural aspects and social properties inherent in your managers and your employees, and are utilised in applying

---

[138] For more see: _www.paramountlearning.co.uk/2010/04/23/six-principle-reasons-why-strategies-fail/_.

hard controls in their daily business activities, such as: tone at the top, understanding of the organisation by the Board, culture, structure of reporting relationships, morale, integrity and ethical values, operational philosophy, trust, etc, as described in the next paragraphs. These are most important, as they fulfil the values espoused by almost all human beings, according to Schwartz and his associates who researched the concept of universal values of more than 25,000 people in 44 countries, and came up with 10 types of universal values,[139] such as:

1 Power
2 Achievement
3 Hedonism (pleasure of living)
4 Stimulation in life
5 Self-direction
6 Universalism (wisdom, justice, peace, inner harmony)
7 Benevolence (honesty, forgiveness, friendship)
8 Tradition (devoutness, moderation, accepting one's portion in life, humility)
9 Conformity (self-discipline, obedience)
10 Security (family and national security, sense of belonging, stability of social order).

Regardless of the type and size of companies, soft controls differ from organisation to organisation, but are typically set at a higher, corporate level, and are associated with the overall governance, mission and morale of your company.

---

[139] As per Schwartz, SH (1992). 'Universals in the Content and Structure of Values: Theory and Empirical Tests in 20 Countries' in Zanna, M (ed.), *Advances in Experimental Social Psychology* (Vol. 25). New York: Academic Press: 1–65, and Schwartz, SH and Bilsky, W (1987), 'Toward a Universal Psychological Structure of Human Values'. *Journal of Personality and Social Psychology*, 53: 550–562.

In addition, measuring efforts like the ethics and integrity, or the philosophy of your company, is not a simple task.

Types of soft controls

The usual types of soft controls are:

1. Tone at the top (SOFT Control 1): Tone at the top refers to how an organisation's leadership creates the tone at the top – an ethical (or unethical) atmosphere in the workplace. Management's tone has a trickle-down effect on employees. If top managers uphold ethics and integrity, so will employees. However, if upper management appears unconcerned with ethics, and focuses solely on the bottom line, employees will be more prone to commit fraud, and feel that ethical conduct isn't a priority. In short, your employees will follow the examples of their bosses. You, as the top manager, can reinforce the aspects of the company's 'tone at the top' ethics attitude to your employees by actions, such as:

1 Discussing and resolving all ethics and integrity issues.
2 Providing examples of behaviour in your daily management duties and oversight activities.

2. Understanding of the organisation by the Board (SOFT Control 2): The Board needs to fully understand the company they supervise and control, so that they are as effective as possible in discharging their duties. This understanding involves both the internal (size, form, strategy, structure, people, policies, procedures, operating style, culture, beliefs, etc.) and external (industry, rules, regulations, market, geopolitical locations, etc.) aspects of the organisation.

You can ensure that your board members attain better organisational understanding by actions, such as:

1 Company ownership or board selection committee selecting and appointing board members on the basis of education, professional background and practical experience.
2 Ensuring that board members attend your critical business operations for a specific period.
3 Providing board members with specialised training courses on very specific issues and areas where the given organisation is active.

3. Structure of reporting relationships (SOFT Control 3): The structure of reporting relationships is usually depicted in an organisational chart. This chart can provide a great deal of information, and may help organisational members understand the overall structure of the company, and its strategy. The organisational chart allows employees, and other stakeholders, to see employee job titles and the reporting relationships in an organisation. The vertical lines demonstrate the reporting relationships of supervisors and their reporting staff. The lateral, or horizontal lines, indicate a working relationship. Managers can improve the elements of the organisation's reporting relationships by actions, such as:

1 Crafting an effective organisational chart and communicating it to all staff.
2 Developing job titles for all employees, and using in all dealings.
3 Reviewing, and improving, both chart and job titles, as the company grows and its demands change.

4. Culture (SOFT Control 4): Culture is the environment that surrounds you at work all of the time. Culture is made up of the values, beliefs, underlying assumptions, attitudes, and behaviours shared by a group of people. Culture is the behaviour that results when a group arrives at a set of – generally unspoken and unwritten – rules for working together. An organisation's culture is made up of all of the life experiences each employee brings to the organisation. Culture is especially influenced by the organisation's founder, Board of Directors, executives, and other managerial staff, because of their role in decision making and strategic direction.

Managers can reinforce the elements of the organisation's culture to their employees by actions, such as:

1 Discussing all cultural issues with employees.
2 Providing examples of behaviour in their daily supervision activities.
3 Involving them in reviewing corporate statements on vision, mission and values.

5. Morale (SOFT Control 5): Morale is 'moral principles or practice'. In business management terms, it describes the capacity of employees to maintain belief in the company they work for, or a general goal and specific objectives set by their superiors. It refers to the level of faith of individual employees in the collective benefit gained by such performance.

Managers must pay special attention in improving morale by actions, such as:

1 Providing opportunities for your employees to make decisions about, and influence, their own work.

2 Providing timely, accurate and proactive responses to their questions and concerns.
3 Treating them as responsible adults, with fairness and consistency.
4 Developing, and publicising, corporate policies and procedures, whilst ensuring that they work effectively.
5 Communicating positively, effectively and constantly with all employees, on all issues (e.g. performance, work details, etc.).
6 Affording all staff the opportunity to grow and develop.
7 Providing appropriate leadership, and a framework of strategy, vision, mission, values and goals.

6. Integrity and ethical values (SOFT Control 6): Integrity is the inner sense of 'holistic sense' ('wholeness') deriving from qualities, such as honesty, truthfulness and consistency of personal character. In a business environment, integrity and ethical values mean that both employees and their managers must interact with each other, in all their business activities, on the basis of integrity, honesty, truthfulness and consistency in the actions they execute, methods and measures they use to monitor performance, principles they activate, and expectations, results and outcomes they manage. Also, in this regard, managers must lead by example, so that their employees follow. Board members and managers can reinforce, and enhance, the elements of the organisation's integrity and ethical values by actions, such as:

1 Crafting and implementing an effective ethics and compliance programme, and communicating it to all staff.
2 Establishing, and functioning the office of compliance and ethics.

3 Providing examples of behaviour in their daily supervision activities.
4 Reviewing, and improving, both the ethics and compliance programme and policies, as the organisation grows, and its regulatory aspects and expectations change.

7. Operational philosophy (SOFT Control 7): Operational philosophy is an explicit (written) or implicit (unwritten) declaration of how a person, group or organisation operates. In business terms, it represents how business activities are conducted by all levels of management in various areas, such as: investments, funding, managing employee relationships, customer transactions, regulatory authorities, risk-taking, quality, profits, ethical standards, environment, etc.

All company managers can reinforce and enhance the operational philosophy of their company by actions, such as:

1 Dealing with all people (internal staff, outside auditors, customers, external suppliers, government authorities, regulators, stakeholders, community, etc.) on the same basis of fairness, and on written and approved rules and codes of business conduct.
2 Crafting, and implementing, effective ethics, human rights and procurement policies.
3 Communicating all company information, to all parties, on the basis of transparency and accountability.

8. Trust (SOFT Control 8): Trust means 'reliance to another person or entity'. Aristotle[140] believed that trust of a speaker by the listener, was based on the listener's perception of three characteristics of the speaker: the intelligence of the speaker (correctness of opinions, or competence); the character of the speaker (reliability – a competence factor and honesty – a measure of intentions); and the goodwill of the speaker (favourable intentions towards the listener). In corporate terms, trust forms the foundation for effective communication, employee retention, and employee motivation, and is a major contributor of the extra effort and energy that people voluntarily invest in work. When trust exists in an organisation, or in a relationship, almost everything else is easier and more comfortable to achieve.

All managers can reinforce the aspects of trust in interacting with their stakeholders, employees, customers, authorities, etc, by actions, such as:

1 Promoting personnel to higher levels of organisational hierarchy, who are capable of forming positive, trusting and caring, interpersonal relationships, with people who report to them.
2 Developing the interpersonal relationship skills of all personnel, and especially those of current managers and employees desiring promotion, by sending them to relevant courses, or by coaching and mentoring programmes.
3 Keeping company personnel informed, as much as possible.

---

[140] For more see: *On Man in the Universe (Metaphysics, Ethics, Politics, Ethics, Poetics)*, Aristotle, Walter J Black, USA (1942).

4 Acting with integrity, and keeping commitments to all participants in the affairs of the business (employees, authorities, customers, board members, stakeholders, etc.).

5 Protecting the interest of all employees in a work group, even those who are absent.

6 Being effective.

7 Listening with respect, sensitivity and full attention.

9. Ethical climate (SOFT Control 9): The ethical climate of an organisation is the shared set of understandings about what is the correct behaviour, and how all ethical issues will be handled. This climate sets the tone for decision making at all levels of the organisation, and in all circumstances, activities and dealings of all participants in the affairs of the company.

All board members and organisational managers can reinforce, and improve, the ethical climate of the organisation by actions, such as:

1 Ensuring that they always maintain a positive and ethical climate in managing and interacting with their employees, their superiors and their customers.

2 Leaving aside and amending, as required, and certain circumstances, their personal self-interest, company profit, operating efficiency, rules, procedures, etc, in order to preserve and improve this ethical climate.

3 Dealing with all stakeholders (employees, external auditors, customers, suppliers, authorities, regulators, community, etc.) on the same basis of fairness, and on written and approved rules and codes of business conduct.

10. Empowerment (SOFT Control 10): Empowerment refers to increasing the spiritual, political, social, racial, educational, economic, or other strength of individuals.[141] Empowerment in corporate environments for employees, means that these employees are supported and enabled to make more, better and larger-scope decisions, without having to refer to someone more senior in the organisation.

All managers can reinforce, and improve, the implementation of empowerment as regards the employees of their organisation, by actions, such as:

1 Giving the authority, and the responsibility, to selected employees, of carrying out specific actions to achieve general corporate goals and specific objectives, and monitoring these results to ensure that these are properly done.
2 Encouraging employees to assume a more energetic and effective role in their work.
3 Involving employees in assuming responsibility for improving the way things are done in their daily work activities.

11. Corporate attitudes (SOFT Control 11): The concept of attitude represents an individual's degree of like or dislike for something (person, place, thing, or event). In a corporate workplace, attitudes play a great role in employees executing corporate tasks, and achieving strategic and operational goals predetermined by senior managers. If they like the organisation, or their manager, or the task, they will perform better, in most cases. If they

---

[141] See also: *Emotional Intelligence: 10th Anniversary Edition; Why It Can Matter More Than IQ*, Goleman, Daniel, Random House (2006).

dislike the organisation, or their manager, or their task, they are bound to perform at a lesser degree.

All managers can improve the corporate attitudes of the employees of their organisation by actions, such as:

1 Using polite and positive language and manners in assigning and managing tasks.
2 Connecting tasks to rewards.
3 Adding variety to tasks.
4 Assigning both liked and non-liked tasks to all employees.
5 Thinking out a solution as regards the difficult task and situation with the person involved.
6 Working out a mutually-agreed solution with the person involved.

12. Competences (SOFT Control 12): Competence means 'sufficiency to deal with what is at hand'. Competence in a corporate environment is the ability, the will, the commitment, the knowledge, the skills and the dexterities of an individual, to perform a job, or task, properly. Managers must manage, and improve, the competences of themselves and their employees, through education, training, coaching, mentoring, etc.

Managers can improve their own competence as well as the competences of the employees of their organisation, by actions, such as:

1 Assessing their skills (managers and employees) via self-evaluation methods, benchmarking, or other tools.
2 Taking specific industry courses themselves (managers) and sending their employees to courses also.
3 Upgrading job-related knowledge, by attending university and professional seminars.

4 Getting involved in coaching and mentoring programmes.
5 Getting certified by a professional association.
6 Getting various organisational functions (e.g. production, IT, etc.) and components (IT security) certified.

13. Leadership (SOFT Control 13): Leadership is 'organising a group of people to achieve a common goal'. Leadership, in a business environment, is manifested in managers exhibiting traits, such as: intelligence, personal effectiveness and efficiency, high level of creativity in resolving issues and problems, adjustment, extraversion, conscientiousness and motivation, which are used for accomplishing goals for the given corporate entity.[142]

Senior managers can improve the leadership qualities of the employees of their organisation by actions, such as:

1 Have a vision and a mission.
2 Be organised to the fullest.
3 Plan effectively.
4 Delegate, by assigning ownership of the work given to employees, and always act with responsibility.
5 Be passionate and enthusiastic, and get employees involved in the decision-making process.
6 Train and coach them, as required, to get the job done well.
5 Handle emotional issues with calmness and fairness.
6 Know your organisation extremely well.
7 Provide a positive and moral example to others.

---

[142] For more, see: *The 7 Habits of Highly Effective People*, Covey, Stephen R, Simon and Schuster (1989), *The Bass Handbook of Leadership: Theory, Research, and Managerial Applications*, Bass, BM and Bass, R, New York: Free Press (2008).

8 Motivate people, and keep clear channels of communication.

14. Employee motivation (SOFT Control 14): Motivation is 'inner or social stimulus for an action' for human beings. In a corporate environment, managers need to motivate employees to do a better job. This is achieved in a corporate setting, according to various thinkers,[143] such as Maslow, Argyris, etc, by managers using various strategies, such as:

1 Providing positive reinforcement
2 Effective discipline and fair punishment
3 Treating people fairly
4 Satisfying employee needs on a cost-benefit case
5 Setting achievable, work-related goals
6 Restructuring jobs/tasks to become more manageable
7 Rewarding people on job performance.

15. Expectations (SOFT Control 15): This is the act, or process, of knowing what is anticipated in a given work situation. This means that managers must consider the issue of expectations in dealing with their employees. Learning what interests and engages employees, can help managers to distribute work in a way that promotes enthusiasm for completing tasks. This will help employees understand the employer's expectations.

All managers can reinforce the aspects of expectations of the employees of their organisation by actions, such as:

1 Meeting with employees on a regular basis to discuss problems, issues, goals and progress.

---

[143] For more, see: *Motivation and Personality*, Maslow, AH, New York: Harper and Bros. (1954), *Toward a Psychology of Being*, Maslow, Abraham, John Wiley and Sons, USA (1998) and *On Organisational Learning*, Argyris, C, Oxford: Blackwell (1992).

2 Promoting enthusiasm for completing tasks.

3 Expressing confidence in each employee's ability, and reinforcing past achievement, so that employee motivation is sustained.

16. Openness and shared values (SOFT Control 16): Openness is the quality of being open.[144] Values represent what a person believes in. In corporate terms, openness and shared values characterise an environment in which decisions are made and communicated to all parties.

Senior managers can improve the characteristics of openness and shared values in their organisation by actions, such as:

1 Appreciating the opinions, skills and knowledge of all employees.

2 Re-examining traditional organisational standards in order to achieve better, and more beneficial, results.

17. Information flow throughout the organisation (SOFT Control 17): Information flow throughout the organisation is usually attained by both informal and formal communication systems.[145] Formal communication is used to distribute, and implement, rules, policies and procedures. All managers, however, must pay attention also to informal communication, as this type of communication may hinder, or ensure the effective conduct of work, in modern organisations.

---

[144] For more, see: 'A meta-analysis of the five-factor model of personality and academic performance', Poropat, AE, *Psychological Bulletin*, 135(2), 322–338 (2009), *Personality Traits*, Matthews, G, Deary, IJ and Whiteman, MC, Cambridge University Press (2003).
[145] For more, see: *Lean Connections: Making Information Flow Efficiently and Effectively*, Harris, Chris and Harris, Rick, Productivity Press (2008).

Senior managers can improve the information flow throughout their organisation by actions, such as:

1 Drafting and implementing a communications policy, by identifying the strategic objectives of the organisation, reviewing current communications practices, identifying the communications audiences, and determining the communications methods and means to be used.

8 Getting executives trained on listening techniques and practices.[146]

9 Ensuring that information (internal and external), critical to achieving the objectives of the company, is identified, regularly collected, and reported to management and stakeholders.

10 Implementing a performance system that identifies, collects, stores, processes, analyses and communicates corporate performance to all approved stakeholders of the organisation.

11 Implementing mechanisms to allow the easy flow of information down, across, and up the company.

Emotional contracting

All of these types of soft controls (SOFT Control 18) (tone at the top, understanding of the organisation by the Board, culture, structure of reporting relationships, morale, integrity and ethical values, operational philosophy, trust, ethical climate, empowerment, etc.), refer to the emotional contracting issue, also referred to as 'the psychological

---

[146] For more in this, see: 'The Executive's Guide to Better Listening', *McKinsey Quarterly*, (February 2012), at:
www.mckinseyquarterly.com/Governance/Leadership/The_executives_guide_to_better_li
stening_2931.

contract'. This is the crucial and powerful link between the organisational performance intent, and the motivations, values and aspirations of the people. This emotional contracting element is sometimes overlooked by organisations and managers, and that is the reason that may explain why people have failed to do what the organisation expected and asked them to do.

In management and organisational theory, many employee attitudes, such as trust, faith, commitment, enthusiasm, and satisfaction, depend heavily on a fair and balanced psychological contract. Where the contract is regarded by employees to be broken or unfair, these vital, yet largely intangible ingredients of good organisational performance, can evaporate very quickly. Where the psychological contract is regarded by employees to be right and fair, these positive attitudes can thrive.[147]

Implementing and evaluating soft controls

Soft internal controls (trust, integrity, values and beliefs, etc.) should be part of the organisational process of strategy setting and ethical environment establishment. Corporate policies and procedures, vision and mission statements, strategic planning, ethics codes, job descriptions, training and coaching of staff, compliance programmes, etc, are the tools, and the hard controls, that help define whether an organisation consistently will do (supposedly) the right thing. An organisation might have written codes of conduct

---

[147] For more, see: *Understanding Psychological Contracts at Work: A Critical Evaluation of Theory and Research*, Conway, Neil and Briner, Rob B, Oxford University Press Oxford, UK (2005), 'The Psychological Contract – Resource Summary' (July 2011): *www.cipd.co.uk/hr-resources/factsheets/psychological-contract.aspx*.

and other value defining type documents (vision, mission, values, social responsibility, etc.), but that does not guarantee whether they are actually followed consistently. Most of the real understanding will not be expressly written in any document, but better evidenced in the day-to-day discharge of everyday duties and interactions. For example, the ethical culture can only rise as high as the tone set by the Board and the senior executive management. If management distributes the message about ethics poorly, or worse yet, delegates the message to subordinate levels, then the effectiveness of the ethical culture is greatly diminished. The best way to reinforce soft controls is to (probably) formalise them.

.

Performance measures and compliance indicators (SOFT Control 20)

Examples of performance measures (SOFT Control 20.1) and compliance indicators (SOFT Control 20.2) that could be used to support and monitor soft controls, are noted next.

Soft controls performance measures: Number of self-assessments, number of improvements after performance reviews, and number of hours on mentoring programmes.

Soft controls compliance indicators: Self-assessment policy for all departments (exist or not), coaching policy followed (or not), and management reports on self-assessments, coaching and mentoring issues produced (or not).

You can monitor your performance in soft controls, in your medium or large company, by monitoring the performance measures and compliance indicators noted above, via the internal process and innovation and learning perspectives of a corporate BSC (*Chapters 10 and 11*), as well as by the use of the GRC information system (EPRM Control 3), as discussed in Chapter 2. You can monitor your performance for your small company, by setting up a small manual or automated system (e.g. by using a spreadsheet application based on BSC).

Relating soft controls to the BMC framework

The controls identified in this chapter (SOFT Controls 1 to 20.2) that can be deployed to protect organisations against fraud, asset abuse, reputational damage, and other risks that they may be faced with, while achieving and improving their performance and compliance objectives and targets, are considered to be part of the fifth level (augment level) of business operational controls of the BMC framework (*see Figure 1: Business Management Controls Framework, Chapter 1*).

Conclusion

Codes of conduct, business values and ethics, and compliance communication programmes, should look beyond legal and regulatory boundaries, to tone at the top, employee buy-in, motivation and promotion programmes, and other factors that influence organisational culture. Statistics, such as percentage of participation, and the number of training modules conducted, are vital for overall programme evaluations, but they should be treated only as indicators.

13: Human Factors in Applying Business Management Controls

The ultimate goals are qualitative – open dialogue and a culture of accountability. With this in mind, some companies have gone beyond traditional training, and elected to rotate business managers through one of their ethics and compliance oversight functions.

This type of on-the-ground experience, engenders ethical behaviour as natural instinct for rising leaders, allowing them to make decisions in cases where clear right or wrong does not exist.

Socrates argued that the determination of good or bad behaviour depended entirely on the integrity of the rational process. Plato argued that to know good was to do good, that doing good was more useful and rational than doing bad, and that one who behaved immorally did so largely out of ignorance. Aristotle argued that ethics was a purely logical outcome of human nature, and it was useful because it was logical.

The design and deployment of controls in organisations is directly impacted by humans who act as the designers, operators, and implementers of these controls.

As people execute transactions and manage business processes with the facilitation of specific controls, both hard and soft (as explained later), they are bound to commit errors, due to various reasons, such as inadequate training, lack of motivation, inaccurate instructions, etc.

The ability of personnel to perform tasks according to expectations, or the competence of personnel, is crucial to every organisation, because of the role it plays in ensuring tasks are carried out satisfactorily and safely. Often assumptions of competence are made based on the adequacy of experience or training, possession of education and professional qualifications, or the availability of an efficient policy and associated procedures.

However, such assumptions may be incorrect, and should not be made. Competence, dexterities, and other required skills of personnel, should be managed and improved, otherwise, poor performance and operational accidents may result. Various human factors issues are important in developing procedures. Also, a variety of documentation is used, including manuals, guidelines, checklists, data sheets, logs, records, work orders, etc. Documentation design can have a major impact on process safety and operability. Procedures that are not followed, guidelines that are not used, diagrams that are misleading, and records that are not completed properly, can all increase the likelihood of accidents.

The simple message to employers from this – and a simple rule for managing this part of the psychological contract – is therefore to focus on helping employees to feel good and be happy, because this, in itself, produces a healthier view of the contract, and other positive consequences. Less, sensible employers who ignore the relevance of employee happiness – or the relevance of the contract itself – invariably find that the psychological contract is viewed more negatively, and staff are generally less inclined to support, and co-operate, with the leadership.

Soft controls recommendation

Recommendation 16: Design good, hard controls and implement them with effective soft controls

The key points to consider in assessing this recommendation for your business environment are:

13: Human Factors in Applying Business Management Controls

1 Communicate constantly your company's ethics and values to all parties.
2 Practise what you preach.
3 Train all participants in the affairs of your company in issues of soft controls.
4 Reward all your employees on performance.
5 Respond, resolve and punish, if needed, all violators.
6 Establish accountability and transparency at all levels.
7 Make decisions on accurate facts and data, with an understanding of all business functions and actions of individuals.

CHAPTER 14: BUSINESS AND IT CONTINUITY MANAGEMENT CONTROLS

'God not only plays dice, He also sometimes throws the dice where they cannot be seen.'

Stephen Hawking, English Physicist (1942–)

Chapter overview: This chapter, the first chapter of Part C: Enhancing Business Operations, deals with business and IT continuity controls, which are ensuring the continuity of your critical business functions and IT systems. Also, several business and IT continuity controls are detailed and one recommendation (Recommendation 17: Prepare for disasters as they can be most devastating to your operations) is offered for your consideration.

Introduction

'I always tried to turn every disaster into an opportunity,' is a famous quote by John D Rockefeller. Research conducted by Professor Daniel Diermeier of the Kellogg School of Management,[148] supports this, and suggests, according to Professor Diermeier, 'that when disaster strikes, a company becomes not just an anonymous provider of goods and services, but a member of the community'. This provides us with the motivation to analyse and present ways and means

---

[148] See article 'Every Disaster is an Opportunity you must Seize' at: *www.forbes.com/2011/04/12/disaster-corporate-opportunity-leadership-managing-japan.html*.

to companies, of all types and sizes, to plan for recovering from disasters, and to get their operations up and running in the quickest time possible.

Corporate governance and business continuity

Business continuity (BC) is one of the fields of study of emergency management, the other fields being, civil defence (or civil protection, or emergency preparedness, or emergency service, etc, depending on country characteristics), crisis management and continuity of government.[149] In plain business language, business continuity (BC) is working out how to stay in business in the event of disaster. It is usually part and parcel of corporate governance in modern organisations, all over the world.

Corporate governance, in general terms, refers to the body of guidelines, systems, policies, procedures and practices, by which private corporations and public organisations are structured and governed.[150] There are various models or frameworks of corporate governance, for all types and sizes of companies (small, medium, large, conglomerates, listed and not-listed, etc.), that serve a set of organisational, economic sector, regulatory and reporting needs, such as: COSO, BIS, COCO, Sarbanes-Oxley, GRI, COBIT®, ITIL®, ISO, TQM, etc.[151]

---

[149] See also: *www.ferma.gov.ng*, *www.publicsafety.gc.ca*, *www.cabinetoffice.gov.uk/ukresilience*, *www.em.gov.au*.
[150] The term 'corporate governance' was coined by COSO. Other organisations, such as CIMA, and ISACA, use the term 'enterprise governance' expanding, however, the basic COSO definition. See: *www.cimaglobal.com/*, and *www.isaca.org*.
[151] See also: *www.oecd.org*, *www.ecgi.org*, and *www.ccgg.ca*.

Establishing a corporate governance controls framework should be done by the Board. The actual, detailed, corporate governance controls, may be developed by the corporate committees (made up of the chief executive officer, chief financial officer, human resources director, etc.). Also, various generic or specific audit programmes and checklists, such as: internal controls framework checklist, business continuity audit review programme, and corporate performance audit programme (contained in this book) may be used to support the design and implementation of corporate governance for your specific company and business environment. There is no single model or framework, however, of good corporate governance that covers both the corporate governance, and the management aspects of the organisation, which could apply to all types of organisation (private, public, etc.) across the world. Each organisation should formulate, and institute, its own corporate governance framework (philosophy, policies, procedures, practices, etc.), for its own strategic and operational control, compliance and reporting needs.

This, however, should be built along the lines of the five, widely-accepted, COSO internal control standards:

1 Control environment
2 Risk assessment
3 Control activities
4 Information and communication
5 Monitoring.

According to COSO, and on the basis of various studies and practical, consulting projects and assignments, the following main corporate governance (CG) controls established for the effective running of enterprises are:

CG Control 1: Board of Director's charter.

CG Control 2: Corporate committees (e.g. audit committee, benefits and personnel committee, IT committee, financial issues committee, and business continuity issues committee).

CG Control 3: Corporate policies, procedures and plans.

CG Control 4: Risk management process and plan.

CG Control 5: Compliance process and plan.[152]

Business continuity and related aspects are the topic of this chapter. Other corporate governance controls are described in other chapters of this book.

Main types of business continuity controls

The main business continuity-related controls (BITC Controls 1 to 7), described next, are:

Business continuity issues committee

The primary purpose of the business continuity issues committee (BITC Control 1) is to provide guidelines, review, and approve, the critical business continuity issues (systems, budgets, plans, etc.) of your company. An example of a business continuity issues committee charter is described next.

---

[152] For examples, and more information on this subject, see: 'Board of Directors' Charter': *www.credit-suisse.com*. Also see: *www.oecd.org*, *www.frc.org.uk*, *www.corporatecompliance.org*, and *www.ccgg.ca*.

Business continuity issues committee charter – Example

Main responsibilities: General guidelines, duties and areas of responsibility of the business continuity issues committee are listed below. The committee shall:

1 Review all the critical business functions, identify the critical ones, and submit recommendations to the Board, so that they will be included in the business continuity planning process, and plan of the organisation.
2 Oversee the business continuity management process.
3 Provide business expertise to all levels of management of the organisation on continuity issues.
4 Ensure that accountability of the organisation is improved in terms of continuity issues.

Membership and organisation: Depending on the organisation size, structure and culture, the business continuity issues committee shall consist of the chief financial officer, and one member from each major department of the organisation.

Business continuity management process

Business continuity management (BCM) process (BITC Control 2) is a corporate process that identifies potential impacts that threaten your company, and provides a framework for building resilience, and the capability for an effective response and recovery which protects the interests of its key stakeholders, corporate reputation and brand name and value creating activities[153] of the specific

---

[153] See also: NFPA 1600 Standard on Disaster/Emergency Management and Business Continuity Programs: *www.nfpa.org* and Business Continuity Institute (BCI) and BS25999: *www.thebci.org*.

organisation. The product of this process is a business continuity plan (described below) and a structure to execute this plan, when needed.

The BCM process includes, as an example, the following steps:

1 **Business resilience planning**: Studying, analysing and planning for managing business resilience issues, such as: supply chain logistics, customer issues, brand name, reputation and other competitive advantage issues, privacy, building redundancy with partners, inventory and offshoring facilities, aligning procurement strategy with suppliers, building honest relationships with your employees, customers, and suppliers, etc.[154]

2 **Identifying the business functions, business data, IT systems and resources**: This involves identifying funds, personnel, facilities, business functions, IT systems, offices, data, filing systems, equipment, partners, etc.

3 **Addressing any special security requirements**: Companies, regardless of type and size, need to support security-rich communication, business transaction processing, and other critical systems and facilities, via a well-defined security strategy for protecting the corporate assets, including the brand image and other intangible assets.

4 **Developing the plan, changing the corporate culture, and assigning roles and responsibilities**.

5 **Testing the plan**.

---

[154] For more on resilience and business continuity, see: *The Resilient Enterprise: Overcoming Vulnerability for Competitive Advantage*, Sheffi, Y, Cambridge, Mass.: MIT Press (2005), *Reorganize for Resilience: Putting Customers at the Centre of Your Business*, Gulati, Ranjay, Harvard Business Press Books (2010), and *Everything you Want to Know about Business Continuity*, Drewitt, Tony, IT Governance Publishing (2012): www.itgovernance.co.uk.

6 **Reviewing the plan.**
7 **Maintaining the plan.**

Business continuity plan

Establishing the business continuity plan (or user contingency plan) (BITC Control 3) is the alternative method of continuing your business operations if IT, or other systems, are unavailable. This should be done by the business continuity corporate committee (made up of the chief executive officer, chief financial officer, human resources director, etc.). Also, various audit programmes and checklists, such as: business continuity audit review programme (described later in this chapter), internal controls framework checklist and corporate performance audit programme (noted in *Chapter 11*), may be used to support the design and implementation of business continuity for the specific organisation.

The events leading up to the use of the business continuity plan would be classified as a major catastrophe. Generally, local problems of a temporary nature are not covered by a contingency plan, with the possible extension of a lengthy full-scale black out of electrical power.[155]

Your business continuity plan should contain, as an example, the following:

---

[155] For more information, see: *Identification of the Core Competencies Required of Executive Level Business Crisis and Continuity Managers,* Shaw, Greg L and Harrald, John R (2004): *www.bepress.com/jhsem,* Business Continuity Institute, *www.thebci.org,* The Standards 'BS25999', 'BS25777' and 'ISO/PAS22399:2007', *www.bsigroup.com/,* Standard 'NFPA 1600 (2007)', *www.nfpa.org,* and ISO27001, 27002, etc. standards.

Business continuity plan – Example

1 Management overview and summary of costs required.
2 Risks covered: A detailed statement of the risks covered, such as rain, fire, storm, earthquake, disease, flood, hurricane, terrorism, utility outage, inventories, supply chain, partner failures, data losses, etc.
3 Specific business resilience issues and considerations.
4 Critical business functions, business data and critical IT applications.
5 Physical security aspects and needs.
6 Contractual arrangements (including any vendor support).
7 Invocation conditions (especially in terms of time).
8 Contingency procedures (including personnel, data suppliers).
9 Key personnel, and required training plans and management structure.
10 Internal organisational conditions and resources required (legal, IT management, users, building facilities, administration, accounting, security).
11 External organisational resources required (insurers, vendors, alternate business processing personnel, telecommunications, public authorities).
12 Testing strategy (concepts review, test each step, practise once per year).
13 Restoration procedures (back to primary site).
14 Insurance (especially to cover any cost of moving data and operating in an alternative way).[156]
15 Performance review and improvement procedure of the plan.

---

[156] See also: Insurance: Lessons from Disaster, Schut, Jan H, *Institutional Investor* (October 1990): pg. 297.

16 Maintenance procedure of the plan.

In many cases and organisations, especially when these organisations operate on the basis of very integrated IT systems, technology and networks, a business continuity plan may be complemented by an IT continuity plan.

IT continuity plan

The information technology continuity plan (BITC Control 4) is the collection of guidelines, rules, policies, standards, procedures, methods, techniques and tools, through which private and public organisations improve their ability to respond when major IT system and facility failures occur, ensuring that critical systems and services do not fail, or that failures are recovered within acceptable process recovery time limits.[157]

Business continuity manager

The business continuity manager (BITC Control 5) is usually responsible for developing, maintaining and managing the company's business continuity programme. This officer will support all activities necessary to enable the organisation to respond to a business interruption.

---

[157] See also: ISO27031:2011 standards, at: *www.iso.org* and *Contingency Planning and Disaster Recovery: Protecting Your Organisation's Resources,* Butler, Janet G and Badura, Poul, Computer Technology Research Corporation (1997).

Some more critical responsibilities are:

1 Develop, and maintain, a corporate-wide business continuity programme that addresses disaster recovery, business recovery and emergency response management.
2 Develop, produce and update business continuity materials and documentation.
3 Plan, and co-ordinate, all business continuity technical and user testing.
4 Work closely with IT to develop/maintain disaster recovery plans for critical systems and applications, and to ensure that internal recovery sites are updated and functioning properly.
5 Maintain, and update, the business continuity corporate website.
6 Perform risk analyses for functional areas, to identify points of vulnerability, single points of failure, and identify risk avoidance and mitigation strategies.
7 Assist in crisis management, and co-ordinate with government emergency management officials (as required) in the event of a business interruption.

IT back-up and restore policy and procedures

The purpose of the back-up and restore policy, and related procedures (BITC Control 6), is to standardise a means of backing up and recovering your computer files and computerised data. This policy contains statements (instructions) about what elements, files and data, related to and managed by information technology, should be copied and restored. Back-up and restore procedures provide detailed instructions on how the back-up and restore operations should function.

The IT management of your company should establish a back-up policy[158] and associated back-up and restore procedures, including the vital records package (see next paragraph).

IT back-up and restore policy: A typical policy would define the types of your application data and software (application, system, etc.) to be copied, the back-up execution schedule (continuous, daily, monthly, etc.), delivering back-up tapes/digital media off-site, the tape/digital media rotation schedule, what physical devices are used to store and perform all of the back-ups, the software packages used to perform and verify back-up and restore operations, the time back-ups of each kind of data are retained, how back-ups are verified, process for requesting and performing restoration of each type of data from back-ups, archival procedure for old back-ups, etc.

Vital records package

All your critical business data should be copied, as per the back-up policy of your company, and should be included in the vital records package of the enterprise. Developing the vital records package (BITC Control 7) should be the responsibility of the IT committee, with the support and assistance of the business functions, and ratified by the Board. The contingency plan and the disaster recovery procedures, as well as the disaster site alternative, will be effectively worthless, unless the organisation has taken

---

[158] For more details, see: *Weaving the Web*, Berners-Lee, Tim, Texere Publishing (2000), *Contingency Planning and Disaster Recovery Strategies*, Butler, Janet, Computer Technology Research Corp. (1994) and FFIEC (3/2003): *Business Continuity Planning Handbook*.

measures to ensure that a copy of its vital records (the vital records package) exists in an offsite, safe location, to enable full disaster recovery.

The vital records package should include, depending on the particulars of each organisation,[159] copies of:

1 All application programs, systems software (including networking software and database management systems), and enterprise architecture components (including the enterprise architecture repository).
2 Statistic reports.
3 Source data for computerised transactions.
4 Original business data recorded on business transactions.
5 Data stored in electronic media, and other critical registers.
6 Security-related logs.
7 Legal proceedings and Board of Director minutes of meetings.
8 Standards and regulations.
9 Corporate policies and procedures.
10 Recent computerised application data.
11 Documentation of all applications, and the enterprise architecture framework information.
12 Contracts (purchasing, maintenance, etc.).
13 Licences.
14 A small stock of pre-printed stationery.
15 System software books (vendor manuals).
16 A small stock of digital storage media (flash disks, diskettes, DVDs, CD-ROMs, tapes, printer cartridges, etc.).

---

[159] For examples, see: *www.csu.edu.au/adminman/tec/policy-vital-records.pdf*, *www.usaid.gov/policy/ads/500/511.pdf*, *www.vitalrecordsprotection.org*.

17 A list of key personnel and their details (addresses, phone numbers, etc.)
18 Documentation of employment contracts for critical staff (managers, IT, finance, etc.).
19 Corporate performance printed reports for the last year, depending on the regulatory framework, such as: balance sheets, transaction listing, budgets, etc.
20 Financial transactions on digital media for the last year (corresponding to corporate performance reports).

Your vital records package should be kept current, and should be updated as per the back-up policy of the company, in order to ensure that the specific organisation can always recover its most critical operations in case of a major disaster.

Business and IT continuity audit tools

The above business continuity controls (business continuity issues committee, business continuity management process, business continuity plan and business continuity manager, etc.) may be supported by various audit programmes and checklists (such as: business continuity audit review programme (BITA Control 1) and IT back-up and recovery procedures audit checklist (BITA Control 2)), which may assist you in planning, establishing and improving your business and IT continuity process for your specific corporate environment. These are detailed in the *Business Management Controls Toolkit*.

Performance measures and compliance indicators (BITC Control 8)

Performance measures (BITC Control 8.1) and compliance indicators (BITC Control 8.2) related to the implementation effort of business and IT continuity controls, are noted next.

Business continuity performance measures: Percentage of critical business functions covered, percentage of critical IT applications covered, number of key personnel trained and available, and number of back-ups per time period.

Business continuity compliance indicators: Business continuity issues committee exists (or not), business continuity management process exists (or not), and business continuity plan exists (or not).

You can monitor your performance in business and IT continuity in your medium or large company, by monitoring the performance measures and compliance indicators noted above, via the internal process and innovation and learning perspectives of a corporate BSC (*Chapters 10 and 11*), as well as by the use of the GRC information system (EPRM Control 3), as discussed in *Chapter 3*. You can monitor your performance for your small company by setting up a small manual or automated system (e.g. by using a spreadsheet application based on BSC).

Relating business continuity controls to the BMC framework

The controls identified in this chapter (Business and IT Continuity Management Controls (BITC Control 1 to 8.2)) that can be deployed to protect your company against potential disruptions, and assist you in recovering from them, while achieving and improving your performance and compliance objectives and targets, are considered to be part of the third level (govern level) of business operation of the BMC framework (*See Figure 1: Business Management Controls Framework, Chapter 1*).

Conclusion

Managers, regardless of their level in the hierarchy of the organisation, are directly responsible for all activities of an organisation, including directing, designing, developing, implementing, supervising, monitoring and controlling the proper functioning of, maintaining, documenting and improving the internal control system. Their specific roles and responsibilities vary, depending on their function in the organisation and the given organisation's characteristics, country, culture, industry-type, and other socio-economic factors and conditions.

They must also be prepared to recover from failures. Unfortunately, the answer is that disaster can strike at any time and it is often an unplanned event.[160]

All businesses need a business continuity strategy; unfortunately, however, most businesses do not even know what a business continuity plan is.

By implementing a business continuity plan, your business will increase its recovery capabilities dramatically. That will mean that you can make the right decisions quickly, cut

---

[160] For a list of major disasters, such as: The AT&T network collapse (1990), The explosion of the Ariane 5 (1996), Siemens and the British passport system (1999), EDS and the Child Support Agency (2004), Airbus A380 incompatible software issues (2006), LA Airport flights grounded due to software problems (2007), etc, see: *www.zdnet.com/news/the-top-10-it-disasters-of-all-time/177729*.

downtime, and minimise financial losses. Preparedness is the key. It gives you added confidence. Having business continuity management (BCM) in place, demonstrates a duty of care to your shareholders, employees, customers, suppliers and community. Consulting experience and research studies show that businesses are far more likely to survive a disaster if they have thought about it in advance, and planned accordingly. All participants in the affairs of the organisation, such as regulators, banks, investors, insurers, customers and suppliers, will take a company that has a business continuity plan, much more seriously. Also, business continuity plans build and strengthen employee confidence in the long run. Employees will more likely appreciate the fact that the business they work for is doing all it can to protect their safety and place of work.

In the end, business continuity is about responsible management. It makes a business a safer place to work and contributes to its long-term financial stability and survival.

According to a quite recent article,[161] with which I totally agree, 'High-profile disasters, such as hurricanes, fires, terrorist attacks, earthquakes and tsunamis, aren't the only kinds of disasters that can cripple an organisation. Even mundane events, such as cable cuts, power outages, computer viruses and equipment failures can jeopardise a company's business survival … Not being prepared can result in overwhelmingly detrimental consequences'.

It is, therefore, every manager's responsibility to ensure business continuity is an integral part of their normal business activity.

---

[161] '18 September 2006' by Ken Horner in the *Computer Technology Review*, see: www.wwpi.com/index.php?option=com_content&task=view&id=1379&Itemid=44.

Recommendation 17: Prepare for disasters, as they can be most devastating to your operations

The key points to consider in assessing this recommendation for your business environment are:

1 Business continuity and disaster recovery is quite a difficult and strenuous process.
2 Establish, implement and ensure the proper functioning of BCM controls identified in this chapter.
3 The management of your company must exhibit the proper culture, stamina and strength, so that they design and test the right disaster recovery strategy for your company.
4 The management of your company must motivate their associates to implement correctly and improve, when required, what has been planned when disaster strikes.

CHAPTER 15: CASE STUDIES: APPLYING BUSINESS MANAGEMENT CONTROLS TO MITIGATE FRAUD AND OTHER RISKS

'No one will find me to have knowingly committed fraud.'

Bernard Ebbers, former CEO of WorldCom, convicted of fraud (US $100 billion, 2005)

Chapter overview: This chapter, the second chapter of Part C: Enhancing Business Operations, presents various risks in selected business functions of your company, such as: overall management, finance, purchasing and IT, and describes how specific business management controls may mitigate these risks in 11 case studies, in a more effective way. Also, several control activities are detailed and one recommendation (Recommendation 18: Develop and implement a minimum set of business management controls to mitigate your risks) is offered for your consideration.

Introduction

The 21st Century, according to the noted management thinker John Elkington,[162] is primarily focused on evolution: corporate, technological, economic, political and, above all, cultural evolution. At the corporate level, organisations will need to operate on the basis of the triple

---

[162] See: *The Chrysalis Economy: How Citizen CEOs and Corporations can Fuse Values and Value Creation*, Elkington, John, Capstone Publishing/John Wiley, Oxford (2001).

bottom-line principle, in order to be more responsible, socially and economically. This principle guides the companies to operate with full regard to values, transparency, environment-safe products and services, symbiotic partnerships, long-term view of developments, and increased corporate governance. But all companies and organisations do not seem to operate on these principles. The international business landscape is full of corporate fraud scandals. Various data and studies have shown (US-FBI and IRS, UK Government, etc.) that most corporate frauds involve falsification of financial information, self-dealing by corporate insiders and obstruction of justice.

This means that at the practical business level, organisations and their management must establish better and more effective performance and compliance controls, and ensure more efficient monitoring of the activities of their organisation. This book describes a set of several types of performance and compliance controls that may be customised and established by each organisation to make it more responsible.

This chapter provides examples of applying business management controls in four major functional areas of an organisation, in a generic sense, and therefore to show in a practical way how these controls can be applied. These areas were selected, as most frauds, lately,[163] are committed within the operating realm of these functions.

For each business functional area the relevant risks are presented, the controls that may mitigate these risks are noted, and two real-life case studies are described where

---

[163] As per FBI, IRS, UK and Australian Government data, *www.acfe.org*, etc.

corporate controls were not applied successfully, or not at all.

These areas are:

Area 1: Overall business management of the organisation

Area 2: Financial management of the organisation

Area 3: Purchasing operations of the organisation

Area 4: Information technology (IT) operations of the organisation.

In addition to the above, three cases of how segregation of duties (SOD) controls may be applied in purchasing operations, IT systems development and operations, and cash handling functions of an organisation, are presented.

Area 1. Business case studies for the overall corporate management function of the organisation

Some of the more critical risks that may appear in the overall corporate management function of the organisation are:

1 Damage to company name and reputation
2 Loss of control of company's activities
3 Loss of property and other corporate assets
4 Loss of market share
5 Loss of research and other critical patents
6 Fraud and abuse of resources.

Examples of various overall corporate management controls to reduce the risks to the overall business management of the organisation, identified in the previous paragraph, are noted next.

15: Case Studies: Applying Business Management Controls to Mitigate Fraud and Other Risks

1 **Corporate management responsibility controls**: Establish management to be responsible to the Board for the company's system of internal controls, operation and risk management processes. *For more also see Chapter 2 (EGOV Controls 1-4. Corporate Management Responsibility).*

2 **Corporate audit responsibility controls**: Establish an internal audit function to operate under a charter with a definite purpose, authority and responsibility of the corporate audit department, and establish the company's audit committee to meet with them several times a year to review the annual corporate audit plan and the results of the internal audit activities. *For more also see Chapter 2 (EGOV Control 6. Corporate Audit Responsibility).*

3 **External audit service controls**: Appoint an external audit service separate and distinct from the company's corporate audit department, under the oversight of the company's audit committee. *For more also see Chapter 2 (EGOV Control 7. External Audit Service).*

4 **Corporate risk management controls**: Establish the company's risk management organisation, policies and procedures, to cover regulatory, legal, property, treasury, financial reporting and internal controls. Also execute international insurance contracts to cover various risks to operations. *For more also see Chapter 2 (RISK Controls 1-3. Corporate Risk Management).*

5 **Corporate organisational structure controls**: Establish a clear organisational structure, with well-defined lines of authority and control responsibilities. *For more also see Chapter 2 (EGOV Control 13. Corporate Organisational Structure).*

6 **Business unit/function management controls**: Make each business/functional unit responsible and accountable for implementing procedures and controls to manage risks within its business. *For more also see Chapter 2 (GOV Control 5. Business Unit/Function Management).*

7 **Strategy controls**: Set up formal operating and strategic planning processes for all businesses and functions within the company. *For more also see Chapter 3 (STRP Control 1. Strategy).*

8 **Policies and procedures controls**: Develop, and implement, policies and procedures for the management of all business functions/units and their activities and operations. Also provide guidelines and limits for approval of capital expenditures and investments. Establish, and implement, security policies and procedures for facilities, plants, offices, property and IT components (hardware, software). *For more also see Chapter 2 (EGOV Control 16. Policies and Procedures).*

9 **Ethics and compliance controls**: Craft, and communicate, standards of business conduct applicable to all employees, develop a compliance organisation and compliance action plan, and manage all compliance issues. *For more also see Chapter 2 (COMP Controls 1-4. Ethics and Compliance).*

10 **Performance management controls**: Establish annual budgeting and periodic reporting systems for all businesses which enable the monitoring of progress against financial and operational performance targets and metrics, and evaluate the organisation against industry, technological and market trends. Also monitor all performance and compliance measures. *For more*

15: Case Studies: *Applying Business Management Controls to Mitigate Fraud and Other Risks*

also see Chapter 2 (EPMR Controls 1-2. Performance Management).

The following two cases illustrate the risks, in question, and the application (or not) of the various controls in real-life situations, and their impact thereof to the particular companies concerned.

Case 1: IBM's share of the computer market (in the 1980s) was reduced due, mainly, to the non-investment in personal computers. In this case, IBM board and senior management, among other things, did not assess, and resolve, the risk: 'lack of forecasting of market demands' and 'industrial and technological trends'. Better execution and monitoring of controls related to 'strategy', 'risk' and 'performance management' (as identified above and in *Chapters 2 and 3*) might have avoided this.

Case 2: A 200-year old bank (Barings) collapsed (1995) due to senior management's practices in investing very large sums in high-risk instruments. In this case, the Board of Barings Bank, was unable, or not willing, to effectively supervise all senior management actions and activities, did not monitor the effective operation of internal controls, was ineffective in monitoring the Bank's critical operations, and allowed deficient internal auditing and risk management practices to be executed. Better execution and monitoring of controls related to 'corporate management responsibility', 'ethics', 'risk', 'policies and procedures', and 'performance management' (as identified above and in *Chapters 2 and 3*) might have avoided this.

Area 2. Business case studies for the financial management function of the organisation

Some of the more critical risks that may appear in the financial management function of the organisation are:

1 Damage to company financial integrity
2 Loss of funds
3 Loss of property and other corporate assets
4 Incorrect postings in the books
5 Incorrect calculation and reports
6 Fraud, theft, revenues not collected, inappropriate refunds given
7 Abuse of resources and mismanaged financial operations.

Examples of various financial management controls to minimise the real, or perceived, opportunities to commit fraud and abuse, and secondly for management to be able to identify, in a timely manner, fraud, or frauds that have been perpetrated, are noted next. More financial controls are described in *Chapter 5*.

FINM Control 1. Financial management responsibility controls: Establish financial management to be responsible, with terms of reference, job descriptions, employment contracts, confidentiality statements, etc, to the Board, for the company's system of financial management controls and for operating the systems, policies and procedures to keep the company in a stable, financial status.

FINM Control 2. Financial standards, systems, policies and procedures controls

1 Establish financial standards.
2 Develop, and implement, financial systems, policies and procedures, for recording all financial activities and

operations in the formal accounts of the company, and for managing cash, receipts and payments to all stakeholders (employees, management, vendors, shareholders, state agencies, etc.) of the organisation.

FINM Control 3. Computerised financial systems controls

1 Develop, and implement, all the required computerised systems to support all functions of the finance department of the organisation.
2 Assign access to all computerised systems on the basis of the tasks assigned to staff.
3 Ensure that back-ups are taken by the IT department of all computerised data, and that these back-ups are tested on a periodic basis.

FINM Control 4.5. Responsibilities and segregation of duties controls: Establish and assign responsibilities to accounting staff on the basis of segregation of duties, for posting and updating accounts, handling cash, cheques and payments, reporting, etc.

FINM Control 4.6. Locked safe controls: Obtain, and use, a locked safe, and keep cash, cheques and other critical documents, reports, contracts, bonds, shares, etc, in this. Establish, and assign, responsibilities to specific staff for controlling this safe.

FINM Control 4.7. Post transactions and update books controls

1 Post transactions to books on a daily basis, at least.
2 Resolve all errors as quickly as possible.
3 Balance inputs to processed items.
4 Balance accounts on a pre-determined period (daily, monthly, etc.).

5 Produce interim financial reports (at least monthly) and audit specific transactions, as needed.
6 Produce and distribute, as authorised, the final company financial reports.

FINM Control 4.8. Manage petty cash controls

1 Control petty cash via a petty cash register, for all incoming and outgoing payments.
2 Assign responsibility of managing petty cash to only one individual, and rotate him (her) on an ad hoc basis.
3 Limit petty cash reserves.
4 Conduct spot audits of petty cash, keeping in mind that it's possible to falsify petty cash records through the use of miscellaneous receipts and other documents.
5 Balance petty cash, at least monthly.

FINM Control 4.9. Manage cheques controls

1 Control cheques via a cheque register for all incoming and outgoing payments.
2 Assign responsibility of managing cheques to only one individual, and rotate him (her) on an ad hoc basis.
3 Conduct spot audits of cheques, keeping in mind that it's possible to falsify petty cash records through the use of miscellaneous receipts and other documents.
4 Compare the cheque register to the actual cheque number sequence.
5 Control the cheque stock, making sure that cheques are kept under lock and key.
6 Deposit cheques daily.
7 Fill in empty spaces on cheques. If the amount line of a cheque is left partially blank, an additional amount may be inserted.

8 Mutilate voided cheques. Be sure to stamp voided cheques 'Void', or tear off the signature line to avoid cashing of the cheque.
9 Review un-cashed cheques. It is possible that an un-cashed cheque is created through a flaw in the system, which could send a cheque to a non-existent supplier.
10 Stamp incoming cheques 'For Deposit Only'.
11 Conduct spot audits of cheques, keeping in mind that it's possible to falsify petty cash records through the use of miscellaneous receipts and other documents.
12 Performing bank reconciliations monthly. This should be done by someone who has no association with accounts payable, accounts receivable or cash receipts.

FINM Control 4.10. Manage accounts receivable controls

1 Confirm accounts receivable balances.
2 Require approval of credits for all customers on the basis of a formal process.
3 Compare cheques received to money posted against accounts receivable.

FINM Control 4.11. Manage accounts payable controls

1 Audit credit card statements.
2 Apply limitations on the amount that can be charged, to keep an employee within spending limits.
3 Verify authorisations with a three-way match of the purchase order, invoice, and receiving report.
4 Review additions to the vendor file. Have someone not associated with accounts payable review all additions to the master vendor file, to avoid payments to fictitious vendors.

5 Require approval on all invoices that do not have a purchase order.

6 Approve all expense statements before payments are made.

FINM Control 4.12. Manage payroll controls

1 Ensure that all payments related to payroll are approved by the human resources or administration department, and the CEO of the company, before any payments are made to the employees.

2 Check the total amount paid by finance to equal the total shown on the payroll report.

3 Ensure that internal audit performs payroll audits on an ad hoc basis, and as required by their annual audit process.

FINM Control 4.13. Manage performance controls

1 Ensure that management reviews budget position reports for budget status.

2 Ensure that management reviews periodic activity reports, to evaluate whether objectives are being achieved.

3 Ensure that systems, policies and procedures provide timely, accurate, and sufficient information for all levels of management.

4 Ensure that the finance department uses ethics, benchmarking and other measures, to evaluate effectiveness and satisfaction by all their internal and external customers.

The following two cases illustrate the risks in question, and the application (or not) of the various controls in real-life situations, and their impact thereof to the particular companies concerned.

15: Case Studies: Applying Business Management Controls to Mitigate Fraud and Other Risks

Case 1: Parmalat (Italy) collapsed (2003), mainly due to high debt and other erroneous or 'not allowed' accounting practices, regarding representation of debt in the financial books and reports of the company. In this case, the Board and top management of Parmalat, was unable, or not willing, to effectively supervise all financial management actions and activities of the company. Better execution and monitoring of controls related to:

1 'Financial management responsibility', 'financial standards', financial performance management'.
2 Overall corporate management controls ('corporate management responsibility', 'ethics', 'risk', 'policies and procedures', as described above and in *Chapters 2 and 4*), might have avoided this.

Case 2: Lehman Brothers (US) collapsed (2010) due to senior management's practices in employing various 'improper' accounting techniques to post false data in their books. The Board and top management of Lehman failed, among other things, in monitoring the accuracy of financial data, the operation of internal controls, internal auditing and risk management practices. Better execution and monitoring of controls related to:

1 'Financial management responsibility', 'financial standards', 'financial performance management'.
2 Overall corporate management controls, such as 'corporate management responsibility', 'external audit service', 'ethics', 'risk', and 'policies and procedures', as described above and in *Chapters 2 and 3*, might have avoided this.

Area 3. Business case studies for the purchasing function of the organisation

The various risks that may appear in the purchasing function of the organisation are:

1 Damage to company name due to improper dealings.
2 Purchases awarded to an employee's relative without proper justification.
3 Loss of funds, property and other corporate assets.
4 Conflict of interest for company staff.
5 Kickbacks received by vendors, overpayment for services or goods, payments for services or goods not received, duplicate payments to vendors, etc.
6 Fraud, theft, or inappropriate purchases awarded.
7 Abuse of resources, adding fictitious vendors, supplier cartels, etc.

Examples of purchasing controls that may be used to minimise the real, or perceived, opportunities to commit fraud and abuse, and secondly for management to be able to prevent and detect, in a timely manner, that a purchase fraud has been committed, are noted next. Other similar controls are described in *Chapter 6.*

PROD Control 2.1: Purchasing management responsibility

1 Establish purchasing management to be responsible for operating the purchasing system, policies and procedures of the company, with terms of reference, job descriptions, authorisation limits for purchases, confidentiality statements, etc.
2 Establish purchasing organisation and allocation of specific duties and responsibilities to staff with job

descriptions, authorisation limits for purchases, confidentiality statements, etc.

3 Implement compliance and ethics controls, including an ethics policy, conflict-of-interest policy, and getting all employees to sign conflict-of-interest disclosure forms.

4 Establish an anonymous whistleblower hotline that employees can use to report doubtful, questionable, or improper purchasing, accounting or auditing matters, and issues that come to their attention.

PROD Control 2.2: Purchasing standards, systems, policies and procedures

1 Establish purchasing standards.

2 Develop, and implement, a system of policies and procedures for purchasing all goods, services and materials required for all activities and operations of the organisation.

3 Issue detailed guidelines and train all staff on making purchases and payments according to the company's standards.

4 Establish a process via which all purchase contracts, before they are awarded to the selected vendor(s), are reviewed and approved by the legal function of the organisation, and ratified by the Board.

5 Ensure that background checks are performed for all vendors before a purchase is awarded. These background checks should be carried out for all vendors (Internet, non-Internet, etc.) and should include verifying all their ownership and shareholder status, registration details, reputation of officers, financial data, criminal and other law cases they might be involved in, etc.

6 Develop, and implement, a purchase file maintenance procedure for filing and maintaining all documentation

related to purchases (RFI, RFP, vendor proposals,
market survey data, evaluation analyses,
correspondence, purchase contracts, copies of invoices,
etc.).

7 Ensure management reviews all purchase transaction
details on a continuing basis, double checking that
vendors are paid as defined in the purchase contract, and
that the amounts are correct. Also, review vendor
payments to ensure that all payments match authorised
invoices and approved purchase orders.

PROD Control 2.3: Computerised purchasing system

1 Develop, and implement, the required computerised
system, and a purchase ledger, to support all functions of
the purchasing department of the organisation.

2 Assign access to the computerised purchasing system on
the basis of the tasks assigned to staff.

3 Audit the vendor files, on a periodic basis, to ensure that
fictitious vendors have not been added.

4 Ensure that back-ups are taken by the IT department of
all computerised purchasing data, and that these back-
ups are tested on a periodic basis.

PROD Control 2.4: Purchasing staff responsibilities

1 Establish and assign responsibilities to purchasing staff,
on the basis of segregation of duties, so that at least two
persons are involved in any purchase.

2 Ensure that background checks are performed by human
resources for all purchasing staff, before their
assignment to a purchasing position.

3 Ensure that persons signing invoices have personally
verified that the items, or services, were received.

4 Ensure that persons initiating purchase orders should not also approve payments, and that persons approving payments should not also handle bookkeeping.

5 Ensure that all payments are supported by an original invoice and an approved purchase order, receipt of goods and services is acknowledged, payment is made on the account and on an original invoice, cheques are made payable to the account of the supplier, and not to 'cash', and that you keep payment records for management and audit purposes.

PROD Control 2.5 Locked safe

1 Obtain, and use, a locked safe, and keep all original purchase orders, contracts, etc. for all purchases of the organisation.

2 Establish and assign responsibilities to specific staff for controlling this safe.

3 Remove purchase-related documentation upon written senior management approval.

PROD Control 2.6: Manage performance

1 Ensure that senior management, and the Board, reviews purchases and respective budgets for all company purchases.

2 Ensure that purchase systems, policies and procedures provide timely, accurate, and sufficient purchase information for all levels of management.

3 Ensure that the purchase department uses benchmarking, and other measures, to evaluate effectiveness and satisfaction by all their internal and external customers.

PROD Control 2.7: Improve performance

1 Ensure that senior management monitors all purchase activity to evaluate whether purchase objectives are being achieved.
2 Ensure that the purchase department is audited by the internal audit function and external auditors of the organisation, both on an ad hoc basis, as well as on an annual basis.

The following two cases illustrate the risks, in question, and the application (or not) of the various controls in real-life situations and their impact thereof to the particular companies concerned.

Case 1: In 2009, the Office of Fair Trading (*www.homeoffice.gov.uk*) imposed fines totalling £129m on 103 construction firms in England. These firms were found to have colluded with competitors to agree over-inflated bids for building contracts with, amongst other organisations, the NHS and British schools (risk: supplier cartel and price fixing).

The Board and top management of each company involved failed, among other things, in monitoring the ethics and compliance issues of their purchasing operations. Better execution and monitoring of controls related to:

1 'Purchasing management responsibility', 'purchasing standards', 'purchasing performance management'.
2 Overall corporate management controls ('corporate management responsibility', 'external audit service', 'ethics', 'risk', 'policies and procedures', as described in *Chapters 2 and 3*), might have avoided this.

Case 2: In the largest Medicare fraud case in US history (July 2010: *www.aarp.org*), US federal agents indicted 94 people (doctors, nurses and owners, and executives of healthcare companies, etc.) in five cities, on charges of submitting more than $251 million in false claims (risk: falsifying patient medical data, failure to comply to rules, standards and regulations.)

The private individuals concerned, as well as the Board and top management of each organisation involved, failed, among other things, in monitoring the ethics compliance issues of their purchasing operations. Better execution and monitoring of controls related to

1 'Purchasing management responsibility', 'purchasing standards', 'purchasing performance management'.
2 Overall corporate management controls ('corporate management responsibility', 'external audit service', 'ethics', 'risk', and 'policies and procedures' as described in *Chapters 2, 3 and 6*), might have avoided this.

Area 4. Business case studies for the IT department of the organisation

The various risks that may appear in the information technology department of the organisation are:

1 Lack of business plan, IT strategy, IT budget, IT security policy, security of computer systems, security of physical environment, etc.
2 Deviations from the company's established procedures.
3 Inadequate separation of duties.
4 Failure to anticipate market trends.
5 Computer systems and software not properly supported.
6 Improper, or inadequate, or non-existent maintenance contracts.

7   No adequate management monitoring and reporting.
8   Inadequate documentation for information systems.
9   Incomplete IT standards, procedures and policies.
10 Unauthorised software packages.
11 Business interruption.
12 Incorrect recording/maintaining/processing of information/data.
13 Not evaluating needs properly and failing to control development costs.
14 Incorrect hardware selection and sizing.
15 Delays in implementation.
16 Inadequate back-up of software and data, and lack of contingency and fall-back procedures.
17 Unauthorised disclosure of confidential information.
18 Loss of extremely valuable information (stored in application systems).
19 Lack of audit trail, etc.

Examples of various **IT controls** that may be used to minimise the real, or perceived, opportunities to commit fraud and abuse, and secondly for management to be able to prevent and detect, in a timely manner, any possible occurrences of IT frauds and abuses of resources are noted next. More controls are described in *Chapter 6*.

IT management responsibility

1   Establish IT management to be responsible for designing and operating the computer facilities, data centre, information systems, policies and procedures of the company, with terms of reference, strategy, vision and mission, etc.
2   Establish the IT organisation and allocation of specific duties and responsibilities to staff with job descriptions, authorisation limits for IT purchases, confidentiality

statements, background checks for all staff, asset controls, IT management reporting, etc. *See also Chapter 6 (IT Administration Controls, Information Technology (IT) Policy, IT Budget, IT Procurement Process Controls, IT Asset Controls, IT Management Reporting Controls, and IT Safe Storage).*

IT strategy

1 Design and develop an IT strategy for the organisation.
2 Design, develop and implement an IT security strategy with the supporting policy and procedures for its effective implementation.

IT development standards, systems, policies and procedures

1 Establish IT standards for developing and running applications, and for the security of all systems, facilities and data. *See also Chapter 6 (Data and Information Security Practices and Controls, IT Security Policy, Password Controls, and Computer Security Incident Controls).*

2 Develop, and implement, policies and procedures for designing, developing, and implementing computerised information systems. *See also Chapter 6 (IT Systems Development Controls, IT Systems Development Methodology, IT System Test Plan, Spreadsheet Controls, IT Operational Controls, and Application Systems Controls).*

3 Design, and develop, IT back-up and recovery procedures.
4 Design, develop and implement documentation standards for all IT systems and operations. *See also Chapter 7 (IT Systems Development Controls).*

15: Case Studies: Applying Business Management Controls to Mitigate Fraud and Other Risks

Development and operation of IT systems

1   Establish, and operate, the computer facilities and data centre to run all required information systems and IT infrastructure of the organisation.
2   Develop, and implement, all computerised, information systems on the basis of a formal and approved systems development methodology.
3   Monitor all computerised operations and resolve any production problems.
4   Ensure that all back-up procedures are executed as designed.
5   Ensure that at least two system programmers manage the computer systems software of the organisation, and that these are controlled and monitored by management.
6   Endure adequate segregation of duties of IT personnel (programmers not responsible for production data and files, system programmers not responsible for application libraries and production files, operators not responsible for application libraries, etc.).
7   Ensure management reviews all IT operations on a continuing basis.
8   Ensure that audit trails are built into all computerised systems and operations.

See also Chapter 7 (IT Systems Development Methodology, IT System Test Plan, Spreadsheet Controls, IT Operational Controls, and Application Systems Controls).

Manage IT performance

1   Ensure that senior management, and the Board, reviews IT purchases and respective budgets for all company IT purchases and projects.

2 Ensure that IT systems, policies and procedures provide timely, accurate, and sufficient information for all levels of management.

3 Ensure that the IT department uses benchmarking, and other measures, to evaluate effectiveness and satisfaction by all their internal and external customers.

Improve performance

1 Ensure that senior management monitors all IT activity to evaluate whether IT objectives are being achieved.

2 Ensure that the IT department is audited by the internal audit function and external auditors of the organisation, both on an ad hoc basis, as well as on an annual basis.

IT safe storage

1 Obtain, and use, a locked fire-safe vault, and keep all original IT purchase orders, IT contracts, IT licences, primary back-up copies, etc. for all hardware and software of the organisation.

2 Establish, and assign, responsibilities to specific staff for controlling this safe.

3 Remove IT related documentation upon written senior management approval.

4 Store all secondary, back-up copies, on a periodic basis and according to the back-up procedure, to the offsite safe, storage location.

The following two cases illustrate the risks, in question, and the application (or not) of the various controls in real-life situations and their impact thereof to the particular companies concerned.

Case 1: In North Bay Health Care Group (US, 2004: *www.cybercrime.gov*), a former accounts payable clerk used her computer to access North Bay's accounting software without authorisation, and in turn, issued various cheques payable to herself and others, to the amount of $875,035. In this case, senior management, among other things, did not assess, and manage, the risks of unauthorised access, inadequate audit trail, and incomplete monitoring of IT transactions, in the most proper way. Better execution and monitoring of controls related to:

1 'IT management responsibility', 'IT standards', 'IT performance management'.
2 Overall corporate management controls ('corporate management responsibility', 'external audit service' , 'ethics', 'risk', 'policies and procedures'), as described in this chapter and in *Chapters 2 and 7*, might have avoided this.

Case 2: Roger Duronio, a former UBS PaineWebber Inc. (2006: *www.ubs.com/us/en.html*) systems administrator, was found guilty of computer sabotage and securities fraud for writing, planting, and disseminating malicious code that took down up to 2,000 servers (risk: inadequate segregation of systems programmers, incomplete monitoring of IT operations). Better execution and monitoring of controls related to:

1 'IT management responsibility', 'IT standards', 'development and operation of systems', 'IT performance management', 'IT performance improvement'.
2 Overall corporate management controls ('corporate management responsibility', 'external audit service', 'ethics', 'risk', 'policies and procedures'), as described in this chapter and in *Chapters 2 and 7*, might have avoided this.

In addition to the above cases studies, the following three cases depict how segregation of duties (SOD) controls may be applied in purchasing operations, IT systems development and operations, and cash handling functions of an organisation.

Segregation of duties (SOD) case studies

SOD case study 1: Application of segregation of duties in purchasing operations

The purchase requisition, purchase ordering, receiving of goods and services, paying the vendor, and general accounting activities, need to be appropriately segregated if all purchase control objectives (avoid fraud, etc.) of the specific organisation are to be met. For example, those personnel who perform the purchasing activities, including those who maintain contact with outside vendors and service suppliers and issue purchase orders, should not perform any receiving of goods and services, execute accounting functions for the goods and services obtained, or carry out payment activities for what has been purchased. One way of applying SOD in purchasing operations and the related functions involved (purchasing, inventory and accounting) is outlined next:

Purchasing function (SEGD Control 4)

Step 1 – Purchase order initiation: Assign to employee 1, upon the written and approved request of a company officer outside the purchasing function.

Step 2 – Purchase order approval: Assign to employee 2 for small consumables. In large value items, employee 2 will take action as indicated next. A committee evaluates the technical and commercial aspects of the various vendor proposals, a vendor is selected, the purchase contract is reviewed and approved by the legal department, and final approval is obtained from the Board, before the purchase order is placed.

Step 3 – Purchasing manager monitors, reviews and authorises all purchase order transactions. Also audits the whole process, on a random basis.

Inventory function (SEGD Control 5)

Step 4 – Confirmation of the receipt of the product(s) or service(s): Assigned to employee 3.

Step 5 – Inventory manager monitors, reviews and authorises all purchase order receipts. Also audits the whole inventory process, on a random basis.

Accounting function (SEGD Control 6)

Step 6 – Accounting system entry and system maintenance: Assigned to employee 4.

Step 7 – Payment to vendor: Employee 5 after matching vendor invoice with purchase order, obtaining approval from inventory function, and getting approval from:

1 Department manager that initiated the purchase request.
2 Accounting manager.
3 Purchasing manager.

SOD case study 2: Application of segregation of duties in IT systems development and operations

The IT system development and operation activities need to be appropriately segregated, if all IT control objectives of the specific organisation are to be met. For example, those personnel who perform the development of the system, including those who write and maintain application software code, should not operate the computerised systems, and should not have access to production data, or execute accounting functions for any IT hardware, software and services obtained, or carry out payment activities for what has been purchased. One way of applying SOD in IT systems development and operations, and the related functions involved (IT systems development, IT systems operations and accounting), is outlined next:

IT systems development function (SEGD Control 7.1)

Step 1 – Identification of a requirement (or change request): Business person or manager.

Step 2 – Authorisation and approval: IT manager, according to IT strategy, budget, corporate considerations and approval of the Board.

Step 3 – Design and development: IT development person 1. If a ready-made software package is obtained, the purchasing process is followed (a committee evaluates the technical and commercial aspects of the various vendor proposals, a vendor is selected, the purchase contract is reviewed and approved by the legal department, and final approval is obtained from the Board, before the purchase order is placed).

Step 4 – Design and development review: IT development person 2.

Step 5 – System acceptance and approval for production: Business manager for the functional aspects of the system, IT manager for the software and other technical aspects of the system. IT system administrator assigns security codes to system's users in accordance with the IT security policy of the organisation, and the business manager's approval that requested the specific IT system.

IT systems operations function (SEGD Control 7.2)

Step 6 – System implementation in production: Application software is transferred to production libraries by the system administrator, on the approval of the IT manager. Computer operations personnel (different staff from application development or system administration) run the system. Business users are responsible for updating the data maintained by the system.

Step 7 – System production monitoring: IT manager monitors the operation of the system to ensure that access rights to the system and its data are not breached (especially through database administration access, user administration access, and other tools which provide back-door access, or supplier installed user accounts), and the back-up and other critical procedures related to the system are executed and tested as planned.

Accounting function (SEGD Control 6)

Step 8 – Accounting system entry and accounting system maintenance: Accounting employee 1 enters the data about the IT system or IT equipment purchased.

Step 9 – Payment to vendor: Accounting employee 2, after matching IT vendor invoice with IT purchase order, obtaining approval from IT, and getting approval from:

1 Department manager that initiated the IT purchase request
2 Accounting manager
3 Purchasing manager.

Step 10 – Comparison, or review of transactions and data: Business manager and staff of the given business function ensure that the data maintained by the system is valid, accurate and reasonable, by reviewing transactions and data appearing in the system's files and generated reports.

This is not an exhaustive presentation of the system development life cycle, but a list of critical development functions applicable to segregation of duties.

SOD case study 3: Application of segregation of duties in cash handling

The segregation of duties is one of several steps to improve the internal control of an organisation's assets. For example, the internal control of cash is improved if the money handling duties are separated from the record keeping duties. By separating these duties, the likelihood of theft is reduced, because it will now require two dishonest people working together to admit to each other that they are dishonest, plan the theft, and to then carry out the theft. One person will have to remove the cash and the other person will have to falsify the records. One way of applying SOD in cash handling is outlined next.

Accounting function – Handling cash and payments (SEGD Control 6.1)

Step 1 – Accounting system entry and accounting system maintenance: Accounting employee 1 enters the data about receiving and depositing remittances.

Step 2 – Initiating, or preparing invoices: Executed by accounting employee 2.

Step 3 – Preparing cheques: Carried out by accounting employee 3.

Step 4 – Reconciling bank accounts and posting the general ledger, or any subsidiary ledger affected by cash transactions: Accounting employee 4.

Step 5 – Authorising payments: Accounting manager.

This is not an exhaustive presentation of the accounting system life cycle, but a list of critical payment functions applicable to separation of duties.

Relating controls to mitigate risks to the BMC framework

The controls identified in this chapter that can be deployed to protect organisations against fraud, asset abuse, reputational damage and other risks that they may be faced with, while achieving and improving their performance and compliance objectives and targets, are considered to be part of the third level (govern level) of business operation of the BMC framework (*see Figure 1: Business Management Controls Framework, Chapter 1*).

Conclusion

The impact of fraud and abuse hits all companies, private and public, non-profit, etc, right in their financial and operational performance and results. The typical organisation across the world, loses 5% of its annual revenue to fraud, according to a latest global study.[164]

While large private corporations and public organisations may be able to withstand a large fraud, a smaller corporation, or a non-profit organisation, may never recover. To survive in today's fierce and competitive marketplace, businesses must be proactive in the fight against fraud, and other types of abuse of resources and corporate assets. Effective internal controls are the corporate mechanisms to prevent, avoid and detect fraud.

Recommendation to mitigate risks

Recommendation 18: Develop, and implement, a minimum set of business management controls to mitigate your risks

The key points to consider in assessing this recommendation for your business environment are:

1 Safeguard all your assets (physical, data, information systems, patents, etc.).
2 Segregate duties in critical functions.
3 Authorise transactions and payments.
4 Execute performance-related audits.
5 Ensure that your management and board monitor your company.
6 Run awareness programmes on controls, to all participants in the activities of your company.
7 Resolve breaches and incidents, while evaluating and improving your implemented controls.

---

[164] See '2010 Global Fraud Report' by *www.acfe.com*.

CHAPTER 16: AUDITING BUSINESS MANAGEMENT CONTROLS

'Appearances are a glimpse of the unseen.'

Anaxagoras, Ancient Greek Philosopher(500–428 B.C.)

Chapter Overview: This chapter, the third chapter of Part C: Enhancing Business Operations, describes the audit process and products, and provides a set of audit programmes and checklists to enable you to evaluate and improve your business management controls. Also, several audit controls are detailed and one recommendation (Recommendation 19: Ensure that internal audit examines all your operations) is offered for your consideration.

Introduction to auditing

The principal objective of auditing (external and internal) is to review, and appraise, the adequacy, reliability and effectiveness of internal control within systems. External auditing relates, primarily, to the annual independent financial audit conducted for the protection of the stockholders of publicly traded companies. Internal auditing relates to the work executed by the internal audit function of the organisation which evaluates the business management controls established by the management of the organisation[165] to: achieve the organisation's objectives,

---

[165] For more on the Internal Audit Process, see: *Internal Auditing: Assurance and Consulting Services,* Reding, Kurt F et al, The IIA Research Foundation (2009),

ensure the economical and efficient use of corporate resources; ensure compliance with established company policies and procedures, and external laws and regulations; safeguard the business entity's assets and interests from loses of all kinds, including those arising from fraud, irregularity or corruption; and ensure the integrity and reliability of corporate information and data.

Types of audit

The various, usual, types of audit are:

1 **Financial** auditing (also called 'statutory auditing'), which involves reviewing the adequacy of internal accounting controls of the organisation in terms of accuracy, completeness and validity of financial information, financial reports, and of the underlying accounting systems and records.
2 **Operational** (performance) auditing, which includes reviewing the strategic and operational performance of the whole organisation, or specific business processes or departments, focusing on the efficiency and effectiveness of these processes, and the associated management controls.
3 **Compliance** auditing, which relates to reviews of compliance or conformity of the organisation with relevant legislation, regulations, standards, internal policies and guidelines.
4 **IT systems** auditing, which pertains to reviews of effectiveness, accuracy and efficiency of IT general (e.g.

Implementing and Auditing the Internal Control System, Chorafas, DN, St. Martin's Press (2001), *www.iia.org* and *www.isaca.org*.

IT organisation, administration, security, etc.) controls, as well as the IT application controls (e.g. accuracy of data and transactions processed and maintained of specific corporate computerised application systems) related to information technology and telecommunications systems, facilities and projects of the organisation.

Other types of audits are: follow-up audits, investigating audits, integrated audits, quality audits, ISO audits, tax audits, IT security audits, continuous audits, due diligence process audits, etc.

The work of all these audits is carried out by internal auditors (EGOV Control 6, *see also Chapters 2 and 12*), on the basis of an audit strategy (EGOV Control 6.1), an audit plan (EGOV Control 6.2), and an audit methodology (EGOV Control 6.3), with specific audit objectives, and with the assistance of audit programmes, audit checklists, test computerised application systems, and computer assisted audit tools and techniques, like CAATTs, etc.[166] Also, individual managers and functions can audit themselves by conducting self-assessments. The major product of internal audit activities is the '**internal audit report**'.

The usual contents of this report (EGOV Control 6.4) are:

1 Executive summary
2 Introduction
3 Audit objectives
4 Audit scope

---

[166] For more on CAATTS, see: *CAATTs and other Beasts for Auditors*, Coderre, David G, Global Audit Publications, Vancouver, Canada (1998).

5 Audit overall opinion
6 Business areas and risks reviewed
7 Detailed recommendations for each area and risk examined
8 Management action plan with agreed action, responsibility, implementation date, status, etc.
9 Annex with audit tests conducted, detail analysis, etc.

You should also establish a procedure (**Management Action Plan of Audit Issues (EGOV Control 6.5)**) to monitor and follow-up on whether the findings, errors, etc, reports by internal and external auditors and other external experts, are resolved successfully, and whether the organisation's internal controls have been corrected or not. The performance of all internal audit activities can be measured by a set of performance measures[167] (e.g. number of audits executed per time-period, number of audit recommendations made, number of management actions taken, etc.), and by the use of a specific internal audit BSC, as well as by the use of the GRC information system (EPRM Control 3), as discussed in *Chapter 3*.

Auditing business management controls

The responsibility for evaluating internal controls, and business management controls as such, rests with the organisation's internal audit function, according to various regulations.[168] Examining, evaluating and auditing business

---

[167] See also: 'Knowledge Report, Measuring Internal Audit Performance', September 2009, at: *www.theiia.org*.
[168] Sox Act, SEC Regulations, etc. See: *www.pwc.com/en_US/us/sarbanes-oxley/assets/final_so_wp_2-boardsac.pdf*, and *www.sec.gov/news/studies/2009/sox-404_study.pdf*.

management controls identified in this book may be carried
out by the following audit programmes and checklists.
These are designed to support the control, review and audit
activities of corporate managers and internal audit
professionals, in assessing business management controls
and how they are established, and operate, in the given
environment of the organisation under audit. These audit
programmes and checklists pertain to various critical
elements of business management controls, such as:

- 'Red flags' (existence of policies and procedures, board
  and management roles, auditing, fines and legal
  breaches, training of staff, personnel supervision,
  personnel adequacy, corporate performance, etc.)
- Organisational controls readiness
- Organisational strategy
- Business management controls culture
- Performance measurement and monitoring system
- Human resource issues
- Performance of the Board of Directors
- Corporate governance and internal controls system
- Compliance controls
- Corporate policies and procedures
- Business records management system
- Financial management system
- Corporate fraud management system
- Internal audit function
- Ethics management
- Soft controls
- IT controls evaluation.

For a more detailed description of these audit programmes
and checklists, see 'Business Management Controls Audit
Checklists' in the *Business Management Controls Toolkit*,

The results of the analysis and the processing carried out on the basis of the data, replies and opinions collected by the use of the above audit programmes and checklists, and by the use of the GRC information system (EPRM Control 3, in *Chapter 2*), may be used to better plan the required, and approved, necessary changes, and potentially improve all issues, activities and aspects audited (organisational controls, performance of the Board of Directors, corporate governance and internal controls system, compliance controls framework, corporate policies and procedures, records management system, IT security, IT procurement, contingency planning, physical and environmental controls, system development and maintenance, data centre operations and software, and data security, ethics, etc.).

Relating audit controls to the BMC framework

The controls identified in this chapter (Audit Controls (EGOV Control 6 to 6.5)) that can be deployed to protect organisations against fraud, asset abuse, reputational damage, and other risks that they may be faced with, while achieving and improving their performance and compliance objectives and targets, are considered to be part of the fourth level (audit level) of business operation of the BMC framework (*see Figure 1: Business Management Controls Framework, Chapter 1*).

Conclusion

The potential benefits of auditing to private and public organisations are great. Consulting practice, research studies and real-life cases[169] have shown that auditing has strengthened the structures and constituent elements of internal control, and has improved the efficiency and effectiveness of all activities of organisations related to: general management, corporate governance, risk assessment and resolution, compliance, provision of services, financial policies and procedures, IT systems, personnel management, corporate administration, quality, etc.

Auditing business management controls recommendation

Recommendation 19: Ensure that internal audit examines all your operations

The key points to consider in assessing this recommendation for your business environment are:

1 Ensure that your audits are carried out by an audit strategy and an audit plan.
2 These (audit strategy and plan) should examine, and assess, all your business policies, procedures, activities and operations of your company, both on an annual basis, as well as on an ad hoc basis.
3 These (audit strategy and plan) must be executed by getting adequate resources (funds, systems, tools, staff, data, etc.) and skills on a proactive and practical cost-benefit basis.

---

[169] See 'Measuring Internal Auditing's Value' report at: *www.theiia.org*, *www.dit.ie/about/internalaudit/benefitsofaudit/*, *www.mncppc.org/Our_Departments/Central_Administrative_Services/internal_audit/aud it_benefits.html*.

4 Execution of audit strategy and plan may be enhanced by providing, in addition to usual audit, opinions, advice and recommendations, where possible, on improving controls and problems identified during the audit assignments of your operations.

CHAPTER 17: CONCLUSION

'Make up your mind to act decidedly and take the consequences. No good is ever done in this world by hesitation.'

Thomas H. Huxley (1825–1895), English Biologist

Chapter overview: This last chapter offers some final thoughts about the role and approach of managers in protecting their company against various threats, while enabling them to achieve the company's objectives. It presents a list of 'red flags' that may provide a warning sign that the specific business entity may be experiencing problems in managing its operations, and offers two recommendations (Recommendation 20: Implement your complete business management controls by focusing on strategic, operational, risk, compliance and governance performance issues of your company, and Recommendation 21: Your company success depends on your decisive actions) for your consideration.

Managers and decision making

Managers are employed to make decisions, good, bad, or of no relevance. A decision is a choice made between alternative courses of action, in a situation of uncertainty. There are various decision-making methods, techniques, models and tools that can assist a manager during the decision-making process, such as:

1   The Vroom-Yetton-Jago decision model

2 The Kepner-Tregoe matrix
3 OODA loops
4 Grid analysis
5 Paired comparison analysis
6 Pareto analysis
7 Decision trees
8 Risk analysis
9 Cost/benefit analysis
10 Break-even analysis
11 Cash flow forecasting
12 Six thinking hats, etc.[170]

What is, however, of paramount importance, is that good decisions should be made quickly, and on the basis of correct data, and accurately, processed information. As professors, Kaplan and Norton, the noted BSC creators, have stated, performance measurement is not to be considered as an alternative solution, but rather as a necessary tool of management practices for the design and implementation of organisational and operational strategy.

Other authors[171] recommend a strategic control model containing:

1 The definition of mission, objectives and strategy.
2 The establishment of organisational structure.
3 The full utilisation of the balanced scorecard (BSC) model for measuring performance, quality, innovation and response to customers.

---

[170] For more on decision making, see: *The Rational Manager: A Systematic Approach to Problem Solving and Decision-Making,* Kepner, Charles H and Tregoe, Benjamin B, McGraw-Hill (1965), *Management Decision Making*, Monahan, G, Cambridge: Cambridge University Press (2000) and *Human Error*, Reason, James, Ashgate (1990).
[171] For example: *Strategic Management Theory: An Integrate Approach,* Hill, Charles W and Jones, Gareth R, South-Western Cengage Learning (2010).

4 The measurement of financial performance.

According to consulting practices on several large and small private and public organisations, the executive management and the Board of Directors of these organisations, use the following approach to facilitate, enable, and resolve the most critical aspects of the management decision-making process:

1 Financial reports (weekly, monthly, annual. etc.).
2 Performance reports based on the BSC model and its four perspectives (financial, customers, internal corporate processes, employee learning and development).
3 Market prices for primary resources and selling trends for the company's products and services.
4 Monthly risk analysis.
5 Performance progress reports for all ongoing projects of the given organisation.

I should also note that the performance of private and public organisations is influenced by:

1 The internal operating environment and the total capacity and availability of corporate resources (e.g. management, organisation, skills, knowledge, dexterities, etc.).
2 The external environment impacting the organisation (e.g. legal, regulatory and institutional frameworks, international guidelines on corporate governance, industry and market operating standards, greater economic and societal frames of reference, competitive forces and socio-economic stability factors, etc.).

Both of these environments, however, are posing several very serious threats, which must be dealt with by all managers, in order to protect their business operations. It is therefore necessary to analyse ways to deal with them, before I offer some concluding remarks about business management controls that may be applicable to your company.

Corporate threats

According to various sources,[172] about 75% of fraud results from employees, while other sources of fraud include customers, management, suppliers, and service providers. In addition, about 55% of fraud (according to the same source) is discovered as a result of strong internal controls. The Association of Certified Fraud Examiners (ACFE) reports that fraudulent activities cost American business approximately 7% of total revenues in 2008.[173]

In addition to this, the ACFE latest report[174] showed that some of their findings are:

1 Occupational fraud is a global problem.
2 Nearly one quarter of the frauds involved losses of at least US $1 million.
3 The typical organisation loses 5% of its revenues to fraud.

These data, as well as similar studies on insider threat attacks,[175] show you which way to go, as a board member,

---

[172] For example, see:
worldacademyonline.com/article/15/301/why_is_forensic_accounting_necessary_.html.
[173] Based on data from 959 cases of occupational fraud (January 2006 and February 2008). When applied to the projected 2008 US GNP, this is about, approximately, $994 billion in fraud losses. See: *www.acfe.com/press-release.aspx?id=4294968565*.
[174] See ACFE 2010 Global Fraud Study.
[175] Cappelli, Dawn et al (2006): 'Common Sense Guide to Prevention and Detection of Insider Threats', CERT/Software Engineering Institute, *www.sei.cmu.edu*.

manager and stakeholder, in leading, and running, organisations, and monitoring, and improving, performance, results and activities in organisations. You need effective business management controls. It is up to you as board member, manager, or other stakeholder, to pay special attention not only to the performance and profitability of your organisation, but also to how your organisation is best protected against damages, losses, thefts of critical assets, potential fines and litigations, abuse of resources, etc. My proposal of a general model to help you improve your situation, for all types and sizes of companies, is described next.

Levels of business operation

The general model of controlling business entities I am proposing, refers to designing and implementing business management controls according to the conceptual approach of the business management controls (BMC) framework (*Chapter 1, Figure 1*) which applies controls at the five levels of business operation, such as:

First level of business operation (organise phase): This relates to setting up the following:

1 Board, management and committee roles, structure and responsibilities.
2 Business functions and resources.
3 Standards, policies and procedures.
4 Internal controls framework and manual.

Second level of business operation (envision phase): This relates to instituting the following:

1 Corporate culture, vision, mission and values.
2 Strategy, goals, objectives and targets.

3 Performance framework and management.

Third level of business operation (govern phase): This relates to implementing the following:

1 Strategy.
2 GRC (governance, risk and compliance) controls.
3 Operational controls (purchasing, finance, IT, data, security, fraud, etc.).
4 Personnel administration, including segregation of duties, compensating controls, etc.
5 Management and compliance reporting.

Fourth level of business operation (audit phase): This relates to carrying out the following:

1 Monitoring controls
2 Internal audits
3 Self-assessments
4 External audits
5 Regulatory audits.

Fifth level of business operation (augment phase): This relates to executing the following activities:

1 Compare organisation to external entities.
2 Conduct studies by external experts.
3 Certify personnel.
4 Certify organisational components (structure, service quality, policies and procedures).
5 Instil corporate social responsibility, including community involvement, etc.
6 Consider, and implement, soft controls.

Are there, however, any 'red flags' that may provide a warning sign that a specific business entity is not doing well, and may turn into a chaotic out-of-control situation?

17: Conclusion

Red flags

The following list may be an example of such 'red flags'. This is based on the auditing and consulting experience of the author, and on discussions and communications with other consultants, auditors, fraud examiners, accountants, and other professionals. No scientific study, however, has been conducted, to provide added evidence and assurance that this list is even relevant, or applicable, in your own corporate environment. It is only provided as an example for information purposes.[176]

1 **Policies and procedures**: Inadequate design, development, implementation, annual review and improvement of corporate policies and procedures.
2 **Board and management roles**: Ineffective oversight exercised by the Board, and insufficient discharge of duties and responsibilities by all senior levels of management.
3 **Auditing**: Audit (internal and external) findings not acted upon within the time-frame agreed, or forgotten all together.
4 **Fines and legal breaches**: Fines imposed by regulators and government authorities on compliance, tax, customs, accounting, performance results, data privacy, environmental, worker safety and health issues, etc, as well as penal and civic code litigations, breaches, etc.
5 **Training of staff**: Inadequate or ineffective supervision of staff activities by management, including guiding,

---

[176] For other examples see: 'Guidance for Directors: Watch for Fraud, Does Canada have a White-Collar Crime Problem?', by Richard Leblanc, 5 March 2012, www.canadianbusiness.com/blog/corporate_control, www.knowledgeleader.com, www.businessweek.com, www.fraudessentials.com, www.wccfighter.com and www.ftc.gov/redflagsrule.

coaching and training, discussing issues and problems, etc.

6 **Personnel supervision**: Inadequate or ineffective execution of personnel administration controls, including segregation of duties, authorisations and approvals, rotation of duties, hiring and dismissal of personnel, due diligence of all staff, vacation taking, etc.

7 **Personnel adequacy**: Inadequate skills, dexterities, knowledge and experience, including professional certifications, for all board members, managers, and critical staff (accountants, auditors, IT resources, etc.).

8 **Corporate performance**: Very high, or very low achievement of strategic and operational objectives, as evidenced by financial and non-financial performance reports and results.

9 **Morale**: Very high, or very low morale of board, management and employees.

10 **Turn-over**: Very high, or very low turn-over of board, management and employees.

11 **Accuracy of data**: Inaccurate data, unsupported or unauthorised transactions, discrepancies and large number of errors in business records, including accounting records, purchase orders, transactions, balances, files, bank accounts, etc.

12 **Conflicts of interest**: Too close a relationship with customers, vendors, competitors, regulators, and other parties involved in the activities of the organisation.

Is this list relevant to you? It is hard to say on an absolute basis. You have to consider these in relation to your operating environment, and how you want to implement business management controls to manage these 'red flag' issues before disaster strikes you.

17: Conclusion

The whole concept of designing and implementing business management controls, such as the ones recommended in this book; and monitoring your company's performance by appropriate performance management systems, is, to enable and facilitate your business entity (small, medium, large, private, public, etc.) to improve both its own activities and operations to attain long-term growth, and the results these have on society.

This may be achieved by creating and executing a set of processes that facilitate your company to navigate from the level of marketing products and services, to the higher level of satisfying, maintaining and enlarging the customer base, and finally to reaching the highest level of providing better products and services, with vision, values, principles and quality that actually improve the whole wide world, as expressed by all people, their communities, and their physical and mental environment.[177]

Business management controls, as described in this book, when designed and implemented effectively, can enable and facilitate your company to achieve its performance targets, and prevent abuse or loss of resources, as well as minimise fraud and errors. They can help ensure accurate and reliable financial reporting, and support your company to comply with laws and regulations, avoiding damage to its brand name, reputation and other consequences. In summary, it can help your business entity survive, get to where it wants to go, and possibly avoid pitfalls and surprises along the way. But business management controls cannot change inherently ineffective boards or managers

---

[177] For more details see: *Marketing Management*, Kotler, P and Lane Keller, Kevin, Pearson-Prentice Hall (2009).

into good ones and, they cannot change the abrupt impact to organisations, by government policy or programmes, actions by market forces or competitors, or socio-economic conditions.

An internal control system, such as the one in this book, no matter how well formulated and operated, can provide only reasonable assurance (probably) to management and the Board, regarding achievement of an organisation's objectives. The likelihood of achievement is affected by limitations inherent in all internal control systems. These include the realities that judgements in decision making can be error-prone, and that breakdowns can occur because of simple errors or mistakes, or collusions, management override capability, resource constraints, and the benefits of controls to their costs, etc. Thus, while business management controls can help an organisation achieve its goals and objectives, it is not a panacea. It should be noted that in order for all these controls to function most effectively and efficiently, and in a beneficial way both to its stakeholders and to society at large, they need, besides human and financial resources, appropriate ethical and regulatory guidelines, rules, management controls, policies, procedures and review tools and techniques, as well as governance, risk, compliance, IT governance, information governance, business data management, strategic and operational controls.

All these business management controls will need to operate in a corporate control environment.

This control environment will be made up, in most cases, of the following major elements:

1 Organisational values and norms (legal, ethical, etc.).
2 Management philosophy and business operating style.

3 Reward and remuneration systems.
4 Human resource development and organisational systems.
5 Organisational structure.
6 Customer support function.
7 Production and services functions.
8 Management systems, policies, procedures and methods.

And as a recent study by Nitin Nohria[178] concluded, the companies that produced superior results, products and services, did so, by instituting and exercising to the fullest, the following management practices:

1 Well-defined and executed strategy.
2 Effective, organisational structure with ethical and innovative culture.
3 Talented human resources, well-led by executive management.
4 Entering new partnerships with customers and other businesses.

Conclusion

In closing, designing and developing all these is quite a difficult and labouring job. Implementing, reviewing, monitoring, evaluating and improving them, is more than difficult. It is strenuous, and requires extraordinary will and vision by all participants. But the results, practice and studies have shown, are more than beneficial.[179] They can

---

[178] For more, see: Nohria, N, Joyce, W and Roberson, B (2003): 'What Really Works', at: *http://harvardbusinessonline.hbsp.harvard.edu*.

[179] For more on management practices see the studies (2005 and 2007) by Bloom, N and others at: *http://cep.lse.ac.uk/pubs/download/CP177.pdf* and *http://cep.lse.ac.uk/management/*.

keep your company effective, efficient, and above all, agile and quick to react to almost all changes. They make your business organisation successful and prosperous.

Business management controls, as detailed in this book and the additional volume, are beneficial and important to you. They can transform your working practices and save you time and money, as they can:

1 Improve your business control practices.
2 Help you develop, customise, assess and implement your own controls better.
3 Show you how to develop more streamlined and successful working practices.
4 Show you how to protect your business operations in a more effective way.

Recommendations for overall business management controls implementation

Recommendation 20: Implement your complete business management controls to add value to your business by focusing on strategic, operational, risk, compliance and governance performance issues of your company

The key points to consider in assessing this recommendation for your business environment are:

1 Design, and implement, business management controls, and compliance and performance measures, to monitor and improve the performance of your company.
2 Pay attention to strategy design and execution.
3 Improve the leadership, structure and culture of your company.
4 Attract, and use, best human talent to serve and innovate.

5 Explore your customer relationships and partnerships with others, when you want to enter new business areas.

Recommendation 21: Your company success depends on your decisive actions

The key points to consider in assessing this recommendation for your business environment are:

1 Avoid delay.
2 Educate and prepare yourself.
3 Train and involve your staff.
4 Take the necessary actions.
5 Review results and improve both yourself and your company.

And we should also pay attention in implementing business management controls of:

1 The golden rules of Pythagoras (570–c. 495 BC): 'Consult and deliberate before you act, so that you may not commit foolish actions', and 'Never do anything which you do not understand'.
2 The quotation by Filolaos (from Croton) the Pythagorean (480–400 BC): 'Succeed in what you want to do with persuasion and not with violence'.

APPENDIX

This appendix contains a list of the business management controls, noted in a summary form in this book and its specific chapters, such as plans, policies, procedures, checklists, etc.

The following list contains the specific controls referenced in each chapter of this book which are described in more detail in the *Business Management Controls Toolkit*.

Chapter 1: Business Management Controls Framework	
Business Management Controls System Manual (BMCF Control 2)	Location in BMC Toolkit: *Manuals* folder

Chapter 2: Enterprise Governance Controls	
Confidential Information Release and Procedures.	Location in BMC Toolkit: *Policy* folder
Corporate Policies and Procedures Manual	Location in BMC Toolkit: *Manuals* folder
Corporate Rewards System	Location in BMC Toolkit: *Plan* folder
Enterprise Governance (EG) Performance Measures and Compliance Indicators	Location in BMC Toolkit: *Performance Measures and Compliance Indicators* folder (with additional EG

	documentation)
Chapter 3: Risk and Compliance Controls	
Risk Performance Measures and Compliance Indicators	Location in BMC Toolkit: ***Performance Measures and Compliance Indicators* folder**
Compliance Performance Measures and Compliance Indicators	
Business Ethics Policy	Location in BMC Toolkit: ***Policy* folder**
Compliance Programme	Location in BMC Toolkit: ***Plan* folder**
Compliance Action Plan	
Chapter 4: Strategic Management Controls	
Business Strategies, Goals and Objectives	Location in BMC Toolkit: ***Documents* folder**
Strategic Management Process Questionnaire	Location in BMC Toolkit: ***Checklists and Questionnaires* folder**
Strategic Plan Contents Audit Programme	
Strategic Alignment Checklist	

Human Resources Questionnaire	
Strategic Performance Measures and Compliance Indicators	Location in BMC Toolkit: ***Performance Measures and Compliance Indicators* folder**

Chapter 5: Financial Management and Accounting Controls

Job Description for Financial Manager, Treasury Manager and Cost Accountant	Location in BMC Toolkit: ***Job Descriptions* folder**
Financial Policies and Procedures Manual	Location in BMC Toolkit: ***Manuals* folder**
Accounting Procedures	Location in BMC Toolkit: ***Procedures* folder**
Financial Performance Measures and Compliance Indicators	Location in BMC Toolkit: ***Performance Measures and Compliance Indicators* folder**

Chapter 6: Customer Sales and Production Controls

Customer Sales Performance Measures and	Location in BMC Toolkit: ***Performance Measures and***

Compliance Indicators	**Compliance Indicators folder**
Purchasing Action Plan and Procedures	Locations in BMC Toolkit: **Plan folder**
Project Cost Accountant Job Description	Location in BMC Toolkit: **Job Description folder**
Customer Service Policy	Location in BMC Toolkit: **Policy folder**
Quality Management Policy	
Production Performance Measures and Compliance Indicators	Location in BMC Toolkit: **Performance Measures and Compliance Indicators folder**
Chapter 7: IT Governance Controls	
IT Strategic Plan	Location in BMC Toolkit: **Documents folder**
Information Technology (IT) Policy	Location in BMC Toolkit: **Policy folder**
IT Security Policy	
Password Policy	
Information Sensitive Policy	
Date Privacy Policy	

Laptops and Smart Devices Controls	
Confidentiality Policy	
Data Classification Policy	
Internet and E-mail Policy	
Social Media Governance Management Plan	Location in BMC Toolkit: *Plan* folder
IT Governance Performance Measures and Compliance Indicators	Location in BMC Toolkit: *Performance Measures and Compliance Indicators* folder

Chapter 8: Business Data Management Control

Files, Documents and Records (FDR) Management Action Plan	Location in BMC Toolkit: *Plan* folder
Data Quality Improvement Procedure	Location in BMC Toolkit: *Procedures* folder
Business Data Management Performance Measures and Compliance Indicators	Location in BMC Toolkit: *Performance Measures and Compliance Indicators* folder

Chapter 9: Business Intelligence and Espionage Controls	
Business Intelligence Policy	Location in BMC Toolkit: *Policy* **folder**
Information Sensitivity Policy	
Confidentiality Agreement	
Business Intelligence and Espionage Performance Measures and Compliance Indicators	Location in BMC Toolkit: ***Performance Measures and Compliance Indicators* folder**
Chapter 10: Business Performance Management Frameworks	
Canada: Management Accountability Framework (MAF)	Location in the BMC Toolkit: ***Performance Frameworks* folder**
GRI Framework	
Chapter 11: Implementing Business Management Controls – All controls are described in this book.	
Chapter 12: Roles and Responsibilities of Participants in Business Management Controls	

Privacy of Information Policy	Location in BMC Toolkit: **Policy folder**
Information Sensitivity Policy	
Roles and Responsibilities of Personnel Benefits Committee, Compliance Committee, Advisory and Regulatory Third Parties and Stakeholders	Location in BMC Toolkit: **Job Descriptions folder**
Performance Measures and Compliance Indicators relates to Management Roles and Responsibilities	Location in BMC Toolkit: **Performance Measures and Compliance Indicators folder**
Chapter 13: Human Factors in Applying Business Management Controls	
Soft Controls Action Plan	Location in BMC Toolkit: **Plan folder**
Performance Measures and Compliance Indicators for Soft Controls	Location in BMC Toolkit: **Performance Measures and Compliance Indicators folder**

Chapter 14: Business and IT Continuity Management Controls	
IT Continuity Plan	Location in BMC Toolkit: *Documents* **folder**
IT Back-up and Restore Policy	Location in BMC Toolkit: *Policy* **folder**
Business Continuity Audit Review Programme	Location in BMC Toolkit: *Checklists & Questionnaires* **folder**
IT Back-up and Recovery Procedures Audit Checklist	
Business and IT Continuity Performance Measures and Compliance Indicators	Location in BMC Toolkit: *Performance Measures and Compliance Indicators* **folder**
Chapter 15: Case Studies: Applying Business Management Controls to Mitigate Fraud and Other Risks – All controls are described in this book.	
Chapter 16: Auditing Business Management Controls	
Internal Audit Performance Measures and Compliance Indicators	Location in BMC Toolkit: *Performance Measures and Compliance Indicators* **folder**

Audit Programmes and Checklists:	
Red Flags	
Organisational Controls Readiness	
Organisational Strategy	
Business Management Controls Culture	
Performance Measurement and Monitoring System	
Human Resource Issues	
Performance of the Board of Directors	Location in BMC Toolkit: *Checklists & Questionnaires* **folder**
Corporate Governance and Internal Controls System	
Compliance Controls	
Corporate Policies and Procedures	
Business Records Management System	
Financial Management System	
Corporate Fraud Management System	
Internal Audit Function	
Ethics management	

Soft Controls IT Controls Evaluation	
Chapter 17: Conclusion – All controls are described in this book.	

ITG RESOURCES

IT Governance Ltd sources, creates and delivers products and services to meet the real-world, evolving IT governance needs of today's organisations, directors, managers and practitioners.

The ITG website (*www.itgovernance.co.uk*) is the international one-stop-shop for corporate and IT governance information, advice, guidance, books, tools, training and consultancy.

Other Websites

Books and tools published by IT Governance Publishing (ITGP) are available from all business booksellers and are also immediately available from the following websites:

www.itgovernance.eu is our euro-denominated website which ships from Benelux and has a growing range of books in European languages other than English.

www.itgovernanceusa.com is a US$-based website that delivers the full range of IT Governance products to North America, and ships from within the continental US.

www.itgovernanceasia.com provides a selected range of ITGP products specifically for customers in South Asia.

www.itgovernance.asia delivers the full range of ITGP publications, serving countries across Asia Pacific. Shipping from Hong Kong, US dollars, Singapore dollars, Hong Kong dollars, New Zealand dollars and Thai baht are all accepted through the website.

www.27001.com is the IT Governance Ltd website that deals specifically with information security management, and ships from within the continental US.

Toolkits

ITG's unique range of toolkits includes the IT Governance Framework Toolkit, which contains all the tools and guidance that you will need in order to develop and implement an appropriate IT governance framework for your organisation. Full details can be found at *www.itgovernance.co.uk/ products/519*.

For a free paper on how to use the proprietary Calder-Moir IT Governance Framework, and for a free trial version of the toolkit, see *www.itgovernance.co.uk/calder_moir.aspx*.

There is also a wide range of toolkits to simplify implementation of management systems, such as an ISO/IEC 27001 ISMS or a BS25999 BCMS, and these can all be viewed and purchased online at: *www.itgovernance.co.uk/catalog/1*.

Training Services

IT Governance offers an extensive portfolio of training courses designed to educate information security, IT governance, risk management and compliance professionals. Our classroom and online training programmes will help you develop the skills required to deliver best practice and compliance to your organisation. They will also enhance your career by providing you with industry standard certifications and increased peer recognition. Our range of courses offers a structured learning path from foundation to advanced level in the key topics of information security, IT governance, business continuity and service management.

Full details of all IT Governance training courses can be found at *www.itgovernance.co.uk/training.aspx*.

Professional Services and Consultancy

The IT Governance Professional Services Team can work with you to guide and support the implementation of your complete business management controls. These typically include social media, cybercrime, privacy, mobile devices, confidentiality, passwords, espionage, business continuity and privacy, and traditional business and stakeholder processes and controls. Our consultants can show you how to add value to your business by focusing on the strategic, operational, risk, compliance and governance performance issues, based on our experience of implementing management systems frameworks, including ISO27001 (information security), ISO20000 (IT service management), and ISO22301 (business continuity).

Our consultants can help you to motivate employee behaviour and evaluate performance using formal, information-based routines and procedures to maintain or alter patterns in organisational activities. This is important to growing concerns that need to better organise and control their many systems, although it also applies to mature organisations that want to streamline and improve their operations for the purposes of cost-containment and to achieve better strategic positioning.

For more information about IT Governance: Consultancy & Training Services for Business Management Controls see: *www.itgovernance.co.uk/consulting.aspx*.

Publishing Services

IT Governance Publishing (ITGP) is the world's leading IT-GRC publishing imprint that is wholly owned by IT Governance Ltd.

With books and tools covering all IT governance, risk and compliance frameworks, we are the publisher of choice for authors and distributors alike, producing unique and practical publications of the highest quality, in the latest formats available, which readers will find invaluable.

www.itgovernancepublishing.co.uk is the website dedicated to ITGP, enabling both current and future authors, distributors, readers and other interested parties, to have easier access to more information allowing them to keep up to date with the latest publications and news from ITGP.

Newsletter

IT governance is one of the hottest topics in business today, not least because it is also the fastest moving.

You can stay up to date with the latest developments across the whole spectrum of IT governance subject matter, including risk management, information security, ITIL® and IT service management, project governance, compliance and so much more, by subscribing to ITG's core publications and topic alert emails.

Simply visit our subscription centre and select your preferences: *www.itgovernance.co.uk/newsletter.aspx*.

CPSIA information can be obtained
at www.ICGtesting.com
Printed in the USA
FSHW021648281219
65194FS

9 781849 284288